The NEW
KITCHEN
GARDEN

The NEW KITCHEN GARDEN

ANNA PAVORD

DK PUBLISHING, INC.
www.dk.com

A DK PUBLISHING BOOK

www.dk.com

To Vanessa, who planted a weed garden

Project Editor Pamela Brown
Art Editor Thomas Keenes
US Editors Susan McClure, Ray Rogers
Editor Constance Novis
Editorial Assistant Claire Benson
Designer Kylie Mulquinn
Design Assistants Rachana Devidayal,
Deborah Swallow

Location Photographer Steven Wooster
Illustrators Valerie Hill, John Lawrence

Managing Editor Susannah Marriott
Managing Art Editor Toni Kay

Production Manager Maryann Rogers
DTP Designer Karen Ruane

First paperback edition 1999
First American Edition, 1996
4 6 8 10 9 7 5

Published in the United States by DK Publishing, Inc.,
95 Madison Avenue, New York, New York 10016
www.dk.com

Library of Congress Cataloging-in-Publication Data
Pavord, Anna.
    The new kitchen garden / by Anna Pavord. -- 1st American ed.
    p.cm
    Includes index.
    ISBN 0-7894-4119-5
    1. Vegetable gardening. 2. Fruit-culture. 3. Herb gardening.
4. Vegetables. 5. Fruit.   6. Herbs. I. Title
SB321.P4   1996
635--dc20   95-44070
                                                        CIP

Reproduced by Euroscan, Nottingham, Great Britain
Printed and bound in Singapore by
Star Standard Industries (Pte.) Ltd.

CONTENTS

FRUIT 116

PLANNING & CULTIVATION TECHNIQUES 150

INTRODUCTION

ORDER, COUPLED WITH PROFUSION, is the hallmark of the best kitchen gardens. If you can add to this a sense of being cut off from the real world, then you are very close to Eden. For the ultimate sense of detachment, you need to have walls, sunny walls, where pears can ripen mellifluously against warm brick. But even without the walls, even in the smallest of spaces, you can recreate a sense of abundance in your own garden by growing trained fruit trees to make living screens between one part of the plot and another, or planting exotic-looking lettuce and frilly parsley among the flowers in your border or windowbox.

SUMMER STRAWBERRIES
Think of the warmth on your tongue of a freshly picked strawberry on a summer's day. This is a fruit for sybarites.

A novice gardener may grow a passable show of flowers. Vegetables signify a deeper level of commitment. To cut yourself off from growing food is to cut yourself off from a long and resonant tradition of gardening to survive. Even if you no longer have to feed yourself from your plot, without fruit and vegetables you deny yourself some of the great pleasures of gardening. Think of the sense of pride you get when sitting down to a supper that you have made entirely with produce from your own plot. You need to make the most of those moments. After the pride comes the inevitable fall, when somebody discovers a caterpillar, mummified, in the artistically arranged spears of broccoli on their plate.

GEOMETRY IN THE PLOT
Spreadeagled on a warm, sheltering stone wall, the apple tree, trained as an espalier, reinforces the geometrical design of this formal plot.

It is only quite recently that vegetables and fruit have been herded into separate areas of the garden and that the kitchen garden has acquired its dreary overtones: overblown cabbages and decaying scarlet runner beans. When, with increasing affluence and ease on the part of gardeners, the first flowers crept out of the physic gardens to decorate cottage plots, flowers, fruit, and vegetables all grew together in happy profusion.

George Eliot set the scene in her novel *Scenes of Clerical Life* (1858): "No finical separation between flower and kitchen garden there; no monotony of enjoyment for one sense to the exclusion of another; but a charming paradisiacal mingling of all that was pleasant to the eyes and good for food. The rich flower-border running along every walk, with its endless succession of spring flowers, anemones, auriculas, wall-flowers, sweet-williams, campanulas, snapdragons and

HAPPY PROFUSION
Tall Verbena bonariensis waves above the purple and green marbled foliage of lettuce. The sumptuous tones are reinforced by the dark leaves of a patch of beets beyond. Stone paths make neat divisions between the plots.

tiger-lilies, had its taller beauties, such as moss and Provence roses, varied with espalier apple-trees; the crimson of a carnation was carried out in the lurking crimson of the neighbouring strawberry-beds; you gathered a moss-rose one moment and a bunch of carrots the next; you were in a delicious fluctuation between the scent of jasmine and the juice of gooseberries." There is no reason why you too should not be in that same state of delicious fluctuation, if you abandon some preconceived notions about the "proper" place of plants.

Perhaps you have a summer jasmine straddling an old fence at the back of a border. Perhaps the border itself has been a source of irritation. Something is wrong with it. You may decide that what it needs is a series of landmarks to punctuate its sleepiness. You could put in acanthus, but how much more fun it would be to use mop-headed standard gooseberries to bob up between the campanulas. Grown on straight yard-high stems, they have the sculptural quality of pieces of topiary, and are particularly enchanting if you leave the berries to hang and ripen until they are as richly colored as amber. Alternately, you could draft in some bold clumps of globe artichokes to liven up the scene. The leaves will bring to the border the drama that it needs, and you will have the buttery bonus of the artichoke heads to look forward to. That is more than an acanthus will ever give you.

You may have two small plots at the end of the garden that you use for vegetables. These grow in straight parallel rows, cabbages next to lettuce, carrots next to parsley. Just by manipulating the rows of vegetables themselves, thinking about contrasts between the shape and texture of their foliage, you can make the plot start to sing. Try setting the frilly leaves of a red lettuce such as 'Lollo Rossa' against the drooping blue flags of leeks. Line up your Savoy cabbages with their swirling foliage next door to the carrots, which have leaves as good as the finest ferns.

There are several other things you can do to improve the appearance of your plot. The first is to choose cultivars that are in themselves more decorative than the norm. There is no need to take this to ridiculous lengths. The prime purpose of a leek is to give comfort on a cold, graceless day when the buses are late and your children more than usually intractable.

CHISELED ARTICHOKES
Every sculptor's dream, the globe artichoke makes a dramatic focal point in mixed plantings of vegetables and flowers. If you do not eat them, the beautifully chiseled buds eventually open into huge, bluish purple thistleheads.

GLOSSY CHARD
Chard is a perfect foliage plant for the kitchen garden. Use the glossy crinkled leaves of a red-stemmed chard next to the feathery foliage that grows above the white bulbs of Florence fennel.

HANDSOME LEEKS
Leeks, planted in a bed of pot marigolds, chives, romaine lettuce, and red-stemmed chard, have been allowed to go to flower, their globe-shaped heads balanced on long, strong stems.

DECORATIVE BEANS
Scarlet runner beans were originally taken to Europe as decorative climbers. Here, a white-flowered cultivar is mixed with the red and white flowers of 'Painted Lady'.

Flavor is the prime criterion of any fruit or vegetable. But you can look for other attributes as well as flavor. Among leeks, for instance, there is an extremely handsome cultivar called 'Bleu de Solaise' (also known as 'St. Victor'), which is hardy and wonderful to eat. You would expect this from an old French variety, but the bonus is its foliage, leaves of a rich purplish blue that you can use to great effect among the pale, frizzed foliage of curly endive. You might think of experimenting with the old-fashioned runner bean 'Painted Lady'. Scarlet runner beans were originally taken from North America to Europe as decorative climbers, rather than as vegetables, and with 'Painted Lady' you can see why. The flowers are neatly bicolored, red and white, charming when grown over an arch, perhaps mixed with the white flowers of a clematis. Even the prosaic Brussels sprout can dress itself up if you want it to. Try 'Rubine', which is suffused with a deep purplish red, the kind of saturated color that looks sumptuous against tall, pale cones of Chinese cabbage.

The other thing you can do is to bring flowers back into the kitchen garden, recreating the "paradisiacal mingling" that George Eliot wrote about. Line the paths with neat clumps of alpine strawberries. Set a ribbon row of pinks behind them, choosing perhaps the blood red flowers of 'Hidcote'. These contrast boldly with their own pale gray, grassy foliage, but they will also strike up an alliance with the strawberries. As you bend to pick a strawberry, the heady, spicy scent of the pinks will be where it needs to be – right under your nose.

The photographs in this book show many different ways of combining fruit, flowers, and vegetables in a single plot. You might like to plant purple-headed alliums among leeks (their cousins), set purple aquilegias with your red cabbage, grow pot marigolds with curly kale, lay down lengths of blue cornflowers in between your fennel and carrots, scatter seed of the California poppy, *Eschscholzia californica,* to sprout among the onions, or use brilliant blue anchusa behind clumps of purple-leaved sage. Certain annual flowers, such as pot marigolds and nasturtiums, have a special affinity with vegetables, for they too can be eaten, the petals of pot marigolds sprinkled over a green salad, the leaves and seeds of nasturtiums used to add extra bite to a sandwich.

GOLDEN HARVEST
One of many vegetables that came into gardens from Latin America, sweet corn has been bred to adapt to cooler climates. Use the tall sheaves to make a summer screen.

THE COLOR OF MARIGOLDS
A low, sprawling bush tomato, its trusses of fruit still to ripen, shares a terracotta pot with clumps of single-flowered French marigolds. Pot marigolds carry the same clear orange into the bed of basil beyond.

George Eliot was writing about a time when the kitchen garden was at its full-blown, spectacular height. At Drumlanrig Castle, in Dumfries, Scotland, during that period, the kitchen garden contained vineries, melon houses, carnation houses, and hothouses for indoor plants. There was also a glass fruithouse that was 500ft (150m) long and 18ft (5.5m) wide. A cast-metal path ran down the middle, with edges raised to make tracks for a railroad car that carted muck into the glasshouse and produce out.

In the 1880s, the house was packed with nectarines and figs, peaches, pears, and plums. Pots of pelargoniums, begonias, and other ormanentals were massed on stepped shelves against the wall. Fourteen gardeners worked for the Duke of Buccleuch at Drumlanrig under the eagle eye of David Thomson, one of the best gardeners of his day. They formed a Mutual Improvement Association and kept careful notes on the subjects they discussed at their meetings: Forcing of the Fig, Cultivation of the Raspberry, Man's Inhumanity to Man.

Our pictures of Glenbervie, another old Scottish garden (see pages 16–17), show that the tradition evoked by George Eliot and enshrined in David Thomson still lives on today. It is a tradition from which we have much to learn. If you are interested in good food, there is an overwhelming reason to grow your own fruit and vegetables. Without good ingredients you cannot expect to produce good food. Commercial growers worry less about the taste of vegetables than the size and uniformity of the crop. When you are growing your own, different standards prevail. To enjoy asparagus, sweet corn, and purple sprouting broccoli at their best, they need to go straight from plot to pot. Some produce such as snap beans, strawberries, and raspberries may be expensive to buy. If you have your own, you can indulge to your heart's content.

These are practical reasons to grow fruit and vegetables at home. The best reason, though, is the pleasure they give, and the beauty they add to the garden. Few trees in spring can match the elegiac performance of a mature pear, pouring out its heart in white blossoms against the blue sky. Few flowers can produce a scent to equal that of a ripe damson plum, drooping intoxicatingly from a tree fanned out against a warm wall. Few foliage plants can match the bravura perfomance of a kale such as 'Chou Palmier', rising in a fountain of nearly black leaves. All these pleasures can be yours. To recreate Eden, just plant, watch, and wait.

BOLD ZUCCHINI
While the zucchini itself is just beginning to swell, you can pick off the flower and use it as a package to fill with a savory rice stuffing. Grow both green- and yellow-fruited cultivars of zucchini in the decorative kitchen garden.

BRIGHTEST BLOSSOM
Safe in the cocoon of a frost-free greenhouse, this peach blooms bravely while the garden outside is still in the grip of winter. A tree needs careful training if it is to flower and fruit successfully in a confined situation such as this.

1

GARDEN
STYLES

IN THIS FIRST PART OF THE BOOK you will find ideas for many
different ways of combining fruit, vegetables, and flowers in your
garden to create effects that may be whimsically nostalgic, as in this
charming display, or strictly formal, as in the design for the salad and
herb plot on pages 36–37. Following each inspiring photograph
is a plan showing how you can interpret each particular style in
your own garden. The plans assume a never-never land where
everything fruits and flowers at the same time. Your own garden
will behave more sensibly, as nature intended. The plans do not take
into account the exact number of cabbages or lettuce that will fit
into a row. For the correct spacings at which they should be
grown, check the information given in Part Two.

EXUBERANT POTAGER

POTAGER, A FRENCH WORD, IS THE NAME for a style of gardening using vegetables as part of a formal design, mixed with flowers, fruit, or whatever else makes them look decorative as well as useful. Villandry, a Renaissance château in northwestern France, has the world's most famous potager. There are acres of it divided into nine equal squares, each containing a different arrangement of formal beds edged with boxwood. The idea has been copied all over the world.

When planning a potager, avoid too many permanent plantings of perennials, which will cut down on your options for change. Interplant vegetables with annual flowers, such as cornflowers or California poppies, and try edging beds with violas instead of boxwood. Use plants to give height. You might use a wigwam of scarlet runner beans, or a clipped bay tree as in the exuberant potager (right) in Kinoith, in southwestern Ireland. Here, nasturtiums partner frilly lettuce on one side of the path, while violas romp with lettuce on the other. A golden hop scrambles over an arbor to make a seat in the shade.

RECREATING THE POTAGER

WHEN CREATING YOUR OWN POTAGER, the first job is to draw a design for the beds. The main danger lies in overcomplication, but a central focal point will help to pull the design together. For this purpose you could use a gazebo, a decorative frame, or a dramatic plant such as a globe artichoke (left, and in plan).

To furnish a potager you need three kinds of plants: some to edge the beds, some to fill them, and some to give height. Plant generously to create an exuberant effect, but avoid the temptation to cram in as many different types of vegetables and flowers as you can. The pattern will be more effective if you restrict your choice. Choose carefully: a potager is intended to display each vegetable like a piece of china in a cabinet. In this plan, there are combinations of vegetables that complement each other in looks or habit – purple-leaved beets make stripes through rows of feathery carrot foliage, and tomatoes sprawl under tall sheaves of sweet corn. Stick to a few edgers and use them to reinforce the symmetry of the layout. Aim, too, for a balance between vegetables and flowers. Here, California poppies (*Eschscholzia*) brighten up the bed where onions are growing and cornflowers mingle with the snap beans.

ZUCCHINI COVER-UP
The big, bold leaves of zucchini rapidly cover the ground, their flowers shining out brightly from beneath. If picked regularly, zucchini have a long season. Follow them with some cut-and-come-again oriental brassicas for fresh salads later in the growing season.

THE KEY ELEMENTS

MARIGOLDS TAKE OVER
Borders of orange pot marigolds (left) keep a bed looking fresh and bright while the vegetables growing inside are picked and replanted. A neatly clipped standard bay tree gives a sense of permanence as well as height.

MARIGOLDS, SWEET CORN & TOMATOES *Pot marigolds edge a mixture of tall sweet corn and low-growing bush tomatoes that require no staking.*

HIGH DRAMA
A wigwam of willow or a wrought iron frame (left), used to support a mixture of scarlet runner beans and sweet peas, will add vertical impact to a bed. In a smaller garden, use it as a centerpiece for the whole potager. It will give just the right feeling of formality.

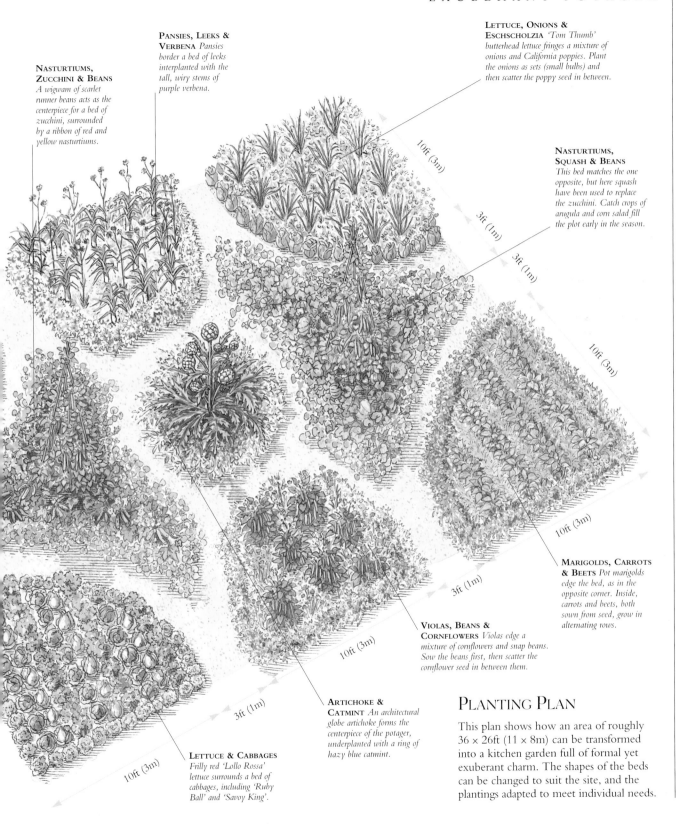

NASTURTIUMS, ZUCCHINI & BEANS *A wigwam of scarlet runner beans acts as the centerpiece for a bed of zucchini, surrounded by a ribbon of red and yellow nasturtiums.*

PANSIES, LEEKS & VERBENA *Pansies border a bed of leeks interplanted with the tall, wiry stems of purple verbena.*

LETTUCE, ONIONS & ESCHSCHOLZIA *'Tom Thumb' butterhead lettuce fringes a mixture of onions and California poppies. Plant the onions as sets (small bulbs) and then scatter the poppy seed in between.*

NASTURTIUMS, SQUASH & BEANS *This bed matches the one opposite, but here squash have been used to replace the zucchini. Catch crops of arugula and corn salad fill the plot early in the season.*

MARIGOLDS, CARROTS & BEETS *Pot marigolds edge the bed, as in the opposite corner. Inside, carrots and beets, both sown from seed, grow in alternating rows.*

VIOLAS, BEANS & CORNFLOWERS *Violas edge a mixture of cornflowers and snap beans. Sow the beans first, then scatter the cornflower seed in between them.*

ARTICHOKE & CATMINT *An architectural globe artichoke forms the centerpiece of the potager, underplanted with a ring of hazy blue catmint.*

LETTUCE & CABBAGES *Frilly red 'Lollo Rossa' lettuce surrounds a bed of cabbages, including 'Ruby Ball' and 'Savoy King'.*

10ft (3m)
3ft (1m)
3ft (1m)
10ft (3m)
10ft (3m)
3ft (1m)
10ft (3m)
3ft (1m)
10ft (3m)

PLANTING PLAN

This plan shows how an area of roughly 36 × 26ft (11 × 8m) can be transformed into a kitchen garden full of formal yet exuberant charm. The shapes of the beds can be changed to suit the site, and the plantings adapted to meet individual needs.

TRADITIONAL KITCHEN GARDEN

THE TRADITIONAL KITCHEN GARDEN, enclosed by walls of stone or brick, is an oasis of order in a chaotic world. Ruler-straight paths divide the space into neat plots, all beautifully dug and weeded. Beans and cauliflowers, onions and peas grow in rows running from north to south to catch the best of the sunlight. Although this is primarily a place for the production of food, flowers are not banished. Broad bands of catmint border paths under garlands of rambling roses; other flowers are grown for cutting. There will undoubtedly be trained fruit trees, spreading their limbs over a sunny wall or perhaps used to make espaliered hedges along the edges of the vegetable plots. When you walk through a door into one of these peaceful places, you jettison any timetable constructed around dentist appointments, car repairs, and the possible arrival or departure of airplanes, and tune into a deeply established pattern of sowing and growing and harvesting and sowing again.

RECREATING THE KITCHEN GARDEN

MOST TRADITIONAL WALLED kitchen gardens are of the size that needs to be divided into smaller areas. This plan shows just one quarter of a garden that has been split into four equal plots. The way the plots themselves are organized is entirely a matter of personal taste. Here, the vegetables are grown in conventional rows, but you might prefer to divide each plot into a series of raised beds, with narrow paths of beaten soil running in between them. Gnarled espaliers are a feature of all old kitchen gardens, creating living screens around the vegetables with their outstretched, lichen-covered branches. Once established, like the fan-trained trees on the walls, they are easy to prune each summer. You could also grow a screen of espaliered apples and pears on two sides of this vegetable plot. Annual flowers, like larkspur, are grown in trellis-patterned beds to provide flowers for cutting. The paths can be of grass, gravel, or aggregate. Once, paths were made of the ash that spewed in vast quantities from the greenhouse boiler. The greenhouse here is emphatically not a space for living, in the manner of a modern sunroom. It is a forcing house, a larder, a growing space, although it will provide welcome shelter in winter and early spring when you can linger there, sowing seeds, and dreaming of the harvest to come.

THE KEY ELEMENTS

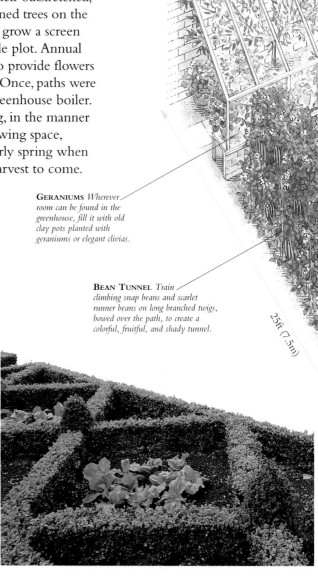

GREENHOUSE *This is an ornamental yet very practical place. A floor laid with tiles or stone is easy to hose down in summer. This helps deter spider mite and whitefly.*

GERANIUMS *Wherever room can be found in the greenhouse, fill it with old clay pots planted with geraniums or elegant clivias.*

BEAN TUNNEL *Train climbing snap beans and scarlet runner beans on long branched twigs, bowed over the path, to create a colorful, fruitful, and shady tunnel.*

25ft (7.5m)

FRAGILE SPRING
The blossoming of peaches and nectarines in early spring is one of the delights of the greenhouse. Once, a greenhouse was essential to be able to produce exotic fruit.

BOXWOOD BORDERS
An edging of boxwood in a geometric pattern is a charming way to arrange the flower border. Each diamond can be used to grow a different type, or color, of flower.

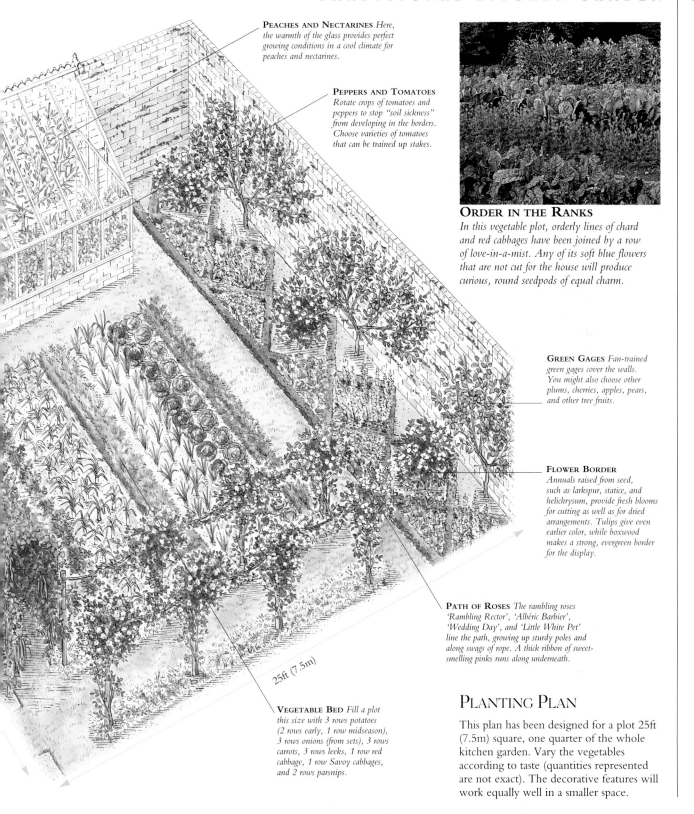

PEACHES AND NECTARINES *Here, the warmth of the glass provides perfect growing conditions in a cool climate for peaches and nectarines.*

PEPPERS AND TOMATOES *Rotate crops of tomatoes and peppers to stop "soil sickness" from developing in the borders. Choose varieties of tomatoes that can be trained up stakes.*

ORDER IN THE RANKS

In this vegetable plot, orderly lines of chard and red cabbages have been joined by a row of love-in-a-mist. Any of its soft blue flowers that are not cut for the house will produce curious, round seedpods of equal charm.

GREEN GAGES *Fan-trained green gages cover the walls. You might also choose other plums, cherries, apples, pears, and other tree fruits.*

FLOWER BORDER *Annuals raised from seed, such as larkspur, statice, and helichrysum, provide fresh blooms for cutting as well as for dried arrangements. Tulips give even earlier color, while boxwood makes a strong, evergreen border for the display.*

PATH OF ROSES *The rambling roses 'Rambling Rector', 'Albéric Barbier', 'Wedding Day', and 'Little White Pet' line the path, growing up sturdy poles and along swags of rope. A thick ribbon of sweet-smelling pinks runs along underneath.*

25ft (7.5m)

VEGETABLE BED *Fill a plot this size with 3 rows potatoes (2 rows early, 1 row midseason), 3 rows onions (from sets), 3 rows carrots, 3 rows leeks, 1 row red cabbage, 1 row Savoy cabbages, and 2 rows parsnips.*

PLANTING PLAN

This plan has been designed for a plot 25ft (7.5m) square, one quarter of the whole kitchen garden. Vary the vegetables according to taste (quantities represented are not exact). The decorative features will work equally well in a smaller space.

IN THE BORDER

OCCASIONAL DRAMA is what you want in an herbaceous border, to wake up the sleepy hordes of daisies and well-bred bellflowers. There is no reason why vegetables and fruit should not provide that drama as easily as flowers. The best borders, as gardeners are told a thousand times, are those that include plenty of good foliage. Only the slightest shift of focus is needed before you reach for a scarlet-stemmed Swiss chard instead of a bergenia, plant a globe artichoke rather than an acanthus, or fill a gap with a frilly-leaved lettuce rather than a hosta. What could be more dramatic spearing through a mound of bright red verbena than the elegant drooping leaves of leeks, especially the French purple-leaved cultivar 'Bleu de Solaise'? So be bold and cast aside inhibition. Liberate your leeks and let their flags fly among your flowers.

SCARLET AFFAIR
The stems of ruby chard glow with a particular brilliance. These have been planted a sensible distance from the path edge so that when the leaves splay out from the center of the plant, they do not get in the way. Kept well-watered, chard makes a striking container plant.

WICKER WORKS
A wicker tripod provides support for scarlet runner beans (purple-splashed snap beans would make a good alternative) between purple Verbena bonariensis *and the fluffy heads of* Thalictrum. *Farther along, feathery bronze fennel is beginning to bloom.*

COLORS OF KALE
*Ornamental kales such as this
have leaves of many colors – pink,
purple, sea green, gray, or cream.
Although it would not be your
first choice for cooking, kale will
make a decorative feature in an
ornamental potager, and it grows
well in pots and windowboxes.*

PARSLEY AND SAGE
*The sage's cool gray foliage makes
a perfect foil for crisply curled
parsley. With their contrasts of
texture and tone, these two herbs
both enliven the front of the
border. Flat-leaved parsley, which
is not such a bright green, would
be less successful.*

DESIRABLE THISTLES
*Globe artichokes and cardoons are both dramatic plants in a border,
but you must not put any other plant too close. Despite being ruthless
smotherers, these plants have great style and presence. If you can bear
not to eat the artichokes, they open out into huge purple thistleheads.*

FORMAL FRUIT GARDEN

A BEAUTIFULLY TRAINED ESPALIER APPLE, with a row of garlic chives at its foot, reinforces the horizontal lines of the stonework on this sunny wall. In colder areas, a wall such as this offers protection for the blossoms against late frosts, and its stored warmth hastens the ripening of the fruit. The charm of trained fruit trees lies in their formal precision. They can be used to great effect, either against a wall or tied to strong parallel wires stretched between posts. Grown like this, both apples and pears will make a protective screen around a fruit garden filled with raspberries, strawberries, and currants. The practical reason for growing soft fruit together is that you can net them all to protect them from birds. Do not believe anyone who tells you that if you plant extra for the birds, both you and they will be happy. They will be delirious at the prospect of more food, but you will be left without a berry to your name. To enhance the decorative air of the plot, you could introduce some sort of arbor at the center. Find a rubber hawk to sit on the top: it may save you the trouble of a net.

MAKING A FRUIT GARDEN

GROUPING FRUIT TOGETHER gives you the chance to arrange it in a decorative yet practical and productive way. The whole plot can be screened from the rest of the garden, as in this plan, by apples and pears trained as espaliers. Winter will reveal the geometry of their bare branches; then follow blossoms and luscious fruit. Raspberry canes are generally planted in wide parallel rows, but in a squarish plot you could plant two lines from corner to corner giving four generous triangles to fill with soft fruit. Put a standard gooseberry in each, staking bushes firmly for they are top heavy, especially when laden with berries. Plant two of the triangles with currants – black currants in one and a mixture of white and red currants (above) in the other – and edge beds with alpine strawberries. That leaves two triangles for growing large-fruited strawberries. Since they rarely crop well after three years, it is essential to keep producing new plants from their runners to grow in fresh ground. Use the two triangles as alternating strawberry beds, and whenever there is a spare patch in one of them, sow an assortment of annual flowers for cutting. For the best crops, mulch the ground regularly with thick layers of compost.

THE KEY ELEMENTS

A DECORATIVE CAGE
If you grow soft fruit in one patch, you can easily use nets to protect it from the predations of birds. Above is a highly ornamental octagonal structure that stays in place all year. The netting is attached to it once the fruit starts to ripen.

STRAWBERRY TIME
It is essential to net strawberries well before the fruit ripens. Here, young, green shrub branches have been bent over the plants, providing a pleasingly natural way of holding the nets in place.

SPRING PEARS
The delicate, white flowers of pears are the most attractive of all tree blossoms. A beautifully trained espalier shows them to perfection. Try to include pears in your garden, whether to screen a fruit plot or herb patch or to decorate a lawn.

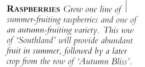

PEARS *Since few pears are self-fertile, plant two varieties to ensure pollination. Avoid planting where frosts may ruin the blossoms and subsequent fruit.*

RASPBERRIES *Grow one line of summer-fruiting raspberries and one of an autumn-fruiting variety. This row of 'Southland' will provide abundant fruit in summer, followed by a later crop from the row of 'Autumn Bliss'.*

STRAWBERRIES *Use two of the triangles for strawberries, starting plants off in one and transferring rooted runners to the other when original plants begin to flag. Renew plants after three years.*

25ft (7.5m)

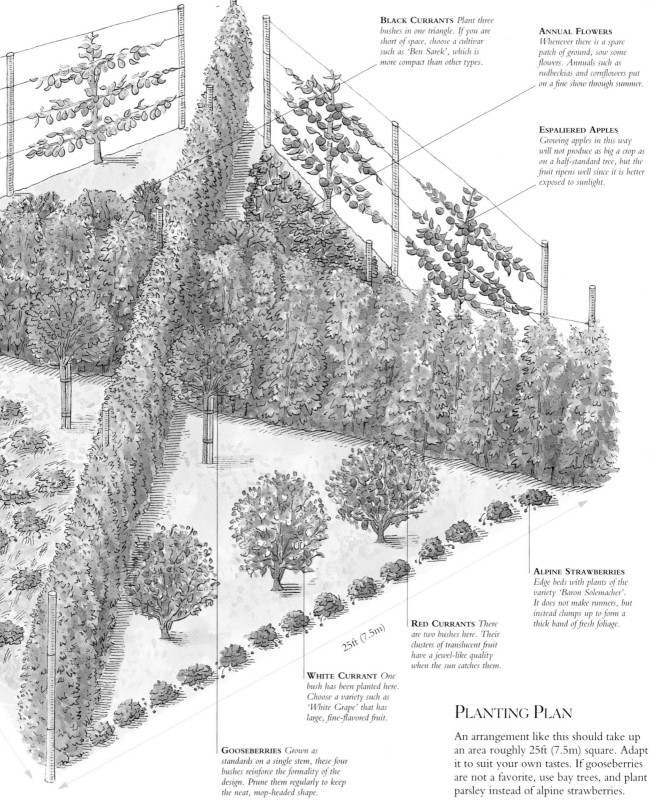

BLACK CURRANTS *Plant three bushes in one triangle. If you are short of space, choose a cultivar such as 'Ben Sarek', which is more compact than other types.*

ANNUAL FLOWERS *Whenever there is a spare patch of ground, sow some flowers. Annuals such as rudbeckias and cornflowers put on a fine show through summer.*

ESPALIERED APPLES *Growing apples in this way will not produce as big a crop as on a half-standard tree, but the fruit ripens well since it is better exposed to sunlight.*

ALPINE STRAWBERRIES *Edge beds with plants of the variety 'Baron Solemacher'. It does not make runners, but instead clumps up to form a thick band of fresh foliage.*

RED CURRANTS *There are two bushes here. Their clusters of translucent fruit have a jewel-like quality when the sun catches them.*

25ft (7.5m)

WHITE CURRANT *One bush has been planted here. Choose a variety such as 'White Grape' that has large, fine-flavored fruit.*

GOOSEBERRIES *Grown as standards on a single stem, these four bushes reinforce the formality of the design. Prune them regularly to keep the neat, mop-headed shape.*

PLANTING PLAN

An arrangement like this should take up an area roughly 25ft (7.5m) square. Adapt it to suit your own tastes. If gooseberries are not a favorite, use bay trees, and plant parsley instead of alpine strawberries.

A RUSTIC MIXED HEDGE

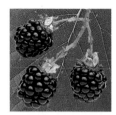

FOR TAKING AWAY the backs of your knees, there is nothing like a slug of sloe gin. In English country areas, sloes are a common component of mixed hedgerows, but there is no reason why they should not be planted elsewhere. They could be part of a rustic mixed hedge, with elder for champagne and wine, cherry plums to make into liqueur, and hazelnuts to nibble along with your drink. Sloes are the fruit of the blackthorn, whose spiny shoots make a hedge that neither animals nor vandals can push through. The wood is dark, a counterfoil to the wreaths of white blossoms that cover it in spring before the leaves come out. Elder grows so easily it is practically a weed, but if you prune out the oldest growths each year it can be kept within bounds. You can make champagne from the flat, creamy flowerheads that appear in early summer; the berries, in early autumn, provide a second excuse for a binge. The cherry plum, or myrobalan, has fruit twice the size of sloes and half as bitter, too fiddly for pies but good for liqueur or wine, which becomes more like port the longer you keep it. Hazels will bear catkins as well as nuts. Once the hedge is fairly well established, you could add to its winemaking potential by planting blackberries at intervals, then training and tying in the shoots.

SLOE WORK
Soused in gin, sloes make a highly intoxicating drink. Pick them in early winter, pull off stems, and prick with a darning needle. Drop into an empty gin bottle with ½ cup (125g) sugar. When it is nearly full, pour in enough gin to cover the fruit, screw on the lid, and let it steep for a year.

THE KEY ELEMENTS

The sloe or blackthorn, *Prunus spinosa*, makes a shrubby sort of tree, rarely more than 12ft (3.5m) tall. Plants are best established when about 12–18in (30–45cm) high. Plant them about 18in (45cm) from their nearest neighbor, preferably in autumn. Elder, *Sambucus nigra*, grows quickly to about the same height and is easily grown from cuttings taken in late autumn. For a more decorative effect, choose the variety 'Aurea', although its golden foliage turns green as summer wears on. The best colored leaves, unfortunately, come from cutting the elder back hard each winter, which means losing the flowers and hence the champagne. The ferny-leaved form *S. nigra* 'Laciniata' does not need such

drastic treatment but is not vigorous. Plant elders about 14ft (4m) apart, and hazels at a similar distance. Both can be kept within bounds if branches are removed from the base at regular intervals. The cherry plum, *Prunus cerasifera*, is more tree-like and taller than the sloe, but you can trim it to size. Its white flowers appear in early spring giving, together with the sloe, a long season of blossoms. Set plants about 24in (60cm) apart. Once the hedge has reached about 4ft (1.2m), add a blackberry or two. Try the variety 'Comanche' for the finest flavor, or parsley-leaved 'Oregon Thornless' for best decorative effect.

HONOR YOUR ELDERS
For the best berries, give elders a site that is reasonably shady and moist, plus an annual mulch of homemade compost.

PLANTING PLAN

This plan shows a range of trees and shrubs that could be used in a hedge about 14ft (4m) long. Choose plants to provide the raw materials for your favorite brews, and adjust quantities according to the length required. If possible, make the planting strip about 3ft (1m) wide and set plants in a zigzag pattern, some at the front and some at the back, to make a hedge that is reasonably thick.

FRESH AS A HAZELNUT

The taste of creamy, fresh hazelnuts, the fruit of Corylus avellana *or* C. maxima, *is unlike anything that has been kept in storage. You will have to race with the squirrels to get them, and the squirrels will probably get there first.*

CHERRY PLUMS *The tree blossoms in early spring with white flowers slightly larger than the sloe's. The fruit is usually ready to pick in late summer. Prune, if necessary, in winter.*

ELDERBERRIES *Soon after the berries hang their heads and ripen, the leaves begin to turn a soft pinkish purple, the color of watered-down wine.*

BLACKTHORN *Planted at regular intervals, this will make a tough, spiny, impenetrable hedge. It needs cutting back from time to time in order to restrict its girth as much as its height.*

SLOES *The blackthorn's small, hard fruit are about the size of a grape and are mostly made up of the pit. They gradually turn purple in late summer but will remain on the tree for a long time.*

HAZELNUTS *Clusters of nuts decorate the hedge from late summer on. In late winter and early spring, it will be hung with delicate catkins.*

ELDERFLOWERS *Spring turns into summer as heads of elderflower light up the hedgerows with lacy patches of cream. As well as making excellent champagne, the flowers give gooseberry jam a delicious muscat flavor.*

BLACKBERRIES *Cultivated types produce larger, earlier, less seedy fruit than wild brambles. Each year, cut out the stems that bore the fruit and tie in the new ones that spring from the base.*

FOXGLOVES *Tallest of the naturalized flowers that grow at the foot of the hedge are the foxgloves in early summer. At ground level, violets, cowslips, and daisies scatter their flowers through the grass.*

VEGETABLE PATCHWORK

VEGETABLES PLANTED IN bold blocks have much more impact than those planted in single rows. This plot, inspired by the paintings of Mondrian, has been divided into a series of rectangular beds of different sizes and proportions to make a vegetable patchwork. In this way you can build up contrasts of color and texture just as you do in a flower border. Sturdy poles have been lashed together to make the outdoor equivalent of a room divider: this one has been supporting a crop of scrambling peas, but it could equally well be used for climbing snap beans or flowers. The annual climber *Cobaea scandens* would give the plot an exotic touch. Tall stems of sweet corn make a living hedge to screen this part of the garden from the lawn beyond, but Jerusalem artichokes could be used in the same way. The main paths are wide and paved and are connected by much narrower routes of beaten soil so that you can get in to pick or weed the vegetables. The beds, none of them too wide to be tended from one path or another, are also practical, since they make it easy to plan a year-to-year rotation of crops.

VEGETABLE PATCHWORK

THIS KIND OF LAYOUT WILL LEND itself to any garden, whatever the size or however awkward the shape. It uses plants that look good in combination with each other and that will supply meals for most of the year. You can vary the quantities or substitute personal favorites. Choose the most decorative vegetables such as bright ruby chard or zucchini with glowing, golden flowers (above). Grow lettuce such as frilly, burnished 'Lollo Rossa' next to the ferny foliage of carrots or the steel-blue ribbons of leeks. Here, the patchwork is made up entirely of vegetables and herbs, but for greater contrast of color, add flowers. Orange pot marigolds could replace one of the beds of parsley, or a stand of cheerful sunflowers could be planted instead of the red-stemmed chard. If you do use flowers, choose annuals rather than more permanent perennials that occupy the ground from year to year. The wide divisions between the beds are proper paths, made from paving slabs or another hard material such as brick. The narrow paths can be left as beaten soil, although on heavy ground you might find a dressing of chipped bark or wood helps to soak up excess moisture. None of the crops in this planting will need support, but you could introduce a screen alongside one of the paths and use it to prop up a crop of peas.

THE KEY ELEMENTS

ACCENT ON SHAPE
Try to make the most of contrasting textures and forms when planning the plot. Above, the spiky, upright leaves of leeks emphasize the soft, rounded shapes of butterhead lettuce.

EXPLOITING YOUR SPACE
Underplant tall growers like sweet corn, right, with ground-huggers such as fiery nasturtiums, whose peppery leaves and red or yellow flowers can be used to enliven a summer salad.

PLANTING PLAN

Designed for a plot roughly 25 × 16ft (7.5 × 4.9m), this plan shows a challenging variety of vegetables and herbs that can be combined in patchwork planting; quantities represented are not exact.

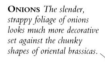

LETTUCE *Use this block to grow a crisphead type that adds texture to the salad bowl and garden alike.*

ONIONS *The slender, strappy foliage of onions looks much more decorative set against the chunky shapes of oriental brassicas.*

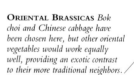

4ft (1.2m)

8ft (2.5m)

ORIENTAL BRASSICAS *Bok choi and Chinese cabbage have been chosen here, but other oriental vegetables would work equally well, providing an exotic contrast to their more traditional neighbors.*

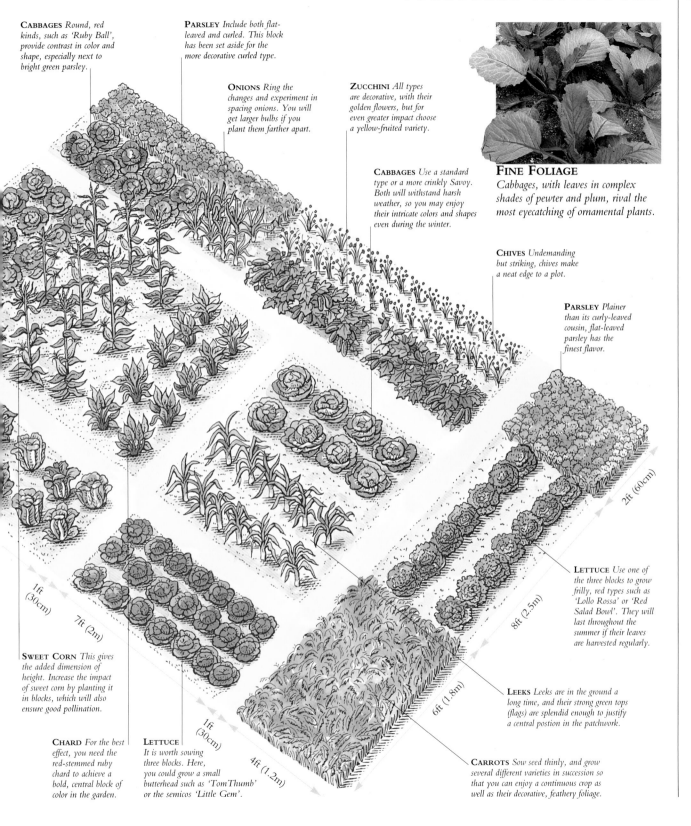

CABBAGES *Round, red kinds, such as 'Ruby Ball', provide contrast in color and shape, especially next to bright green parsley.*

PARSLEY *Include both flat-leaved and curled. This block has been set aside for the more decorative curled type.*

ONIONS *Ring the changes and experiment in spacing onions. You will get larger bulbs if you plant them farther apart.*

ZUCCHINI *All types are decorative, with their golden flowers, but for even greater impact choose a yellow-fruited variety.*

CABBAGES *Use a standard type or a more crinkly Savoy. Both will withstand harsh weather, so you may enjoy their intricate colors and shapes even during the winter.*

FINE FOLIAGE

Cabbages, with leaves in complex shades of pewter and plum, rival the most eyecatching of ornamental plants.

CHIVES *Undemanding but striking, chives make a neat edge to a plot.*

PARSLEY *Plainer than its curly-leaved cousin, flat-leaved parsley has the finest flavor.*

LETTUCE *Use one of the three blocks to grow frilly, red types such as 'Lollo Rossa' or 'Red Salad Bowl'. They will last throughout the summer if their leaves are harvested regularly.*

LEEKS *Leeks are in the ground a long time, and their strong green tops (flags) are splendid enough to justify a central postion in the patchwork.*

CARROTS *Sow seed thinly, and grow several different varieties in succession so that you can enjoy a continuous crop as well as their decorative, feathery foliage.*

SWEET CORN *This gives the added dimension of height. Increase the impact of sweet corn by planting it in blocks, which will also ensure good pollination.*

CHARD *For the best effect, you need the red-stemmed ruby chard to achieve a bold, central block of color in the garden.*

LETTUCE *It is worth sowing three blocks. Here, you could grow a small butterhead such as 'TomThumb' or the semicos 'Little Gem'.*

1ft (30cm), 7ft (2m), 1ft (30cm), 4ft (1.2m), 6ft (1.8m), 8ft (2.5m), 2ft (60cm)

DECORATIVE COMBINATIONS

SHAPE, FORM, COLOR, AND TEXTURE are the attributes you have in mind when combining plants in a flower border. You put together those that will enhance each other's characteristics, perhaps using a broad-leaved hosta to set off the elegant fronds of a fern. Vegetables, herbs, and fruit are no less diverse in their qualities. Of course we grow them to eat, but while they are growing we can heighten our pleasure by combining them in equally telling ways. For hosta, think cabbage. For fern, think carrot. Edge the onion bed with violas and pepper the patch with leeks. If you leave the leeks in place, they will eventually go to flower, producing huge, silvery heads like those of an allium. That is not surprising, for alliums is what they are.

STRAWBERRY BAND
Alpine strawberries make a broad, low edging for a bed of spiky lavender. Choose a variety such as 'Baron Solemacher' that clumps up rather than sends out runners. The strawberry is not evergreen, but the leaves stay fresh over a long period.

VERSATILE LEEKS
Instead of being harvested, these leeks have been allowed to go to flower, the silvery lilac globes balanced on strong, hollow stems. Pot marigolds have self-seeded between lettuce and Swiss chard, while golden marjoram makes a striking contrast with purple sage.

CABBAGES ARE KINGS

For form, color, and texture, you can scarcely find a better plant than a cabbage. Swirling skirts of leaves surround the tightly folded hearts of these red cabbages, protected by tall screens of Verbena bonariensis, *a short-lived, strong-stemmed perennial.*

VIOLAS AND LETTUCE

The long, elegant fingers of an oak-leaf lettuce brush against the irrepressible Viola *'Tricolor'. This viola is ideal along the margin of a path because, although it is exuberant, it does not get too big or straggly. More aggressive plants will attack your ankles.*

RED SPROUTS WITH YELLOW POPPIES

The late-maturing Brussels sprout 'Rubine' has sprouts as richly dark as its leaves, well set off here by the bright blooms of the California poppy, Eschscholzia californica. *This is an annual that will perpetuate itself by self-seeding wherever there is a patch of bare soil.*

SALAD & HERB GARDEN

A SALAD PLOT COMBINED with a scattering of the most useful culinary herbs – parsley, chives, mint, and coriander – will, with a little planning, provide a long succession of crops for a gourmet gardener. Lettuce in all its forms – romaine, loose-leaf, butterhead, and crisphead – provides the bulk of the planting, but for a smooth sequence you need a small back-up plot or greenhouse to raise seedlings for transplanting into the beds at the appropriate time. Other salad crops might include arugula, mizuna greens, corn salad, and chicory.

This small formal area, part of a much larger garden, has the benefit of a sheltering stone wall. This gives crops an early start to the season. A pot planted with scarlet runner beans and variegated horseradish forms the centerpiece and the contrast in foliage colors has been extended to the edgings, a mixture of plain and variegated boxwood.

For extra ornamental effect, let flowers such as nemophila (baby blue eyes), pink opium poppies, and purple *Verbena* 'La France' grow among the salad leaves. The poppies will self-seed, but the others need to be replaced.

MAKING A SALAD & HERB GARDEN

IN A FORMAL DESIGN SUCH AS THIS, you need to think carefully about a suitable centerpiece. You could use a wigwam of scarlet runner beans or sweet peas, or a big clay pot of geraniums with scented leaves. You could also use a tall architectural plant like angelica, as opposite, or fennel. Angelica is splendidly statuesque with bright, light green foliage. It is biennial and in its second year sends up huge, rounded flower heads of pale yellow–green. There is a dramatic purple-stemmed relative called *A. gigas*. To add a little color, a few purely ornamental flowers – pink opium poppies (left), blue nemophila, and purple verbena – have been sprinkled among the red and green lettuce. Edging plants need to be compact. Floppy foliage will swish wetly around your ankles or smother crops. Boxwood, as shown on the previous page, is a traditional edging plant, but it needs fertilizing or it will drain the soil of nutrients, depriving plants nearby. The two edgings used in this design are less demanding: germander and violas. Germander, *Teucrium chamaedrys,* is an evergreen subshrub rarely more than 9in (23cm) high. The little oval leaves are deep shining green on top, gray underneath, and the tiny bright pink flower spikes last from mid- to late summer. When they are finished, clip the plants lightly to keep the edgings neat.

PLANTING PLAN

This is a salad-lover's garden, designed to extend the season for picking fresh leaves for as long as possible. It measures just over 24ft (7m) square, but a simplified version could fit into a smaller space or the beds could be used for another range of crops.

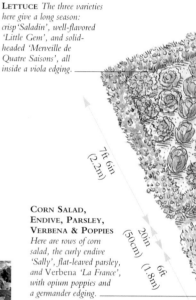

LETTUCE *The three varieties here give a long season: crisp 'Saladin', well-flavored 'Little Gem', and solid-headed 'Merveille de Quatre Saisons', all inside a viola edging.*

CORN SALAD, ENDIVE, PARSLEY, VERBENA & POPPIES *Here are rows of corn salad, the curly endive 'Sally', flat-leaved parsley, and Verbena 'La France', with opium poppies and a germander edging.*

7ft 6in (2.2m)

20in (50cm)

6ft (1.8m)

THE KEY ELEMENTS

LETTUCE PAGODA
When red 'Lollo Rossa' lettuce is past its best for eating, it becomes even better looking and grows into a decorative pagoda. Here, it rises out of a bed of nasturtiums and green lettuce.

SALAD DAYS
Lettuce comes in so many shapes and colors that it is easy to plan a pretty yet practical salad patch. Mix seed of green and red loose-leaf varieties to achieve a striking speckled effect. Put them next to a neat butterhead type.

HEAVENLY ANGELICA
The round green flower heads look magnificent in summer atop their towering stems. Later, the seed pods can be dried for decoration. The stems can be crystallized and used on cakes and in sweet dishes.

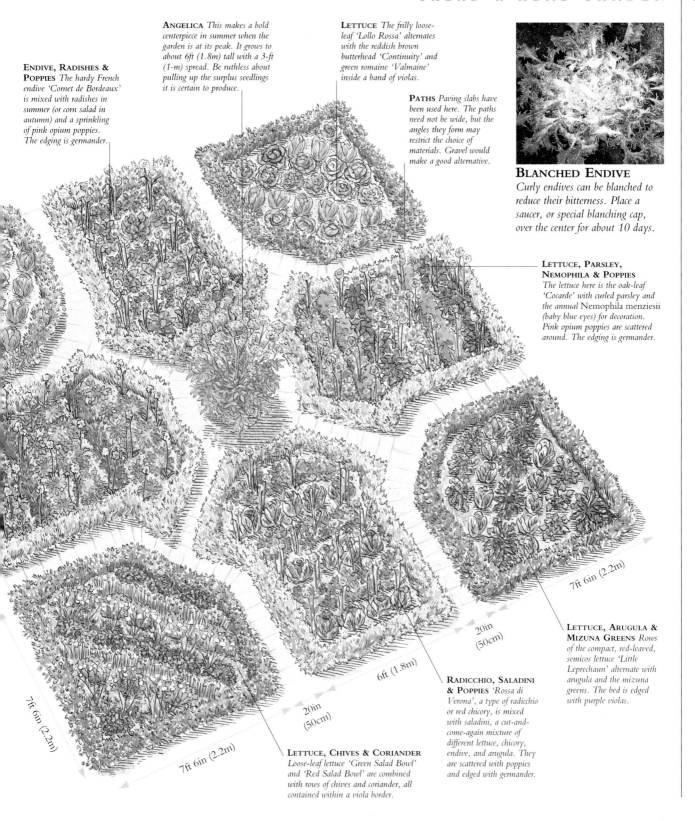

ENDIVE, RADISHES & POPPIES *The hardy French endive 'Cornet de Bordeaux' is mixed with radishes in summer (or corn salad in autumn) and a sprinkling of pink opium poppies. The edging is germander.*

ANGELICA *This makes a bold centerpiece in summer when the garden is at its peak. It grows to about 6ft (1.8m) tall with a 3-ft (1-m) spread. Be ruthless about pulling up the surplus seedlings it is certain to produce.*

LETTUCE *The frilly loose-leaf 'Lollo Rossa' alternates with the reddish brown butterhead 'Continuity' and green romaine 'Valmaine' inside a band of violas.*

PATHS *Paving slabs have been used here. The paths need not be wide, but the angles they form may restrict the choice of materials. Gravel would make a good alternative.*

BLANCHED ENDIVE
Curly endives can be blanched to reduce their bitterness. Place a saucer, or special blanching cap, over the center for about 10 days.

LETTUCE, PARSLEY, NEMOPHILA & POPPIES *The lettuce here is the oak-leaf 'Cocarde' with curled parsley and the annual* Nemophila menziesii *(baby blue eyes) for decoration. Pink opium poppies are scattered around. The edging is germander.*

LETTUCE, ARUGULA & MIZUNA GREENS *Rows of the compact, red-leaved, semicos lettuce 'Little Leprechaun' alternate with arugula and the mizuna greens. The bed is edged with purple violas.*

RADICCHIO, SALADINI & POPPIES *'Rossa di Verona', a type of radicchio or red chicory, is mixed with saladini, a cut-and-come-again mixture of different lettuce, chicory, endive, and arugula. They are scattered with poppies and edged with germander.*

LETTUCE, CHIVES & CORIANDER *Loose-leaf lettuce 'Green Salad Bowl' and 'Red Salad Bowl' are combined with rows of chives and coriander, all contained within a viola border.*

7ft 6in (2.2m)

7ft 6in (2.2m)

7ft 6in (2.2m)

20in (50cm)

6ft (1.8m)

20in (50cm)

20in (50cm)

COTTAGE GARDEN

PROFUSION AND A CERTAIN CAREFREE randomness should be the order of the day in a cottage garden. Here, vegetables are kings of the castle while flowers grow in a jumble in small patches wherever space can be found. Paths are narrow so that as much room as possible can be used for the production of food and are covered in straw to stop the ground from getting muddy. Shallots have been laid out to dry on one side of the path; strawberries line the other. Hedgerows yield the hazel, willow, and privet needed to make the screen, nearly submerged beneath tumbling hops, and the wigwam that will support a crop of scarlet runner beans. True cottage gardens were made by instinct and fueled by necessity. Seed for the following season would be saved from the best of the year's crops. By this means, cottage gardeners gradually developed strains of vegetables that suited their particular growing conditions.

Nowadays, they are more likely to have introduced the occasional foreign flavor. Here, the feathery leaves of Florence fennel, a relative newcomer, nudge a more prosaic crop of parsnips.

RECREATING THE COTTAGE GARDEN

IN THIS PLAN FOR A STYLIZED cottage garden, a meandering path makes its way past beds of vegetables, bordered and interspersed with flowers, to the simple woven seat that occupies a sheltered sunny corner. A second path leads in through an arch in a willow screen covered with hops and blackberries. Next to it, a stand of hollyhocks makes a welcoming entrance. Protecting the garden from cold winds is a mixed hedge of elder, hazel, honeysuckle, ash, willow, and hawthorn. The honeysuckle is there for its heady scent; the rest provide nuts and berries and sticks for the garden. In front of the hedge, a succession of biennials – foxgloves, honesty, mulleins, and evening primroses – will seed themselves from year to year. In the lefthand corner, a fine topiary peacock gazes blandly at the view. In the other corner, next to the seat, a pear tree is planted for its bountiful white blossom and tempting fruit, while a moss rose provides sweetly scented flowers for a buttonhole. The paths are of beaten soil covered with straw, which is inexpensive and easy to find in the country. The crops either side are mostly traditional. There is a big bed of peas and potatoes, both of which can be stored for winter use. The wigwam of beans rises from a sprawling patch of tomatoes and summer squash, while other beds contain onions, leeks, parsnips, cabbages, Brussels sprouts, and curly kale.

TOPIARY PEACOCK
Yew is the best plant to use for large clipped shapes like this.

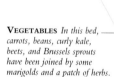

VEGETABLES *In this bed, carrots, beans, curly kale, beets, and Brussels sprouts have been joined by some marigolds and a patch of herbs.*

20ft (6m)

TOMATOES, SUMMER SQUASH & ONIONS *Use indeterminate tomatoes that do not require staking. The summer squash leaves will keep down weeds. Next to them, the onions need a space of their own.*

THE KEY ELEMENTS

ONION ARCH
The arch, which forms part of the woven willow screen, can be put to all kinds of additional uses. Here it has been adorned with a rope of onions that are finishing drying in the sun.

HANDSOME CURLY KALE
Curly kale should find a place in every cottage garden. It has a long season, can be picked in cold weather, and rarely fails to produce a handsome head of crinkled leaves.

PLANTING PLAN

With its easy informality, a cottage garden is the most adaptable of styles. This mix of vegetables, flowers, fruit, topiary, and quirky furniture fills an area 20 × 25ft (6 × 7.5m). Draw on the ideas to fill a space any size or shape.

BOUNDARY HEDGE *A mixture of useful species includes willow and hazel for sticks and honeysuckle for scent.*

PEAR TREE, ROSE & FLOWERS *A pear tree shades the seat and bears inviting fruit, while in front is an old-fashioned moss rose and space for growing annual flowers. A mixture of biennials lines the foot of the hedge.*

TAKE A SEAT

A seat, made from willow and hazel, has a natural, easy charm — the ideal place to rest weary limbs and watch the sun go down.

BLACKBERRIES & HOPS *These cover a screen woven from willows cut from the hedge. Choose a blackberry variety such as 'Oregon Thornless' that has pretty, finely cut leaves.*

VEGETABLES *Lettuce, leeks, parsnips, and red cabbage fill this bed, together with Florence fennel, a recent arrival in the cottage garden patch.*

PATH EDGINGS *Strawberries and English daisies line the paths. In the center they are joined by patches of nasturtiums.*

HOLLYHOCKS *The tall flower spikes, in the colors of an old tapestry, make a picturebook entrance at the side of the arch.*

PEAS & POTATOES *These were both staples of a cottager's diet. The peas would have been dried before being stored for the winter. Now they will be stashed in the freezer.*

PATHS *Made of beaten soil, these are covered with straw that can be raked up each season, put on the compost pile, and replaced with a fresh layer.*

BEAN WIGWAM *The wigwam is made of willow gathered from the hedge and is used to support a crop of scarlet runner beans.*

25ft (7.5m)

BOLD SUMMER SQUASH

Summer squash, growing larger and larger by the minute, put on a bold display, although they can soon outgrow their allotted corner.

THE CITY LARDER

EVEN IF YOU LIVE with your head in the clouds, 17 floors up in an apartment building, you may still be able to surround yourself with the fruits of your own labor by making a mini-kitchen garden in pots and grow bags on a balcony. Hungry vegetables, such as Brussels sprouts and celery, will never be happy growing in these conditions, but lettuces, tomatoes, peppers, and eggplants adapt well to life in the concrete jungle. Zucchini, snap beans, and cucumbers are other possibilities, together with cut-and-come-again salad crops that can be sown at frequent intervals through the season. Even hanging baskets can be used: certain tomatoes will produce a crop happily in a basket, provided you attend to the feeding and watering diligently. In a hot, dry summer you may have to water containers twice a day. Herbs such as marjoram, savory, sage, and thyme thrive in terracotta pots. Parsley and chives need a little more attention because both hate to dry out. Basil can be grown in small pots on a sunny windowsill, where it will flourish if given regular liquid feedings. An indoor windowsill is ideal, too, for crops of mustard, which can be sown on damp paper towels laid in trays. This is also the place to set up a little production line of sprouting beans. Fresh, they add crunch to salads or you can stir-fry them in a wok.

TUMBLING TOMATOES
These tomatoes droop and sprawl, a useful habit when growing in a hanging basket. Mix in some striped French marigolds to add interest while the fruit is still green, although once the tomatoes start to ripen they will have enough color of their own.

THE KEY ELEMENTS

An assortment of barrels, pots, baskets, and grow bags will transform a small space into an attractive yet efficient growing area. Most of the crops in this plan are in grow bags: one contains tomatoes and lettuce, another snap beans, a third cut-and-come-again salad crops. On an exposed balcony, you may need to put up heavy net inside the railings to filter the wind. Grow bags are very shallow and therefore dry out very quickly. You need to be methodical about watering and feeding. A concrete floor makes a cold base. Insulate the grow bags by slipping some polystyrene tiles under them. Tomatoes are greedy, so they should have the first turn in a grow bag. You can use it a second time for a less demanding crop, such as lettuce. Ease the roots of the previous crop out and fork the compost over. Do not feed new plants until they are well established, or you may get a build-up of unhelpful salts that will eventually retard growth rather than promote it. You can easily grow basil plants on a windowsill, where they will get plenty of light. From time to time, soak the pots in the sink, adding a few drops of liquid fertilizer to the water. Even the most hastily made salad or dish of pasta is improved by a whiff of basil.

JUMBO DISPLAY
For the greatest impact you need a profusion of plants in pots of every shape, height, and size. Grow scented geraniums to perfume the air, as well as culinary herbs, such as sage. In a crowded space all plants will need special attention.

PLANTING PLAN

This plan shows how a mouthwatering range of vegetables, fruit, and herbs can fit into a balcony only 7 × 5ft (2 × 1.5m). The growing methods used here can be adapted to the smallest of spaces, from roof gardens to minute backyards. Even the windowsill inside has been put to productive use, with pots of aromatic basil and jars of sprouting seeds.

AN EDIBLE WINDOWBOX
Just lean out of the window to pick the lettuce, strawberries, tomatoes, and cabbages that have been included in this planting, designed to make the best possible use of limited space.

BASIL, SPROUTING BEANS & MUSTARD *Fill the windowsill inside with jars of sprouting beans such as mung beans, trays of mustard, and pots of basil.*

BALLERINA APPLE TREE *On this new type of tree, the fruit forms directly on a single upright stem. It is ideal for a site like this, underplanted with spring bulbs and trailing lobelia.*

TOMATOES *Choose an indeterminate variety whose cherry-sized tomatoes will cascade from the basket. If you remember to water and feed them regularly you will be rewarded with a delicious crop.*

TOMATOES *Plant tall types in grow bags. Instead of using stakes, train them up the railings or tie them to a frame.*

CUT-AND-COME-AGAIN SALADS *Sprinkle a mixture of arugula, mizuna, and saladini seed into a grow bag and keep cutting the leaves as they sprout.*

PARSLEY *The tightly curled kind is the easiest to grow in a pot. It will do best in a shady corner where the pot is less inclined to dry out.*

SWEET PEPPERS *These will thrive in a pot, given shelter and sun. Raise seedlings indoors, or buy ready-grown plants to plant into large containers.*

HOT PEPPERS *As with sweet peppers, the best crops in cool climates often come from pot-grown plants. Choose a variety like 'Yellow Cayenne' or the prolific 'Apache', which will bear up to 100 hot peppers.*

SNAP BEANS *Use bush varieties. In midspring, sow individual seeds into 3-in (7-cm) pots, indoors. The plants should be ready to set out in a grow bag in late spring. Up to 12 plants will fit into one bag. Make sure that they are always watered well.*

PURPLE SAGE & CHIVES *Chive flowers look especially good next to the purple leaves of sage. Trim the sage regularly to stop it from getting straggly.*

LETTUCE *Grow an oak-leaf type around the tomatoes, and pick the leaves a few at a time.*

CALIFORNIAN COURTYARD

LEMONS AND TERRACOTTA POTS are the quintessential elements of a warm, sunny courtyard: the kind of garden you might create in southern California, on the shores of the Mediterranean, in western Australia perhaps, or in any other place where the winters are kind and hard frosts are as rare as sunshine in Siberia. A courtyard by its very nature will be a sheltered place, probably enclosed on two sides by the arms of the house to which it belongs. Here, a retaining wall, pierced with railings through which a patch of sunflowers peer, will break the force of winds coming from any other quarter. The paving that covers the courtyard is randomly laid, with sufficient cracks to encourage the growth of creeping thymes, marjoram, or camomile. Flowers, such as monkey-faced violas or the little Spanish daisy, *Erigeron karvinskianus*, can also seed themselves between the slabs. Although the area will probably be used primarily as an outdoor room, with chairs for lounging and a shady arbor for meals, there is still plenty of space for fan-trained peach trees, nectarines, and figs. If, when drawing up your own plan, you can add a small wall fountain, perhaps a benign lion's mask dripping into a stone trough beneath, you will be getting very close to Eden, California style.

THE TANG OF LEMONS
The fruit on a citrus tree looks curiously unreal, as though it might have been modeled from wax. Lemons can take up to a year to ripen. When they finally turn from green to yellow, the following season's flowers are beginning to open their thick, white petals and scent the air.

THE KEY ELEMENTS

The courtyard in the plan opposite contains two separate areas, linked by a long, low step. The area by the house is paved with large, random stone slabs, and the lower level is covered in gravel. Pots are an important feature: three handsome lemon trees in pots march along the stone curb. Bay trees in pots stand on either side of the railings, let into the retaining wall to give a view of the landscape beyond. A pomegranate sits in a large pot by the house, while in the sunny graveled area, massed lavender fills another swagged terracotta container. Shallow pots of fleshy-leaved aeoniums or sempervivums can be grouped wherever there is space. One door from the house opens directly into a shadowy arbor, made from rough poles lashed together with a vine trained up and over it to make a green, living roof. A passionflower, *Cobaea scandens,* and summer jasmine bring extra color and scent to the sitting area. A whole series of flowers colonizes the gravel and enjoys this sunbaked patch. Sunflowers fill the space between the bay trees, while iris, agapanthus, and gazanias sprawl in relaxed clumps elsewhere. In spring, the area is carpeted by dwarf bulbs – species tulips, crocus, and bright 'de Caen' anemones.

POTTED HIGHLIGHTS
Citrus trees in handsomely decorated pots give a garden a decidedly Mediterranean air. In a frost-free courtyard, lemons can be left outside all year. They do not need regular pruning, but you can trim them to shape if necessary.

PLANTING PLAN

The shape and exposure of your courtyard will, to some extent, determine the choice of plants. This plan shows just one way of creating a relaxing garden filled with fruit and the scent of herbs and flowers.

FLOWERS *Choose flowers such as iris and agapanthus that positively like to bake and will not droop if they spend a week without water.*

NECTARINE *Trained fruit trees in a courtyard can be used like wall-hangings in a room. Through the seasons a nectarine will provide a decorative sequence of flowers, foliage, and then fruit.*

LAVENDER *Plant one of the taller sorts, such as Lavandula angustifolia, for maximum effect and place it so that you can catch its aroma whenever you pass. Cut it back hard after it flowers to keep it in good shape.*

SUNFLOWERS *With their golden heads always turned toward the sun, a group of sunflowers put on a bold show through the railings. When the flowers have finished, dry the heads. The seeds can be eaten raw or roasted.*

BAYS *Two bay trees, trimmed into neat balls at the top, are placed on either side of the railings. Planted in large, simple terracotta pots, their clear-cut outlines stand out well among the more complex shapes of other plants in the courtyard.*

PEACH *A fan-trained peach will produce a first-rate crop in such a warm, sheltered spot. An apricot would be equally at home.*

FLAGSTONES *Tiny violas, daisies, and aromatic thyme and marjoram creep among the large, randomly laid paving stones.*

ARBOR *Formed by a grapevine scrambling over a lattice of rough wooden poles, the arbor makes a relaxed eating area. A passionflower, Cobaea scandens, and summer jasmine climb the three support poles at the front.*

ON THE VINE

Grapes are the ideal plant to shade a sunny terrace, their soft, refreshing leaves creating a cool, dappled light. Trained over a lattice roof, the bunches of fruit will hang temptingly through the crisscross of wooden rafters.

POMEGRANATE *This small tree will have clusters of showy scarlet flowers all summer long. Its fruit, ready in autumn, can be used to make a delicious jelly.*

WISTERIA *The variety chosen here has white flowers, giving the courtyard a cool elegance in the heat of the sun.*

FIG *A fan-trained fig tree not only provides melting, sensuous fruit, but also clothes the wall with splendid architectural foliage.*

LEMON TREES *The row of three lemon trees in pots signals the change in levels between the paved area and the semicircle of gravel.*

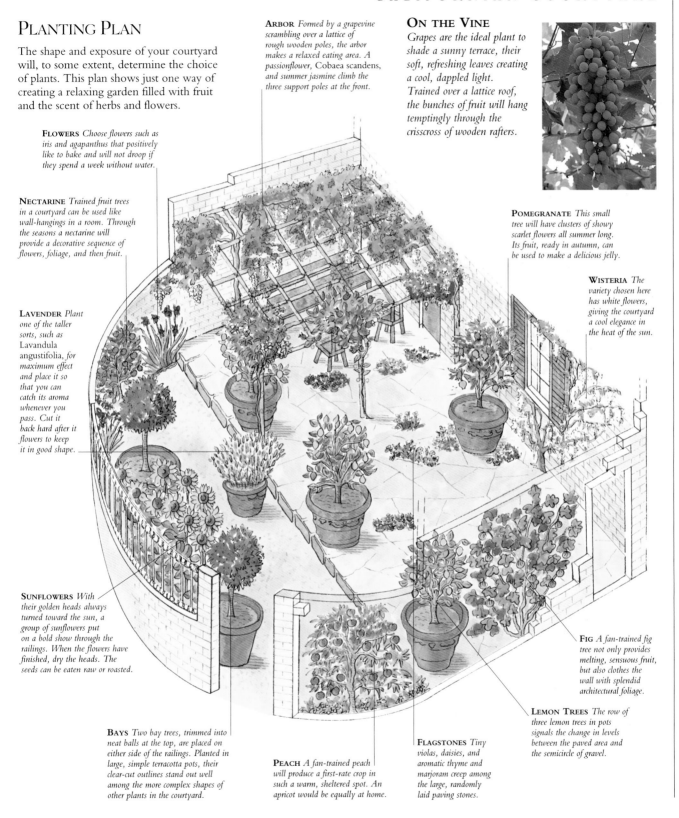

FORMAL HERB GARDEN

WHEN WE PLANT HYSSOP, the aromatic herb that flowers in midsummer in blue, white, and pink, how many of us really believe we are going to brew hyssop tea or produce hyssop honey? But we like the idea that one day we might, and it makes a pretty addition to the herb garden. Growing hyssop reassures us that we have not entirely cut ourselves adrift from a tradition of folk knowledge and thrifty housekeeping. In the big formal herb garden in Kinoith, Ireland, herbs grown for their looks, like hyssop and bergamot, are mixed with culinary types, such as sage. Massive buttresses of purple-leaved sage prop up a showy cardoon, and nasturtiums cavort at the feet of a monumental stand of lovage. The low boxwood hedges that edge the beds emphasize the garden's formal layout and provide frames for the plants inside. Evergreens, such as boxwood and sage, offer year-round interest and form. Three different kinds of sage, an excellent foliage plant in or out of an herb garden, are used in the plan on the following pages, where the emphasis is on herbs that are not just decorative but are indispensable to an avid cook.

MAKING AN HERB GARDEN

THE MOST USEFUL HERBS are those needed for cooking: thyme, basil, parsley, sage, and their kind. This design for a formal plot is planted with a collection for the kitchen, though if you wanted to create a bolder, more decorative effect, it would be easy to introduce some flowering herbs, such as bright blue hyssop, hazy lavender, or pink germander. The beds are edged alternately with tightly curled parsley and chives (left) and mop-headed standard roses mark the corners. In the center is a clipped bay tree, but it could be a small fountain with a simple jet of water, a statue, or an urn tumbling with scented geraniums. Herbs can be split roughly into two kinds: the Mediterranean aromatics, such as thyme, rosemary, and marjoram, which like hot sun and grow in poor soil; and others, such as mint, borage, and parsley, which need a cooler, richer soil in order to thrive. If one side of your projected herb patch is much warmer than the other, save it for the Mediterranean sunseekers. Paths in an herb garden need only be wide enough to shuffle along to pluck and weed. Brick, laid on edge, always looks satisfying. Gravel, as used here, is simple to use but needs low wooden edgings to keep it from shifting onto the soil. If the ground is not too mucky, leave the paths as bare beaten soil.

PLANTING PLAN

This mixture of annual herbs – which you can vary from season to season – and more permanent plants to give height and form has been chosen to fill a plot roughly 8ft 4in (2.6m) square. However, the design can be expanded or shrunk to fill whatever space is available.

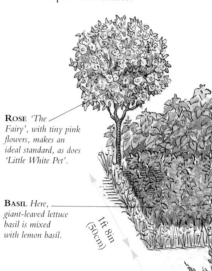

ROSE 'The Fairy', with tiny pink flowers, makes an ideal standard, as does 'Little White Pet'.

BASIL Here, giant-leaved lettuce basil is mixed with lemon basil.

1ft 8in (50cm)

1ft (30cm)

MINT In this bed, spearmint grows with gingermint, variegated applemint, and purplish eau de cologne mint.

3ft (1m)

THE KEY ELEMENTS

SAGE COMPANIONS
The deep velvety leaves of purple sage combine well with amber and yellow. For extra color, add orange pot marigolds or, as here, grow sage next to the golden pea flowers of dyer's greenweed (Genista tinctoria).

CHIVE EDGINGS
Lining paths with chives will give a continuous supply. Cut down the edgings in turn so that one will have just been harvested, the second resprouting, the third nearly ready, and the fourth at its peak.

MIXED MINTS
Mints have a bad name for putting themselves where they are not wanted. Plant a mixture of plain and variegated varieties in a bed together, where they can battle it out with each other.

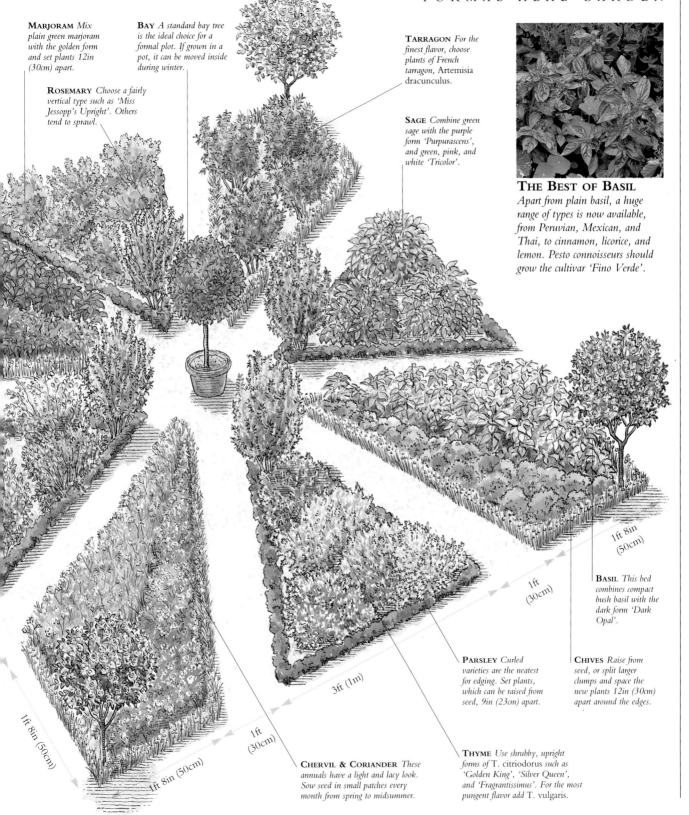

MARJORAM *Mix plain green marjoram with the golden form and set plants 12in (30cm) apart.*

BAY *A standard bay tree is the ideal choice for a formal plot. If grown in a pot, it can be moved inside during winter.*

ROSEMARY *Choose a fairly vertical type such as 'Miss Jessopp's Upright'. Others tend to sprawl.*

TARRAGON *For the finest flavor, choose plants of French tarragon, Artemisia dracunculus.*

SAGE *Combine green sage with the purple form 'Purpurascens', and green, pink, and white 'Tricolor'.*

THE BEST OF BASIL

Apart from plain basil, a huge range of types is now available, from Peruvian, Mexican, and Thai, to cinnamon, licorice, and lemon. Pesto connoisseurs should grow the cultivar 'Fino Verde'.

1ft 8in (50cm)

1ft (30cm)

BASIL *This bed combines compact bush basil with the dark form 'Dark Opal'.*

1ft 8in (50cm)

3ft (1m)

1ft (30cm)

PARSLEY *Curled varieties are the neatest for edging. Set plants, which can be raised from seed, 9in (23cm) apart.*

CHIVES *Raise from seed, or split larger clumps and space the new plants 12in (30cm) apart around the edges.*

1ft 8in (50cm)

1ft 8in (50cm)

1ft (30cm)

CHERVIL & CORIANDER *These annuals have a light and lacy look. Sow seed in small patches every month from spring to midsummer.*

THYME *Use shrubby, upright forms of T. citriodorus such as 'Golden King', 'Silver Queen', and 'Fragrantissimus'. For the most pungent flavor add T. vulgaris.*

2

GROWING VEGETABLES, HERBS & FRUIT

THE FOLLOWING PAGES give all the information you need to be able to grow a wide range of vegetables, herbs, and fruit to combine with flowers in a decorative kitchen garden. Cultivation techniques include full instructions on choosing the right place for each crop, advice on sowing, transplanting, thinning, and harvesting, as well as highlighting likely pests and diseases. There are details, too, for pruning and training fruit. You may already know which types of vegetables and fruit you want to grow. If you are not sure, you will find plenty here to inspire you.

VEGETABLES & HERBS

IF ON A MAP OF THE WORLD you drew
lines showing how different foods had traveled
from their countries of origin, you would end
up with a pattern more complex than a
spider's web. Before the discovery of the
Americas, the vegetable diet in Europe relied
heavily on peas and beans. The New World
proved a happy hunting ground, with corn
and tomatoes as well as potatoes enriching
gardens on both sides of the Atlantic. Some
vegetables traveled in the opposite direction.
In the pages ahead you can learn how to grow
more than 50 different vegetables and 20
different herbs. Stars highlight the best plants
for a decorative kitchen garden.

Leaf & Salad Vegetables

These include some of the lushest vegetables in the kitchen garden: winter cabbages in red and plum, crisp oriental brassicas, elegantly curled kale. Among this group you will find the ingredients for summer salads: frilly lettuce and peppery arugula, as well as a host of other leafy delights such as watercress, purslane, and mizuna. Many leaf vegetables are high in vitamins.

Fruiting & Flowering Vegetables

Warm oranges, yellows, and reds characterize the showiest members of this tribe, pumpkins and squash. Along with zucchini and cucumbers, they belong to the diverse family of cucurbits, originating in South and Central America. Tomatoes belong in this group, too, as does sweet corn. And here you will find the most dramatic vegetables – the artichoke and the cardoon, whose sculpted leaves rise from the ground in fountains of silver-gray.

Podded Vegetables

The pea and bean family produces two types of food, seeds and pods. You eat either or both, depending on when you gather the crop. This is not a large group, but in nutritional terms it is an important one, and the climbing members can be used to great decorative effect.

Bulb, Stem & Root Vegetables

Although this group does not include the most eyecatching vegetables, it contains some kitchen staples, such as onions, potatoes, garlic, and carrots, and one or two gourmet treats, such as asparagus. Leeks and carrots, in particular, can be grown with flowers to create some superb combinations.

Herbs

All the most useful herbs are here, divided into annuals, which must be sown each year, and perennials that will provide years of pleasure.

STAR PLANTS

❀ Especially decorative plants (see also page 200)

KEY TO CULTIVATION CHARTS

- ⚘ Sow inside
- ⚘ Sow outside
- ➤ Transplant
- ⚐ Harvest

The charts on the following pages give recommendations for cool climates; consult your Cooperative Extension Service for specifics in your area.

LEAF & SALAD VEGETABLES

SHOCK WAVES SPREAD THROUGH the florists' world back in the 1950s when the renowned flower arranger Constance Spry first put cabbage leaves among her delphiniums. But she saw what vegetable gardeners had always known: for texture, form, substance, and diversity, there is nothing like a cabbage leaf. Unless it is a lettuce leaf. These two vegetables provide endless opportunities for the gardener. For rich combinations seek out the black kale, sometimes called 'Chou Palmier', with narrow, upright leaves that are as sumptuously textured as tapestry. Combine it with wobbling heads of allium, purple iris, or deep blue columbines. Plant bronze fennel between rows of red cabbage, and sprinkle cornflowers among the endives.

CRIMPED KALE

The superbly handsome kale 'Chou Palmier', with its dark fronds, grows like a miniature palm tree. The texture, bubbly and finely crimped, is like that of a Savoy cabbage, and in France this kale has long been grown as an ornamental plant.

IN THE PINK

Pinks and purples complement each other in this planting that includes young plants of the cabbage 'Red Drumhead', the frilly rosettes of the lettuce 'Lolla Rossa', and the flowering heads of chives. Curly-leaved parsley and parsnip foliage fill in the spaces.

BRIGHTEST CHARD

Cold weather turns the green leaves of ruby chard to a shining purple that makes a dramatic setting for the bright red midribs. Try to arrange them so that light shines through the leaves. Keep them away from other strong tones to enjoy the singing color of the stems.

OUT OF THE EAST

Bok choi, seen here with young flowering shoots, is one of many Oriental vegetables that are increasingly being grown in Western gardens. Its shiny leaves, crunchy stems, and its flowerheads, which may be produced in the first year of growth, are all edible.

THE RED AND THE GREEN

Dark loose-leaf lettuce has been allowed to run to seed, making spires among the chunky shapes of green loose-leaf lettuce. The lettuce patch is surrounded by a thick border of nasturtiums. Here, the variety 'Alaska' has been chosen for its cream-and-green marbled leaves.

CABBAGES *Brassica oleracea* Capitata Group

CABBAGES HAVE AN IMAGE PROBLEM – they are considered inexpensive grocery staples. But once you have grown your own, they start to assume personalities. Where space is limited, the small-headed, early kinds are the ones to go for when too many other plants cry out for room to grow in the garden in summer. For the pleasure of looking at them as well as eating, you need a Savoy, with leaves more intricately puckered than smocking. The outer leaves make a chiseled, swirling skirt around the core. Red cabbages are less tactile, but the plum and gray coloring is beautiful.

Cultivation

For quick-cropping spring cabbages, try some succulent and tender early cabbages, which you plant in spring and harvest in summer. For cabbages with more body, try later cabbages, such as the lovely Savoy types or dense-headed and hardy, long-keeping cabbages. Long-keepers will store nicely out in the garden in mild fall and winter weather. In cold climates, bring them into a root cellar for winter storage.

SITE AND SOIL All brassicas are hearty eaters. They like ground that is rich and fertile, amended with well-rotted manure before planting. The ground need not be deeply dug before planting because cabbages prefer firmness around the roots. Cabbages will not thrive in shade or in soils where the pH less than 7.

SOWING You can buy transplants in early summer, letting someone else shoulder the responsibility of raising the cabbage plants from seed. However, you will then have to accept someone else's choice of varieties, and these may not be the most decorative. Sow seed in flats (see page 168). Transplant them to grow on in individual pots before planting them outdoors (see page 169).

THINNING AND TRANSPLANTING When the weather becomes mild in spring, harden off and transplant the seedlings into the garden. Set them about 24in (60cm) apart, planting them more deeply in the ground than they were growing in the flat (see page 171). Water them in well. When the water has drained away, firm the soil around the plants with your feet.

ROUTINE CARE Late cabbages will need to sit a long time in the ground working up to their grand harvest performance.

Extra rations, particularly nitrogen, should be offered to the cabbage plants during the long growing period.

YIELD AND HARVESTING The size of the heads varies enormously depending on growing conditions. Heads may weigh anything from 1lb (500g) to 3lb (1.5kg) each. Cut early cabbages as soon as they fill out. Late cabbages can wait into fall before harvesting.

PESTS AND DISEASES Clubroot is the worst problem (see page 193). You can try to prevent it by growing cabbage plants on a different patch each year. Do not compost cabbage plants. Liming helps: clubroot is less of a problem on alkaline soil (see page 161). Caterpillars are easily dealt with using an insecticide such as Bt. Use floating row covers to prevent root maggots (see opposite and pages 166 and 193).

RECOMMENDED CULTIVARS

SAVOY
'Julius': *early, vigorous, bright green heads.*
RED CABBAGE
'Super Red': *early and compact.*
EARLY CABBAGE
'Early Jersey Wakefield': *classic with 5-in (12-cm) heads.*
LATE CABBAGE
'Storage No.4': *firm-headed for fall harvest.*

	SPRING			SUMMER			AUTUMN			WINTER		
	Early	Mid	Late	Early	Mid	Late	Early	Mid	Late	Early	Mid	Late
	🌱	➡	➡	✂	✂							
	🌱	➡	➡				✂	✂				
☐ Early cabbage						☐ Late cabbage						

LATE CABBAGE
'Storage No.4'

❀ **SAVOY CABBAGE**

❀ **RED CABBAGE**
'Super Red'

❀ **'JANUARY KING' CABBAGE**

ROOT MAGGOTS
Place a circle of carpet padding around young plants to prevent the cabbage maggot from laying its eggs next to the stem. The maggots feast on the roots after hatching.

ORIENTAL BRASSICAS

BOK CHOI, CHINESE CABBAGE, KOMATSUNA, MIZUNA GREENS, and oriental mustards are still strangers in the average garden. Chinese cabbage, in fact, looks rather like a chunky lettuce, while mizuna greens, a relative of European cabbages and sprouts, has such delicately divided leaves that it is pretty enough to use as a foliage plant in its own right. Mix it in a barrel with trailing lobelia or set it among the bright yellow flowers of French marigolds. You could plant up a whole container of oriental specialties: white-flowered Chinese chives, mizuna greens, coriander, a Chinese cabbage, and perhaps some chrysanthemum greens. These look like ordinary garden chrysanthemums, but it is the leaf that you eat.

Cultivation

The easiest way to grow oriental vegetables in a decorative kitchen garden is as a cut-and-come-again crop, sometimes called oriental mesclun. Sow seed of bok choi (*Brassica rapa* var. *chinensis*), loose-leaf Chinese cabbage (*Brassica rapa* var. *pekinensis*), mizuna greens (*Brassica rapa* var. *nipposinica*), and komatsuna, also known as mustard spinach (*Brassica rapa* var. *perviridis*), mixed together in roughly equal quantities, and cut it at seedling stage. For extra variety, add an ornamental lettuce such as 'Red Salad Bowl' and oriental mustards (*Brassica juncea*) to give spice to the mix. Most oriental greens are fast growing and will provide a speedy spring crop. Late summer and autumn sowings (the later ones in a cold frame in northern climates) will provide a succession of baby leaves in autumn and winter.

SITE AND SOIL Oriental brassicas need fertile, moisture-retentive soil and an endless supply of water.

SOWING Cut-and-come-again crops can be sown over a long season from spring until autumn (see pages 170–71). Broadcast the seed over a bed or sow in wide furrows. For individual crops, sow seed in rows, little and often, about ½ in (1cm) deep, scattering it thinly. Or you can sow groups of 3–4 seeds at 4-in (10-cm) intervals along the row and then thin to leave the strongest seedling. The earliest sowings do best under a floating row cover (see page 166) to warm the soil. Avoid sowing bok choi or Chinese cabbage too early since they tend to bolt. Low temperatures when seeds are germinating or lack of moisture as the plants are growing are likely causes.

THINNING Thin seedlings as necessary (see page 171). Cut-and-come-again crops need little thinning. Leave plenty of space, up to 12in (30cm), between large vegetables that are growing in rows.

ROUTINE CARE Keep plants well watered at all times. This will also encourage fresh growth on cut-and-come-again crops.

YIELD AND HARVESTING In ideal conditions, bok choi may be ready to pick 6 weeks after sowing, komatsuna after 8, Chinese cabbage after 8–10, and mizuna greens after 10. Oriental mustards take 6–13 weeks. Harvest promptly: they do not stand long in an ideal state. You can usually start picking cut-and-come-again crops after a month and then take 3 later cuts. Cut above the base of the leaves (see page 63) to ensure the plants resprout.

PESTS AND DISEASES Unfortunately, the cabbage maggot is just as partial to Eastern brassicas as it is to Western ones, so take precautions (see pages 57 and 191).

RECOMMENDED CULTIVARS

There are few cultivars for most of these vegetables, with the following exceptions.
CHINESE CABBAGE
'Blues': *slow-bolting and disease tolerant for spring and fall crops.*
'Kyoto No.3': *late cabbage for storage.*
'Santo': *good for cut-and-come-again crops.*
BOK CHOI
'Mei Quing Choi': *fast-maturing miniature.*

✿ BOK CHOI

CHINESE
CABBAGE

ORIENTAL
MUSTARD

KOMATSUNA GREENS

*Komatsuna greens, or mustard spinach, have
the flavor of cabbage combined with spinach.
They grow well in a range of temperatures and
are less inclined to bolt than Chinese cabbage.*

✿ MIZUNA GREENS

*Mizuna greens are wonderfully versatile. They
are pretty enough to fill beds in a potager or line
the edges of paths, and they grow well in
temperatures from summer heat to winter cold.*

BRUSSELS SPROUTS & KALE
Brassica oleracea Gemmifera & Acephala Groups

SPROUTS AND BRUSSELS GO TOGETHER like tea and China. The Belgians discovered the first sprout plant around 1750 and have made sure the rest of the world does not forget it. One sprout plant tends to look much like another, but there is a reddish-green type called 'Rubine' that can be used to decorative effect in the garden. Kales are the oldest kind of cabbage and are sometimes dismissed (unfairly) as cattle fodder. They are bulky, hardy vegetables that grow briskly and linger in the garden despite cold weather, allowing you to harvest fresh greens deep into fall or even winter. Kale does not make a head, as a cabbage does; instead, the leaves splay out like a palm tree. The curly kinds can be used as tall foliage plants in a border. Experiment with the handsome 'Russian Red' or the stunning pink-leaved 'Flowering Kale'.

BRUSSELS SPROUTS 'Prince Marvel'

⚜ KALE 'Dwarf Green Curled'

Cultivation

Both are handsome vegetables and add a dramatic touch to the kitchen garden. Set them in the same bed so they can be left undisturbed all season.

SITE AND SOIL Brussels sprouts do best in medium to heavy soil that is well drained and not recently manured. Too much nitrogen makes the sprouts very loose and elongated. The pH should be around 6.5. Kale will tolerate poorer soil.

SOWING Start Brussels sprouts plants indoors under lights in late spring, 4–6 weeks before transplanting outside. Indoor-sown kale seedlings must be set outside in mid- to late summer. In areas with long growing seasons, direct sow Brussels sprouts, but allow them 4 months or so to mature. Direct sow kale starting 3 months before the first fall frost. Set kale and sprout seed in shallow furrows in a seedbed, just under ½in (1cm) deep.

TRANSPLANTING Plant out Brussels sprouts seedlings in their final position in early summer, 24in (60cm) apart each way. For smaller sprouts, reduce the spacing. Thin direct-sown Brussels sprouts to similar spacing. Thin direct-sown kale plants to 12in (30cm) apart or 30in (75cm) for tall types. Water plants well.

ROUTINE CARE Hill up soil around the stem bases (see page 167), to keep the plants stable.

YIELD AND HARVESTING Expect about 2lb (1kg) of sprouts from a single plant and the same weight of shoots or young leaves from kale. Sprouts can be picked from early autumn until the new year. Start picking from the bottom upward. Kale can be cropped from late autumn to early spring.

PESTS AND DISEASES The worst problem is clubroot (see page 193). Aphids may also hide in the sprout buttons (see page 190).

RECOMMENDED CULTIVARS

BRUSSELS SPROUTS
'Oliver': *extra-early with large sprouts.*
'Prince Marvel': *hardy and productive.*
KALE
'Flowering Kale': *turns beautifully white or pink in fall.* **'Dwarf Green Curled'**: *wide-spreading, curly leaves.* **'Pentland Brig'**: *masses of succulent shoots in late winter.*
'Russian Red': *purple leaves with red ribs.*

SPRING			SUMMER			AUTUMN			WINTER		
Early	Mid	Late	Early	Mid	Late	Early	Mid	Late	Early	Mid	Late
	🌱	➡				✂	✂	✂	✂	✂	
	🌱		🌱	➡	➡						
✂							✂	✂	✂	✂	✂

☐ Brussels Sprouts   ☐ Kale

SPINACH *Spinacia oleracea*

SPINACH HAS TWO USEFUL ATTRIBUTES. It will grow in light shade if the ground is moist, and it is also very fast. True spinach is an annual, and the one aim of an annual is to set seed and perpetuate itself. In hot, dry conditions, this works against the spinach fancier. Instead of pausing to produce a feast of leaves, the plant races on up to maturity, leaving only an unusable crop of creamish-green seed.

Cultivation

Little and often is the best way to sow spinach. It is most likely to succeed in rich, damp soil in cool conditions. Feast on it in spring and autumn (or winter in mild climates), and do not expect much from the summer crops. On hot, dry soils, New Zealand spinach (a different, nonhardy species with smaller, fleshy leaves) is more likely to succeed. These are the greens that the intrepid 18th-century voyager Captain Cook collected in New Zealand to prevent his sailors from getting scurvy.

SITE AND SOIL Spinach is a great gobbler of nitrogen. Ground can scarcely be too rich for it. It tolerates light shade, but not dryness. New Zealand spinach is more tolerant of dry, poor conditions.

SOWING For an early crop, sow seed every 2–3 weeks from early to late spring, setting it not more than ⅝in (1.5cm) deep in rows 12in (30cm) apart. For a late crop, sow late summer to early autumn. Sow seed of New Zealand spinach ½in (1cm) deep in rows 15in (38cm) apart.

THINNING Thin early spinach to 6in (15cm) between plants, and late crops to 9in (23cm). Thin New Zealand spinach seedlings to 8in (20cm) apart.

ROUTINE CARE Spinach must never be short of water, and on infertile soils extra feeding is beneficial. In exposed areas, winter crops may need cold frames.

YIELD AND HARVESTING Expect about 5–10lb (2.5–5kg) from a 10-ft (3-m) row.

SPINACH 'Space'

NEW ZEALAND SPINACH

PESTS AND DISEASES Downy mildew is the most prevalent disease (see page 193). Thin plants to allow good air circulation.

RECOMMENDED CULTIVARS

New Zealand: *named cultivars not available.*
'Space': *smooth-leaved, mildew resistant.*
'Tyee': *bolt-resistant, mildew-tolerant foliage.*

	SPRING			SUMMER			AUTUMN			WINTER		
	Early	Mid	Late	Early	Mid	Late	Early	Mid	Late	Early	Mid	Late
	⚘	⚘	⚘		⚘	⚘						
		✁	✁	✁		✁	✁					
		⚘	⚘		✁	✁						

☐ Spinach   ☐ New Zealand spinach

IN THE KITCHEN

Spinach can be used in many different ways: in a soufflé, served as a simple purée, or combined with spices as a tangy stuffing. This recipe is excellent inside a boned and rolled shoulder of lamb. You can also pile it into an earthenware dish and roast it in the oven alongside a chicken.

SPINACH STUFFING
Serves 4

½ large mild Spanish onion, finely chopped
2 tbsp (30g) butter
8 cups (250g) spinach, washed
½ lb (250g) sausage links, skin removed
1 egg, beaten
1 tbsp parsley, finely chopped
salt and black pepper
nutmeg and mace, to taste

1 Sauté the onion gently in the butter until it has become soft and transparent.

2 In another pan, cook the spinach until it is limp (it will cook in the moisture remaining on the leaves after washing), then chop finely.

3 Combine the onion and spinach with the sausage meat, egg, parsley, salt, pepper, and spices in a large bowl, and mix well. Use it to stuff a boned shoulder of lamb, spreading the stuffing over the flattened-out meat. Roll it up like a jelly roll and secure it firmly with skewers or string.

CULINARY NOTES

❧ When cooking spinach, use no more water than remains on the leaves after washing. After cooking, press the leaves in a colander to remove any excess moisture.

❧ A little grated nutmeg enhances the flavor of cooked spinach particularly well.

LETTUCE *Lactuca sativa*

OF ALL DESIGNER VEGETABLES, lettuce is the most versatile, because it presents itself in so many different guises and adapts itself to so many uses in the garden. The ferny, frilly, loose-leaf kinds can be used as foliage plants between bright groups of annual flowers or to make a salad garden with multicolored pot marigolds in a windowbox. You can use a variety such as 'Red Salad Bowl' to line paths or edge a raised bed, a small butterhead like 'Tom Thumb', all heart, to fill beds in a modest knot garden, and crisp and crunchy 'Rosalita' to frame tomatoes in a grow bag.

Cultivation

There are four types of lettuce to choose from: soft butterheads, upright romaine, dense crispheads, and long-lasting loose-leaf varieties. Differences between them have as much to do with texture as with taste and it is useful to grow several kinds, bearing in mind that romaine types take longer to mature than butterheads, and loose-leaf varieties can be cut at an earlier age. Seed keeps from one year to the next so it is not too expensive to experiment.

SITE AND SOIL Lettuce grows best on soil that is light and fertile, but retains moisture. It does not mind partial shade.

SOWING If you sow seed every 2 weeks, you should have a nonstop supply from spring until autumn in cool climates or fall, winter, and spring in warm climates. But unpredictable weather can cause unpredictable crops. In hot weather, germination is erratic; in drought, growth is sluggish. Little and often is the best way to sow seed, directly outside (see page 170), ½in (1cm) deep, in rows 6in (15cm) apart for small cultivars like 'Little Gem', 12in (30cm) apart for large types like 'Lollo Rossa'. Or, you can start seedlings indoors 3 weeks before planting out. Autumn and winter crops require a cold frame or greenhouse.

THINNING Thin small cultivars to 6in (15cm) apart and large types to 12in (30cm) apart. Make the first thinning about a month after sowing when seedlings are 2in (5cm) tall (see page 171). Thinnings transplant well at the start of the season. Once it turns hot and dry, it is hard to persuade them to settle.

ROUTINE CARE Lettuce needs plenty of water while growing, but not too much feeding: scientific tests have shown that excess nitrogen makes it bitter. Water in the morning rather than the evening, when leaves dry off quickly and are less prone to attacks of downy mildew.

YIELD AND HARVESTING A 10-ft (3-m) row gives roughly 10–20 lettuces. Harvest loose-leaf types a few leaves at a time.

PESTS AND DISEASES Slugs, aphids, cutworms, downy mildew, and root rot can all be problems (see pages 190–93).

RECOMMENDED CULTIVARS

BUTTERHEAD
'All the Year Round': *very long season.*
'Tom Thumb': *small but large-hearted.*
ROMAINE (COS)
'Parris Island Cos': *classic long, stiff leaves with creamy hearts.* **'Little Gem'**: *fast-growing semicos, the best of its kind.*
'Rosalita': *red-tipped leaves on early heads.*
CRISPHEAD
'Iceberg': *crunchy texture and long-lasting.*
'Ithaca': *extra-reliable in fertile soil.*
LOOSE-LEAF
'Lollo Rossa': *frilly with red-fringed leaves.*
'Red Salad Bowl': *lasts a long time.*

SPRING			SUMMER			AUTUMN			WINTER		
Early	Mid	Late	Early	Mid	Late	Early	Mid	Late	Early	Mid	Late
🌱	🌱	🌱	🌱	🌱							
	➡										
					✂	✂	✂				
🌱	🌱	🌱									
	➡		🌱	🌱							
					✂	✂	✂	✂			

☐ Other lettuce   ☐ Loose-leaf lettuce

IN THE KITCHEN

John Parkinson, the 17th-century granddaddy of all garden writers, recommended lettuce for "Monkes, Nunnes and the like of people . . . to keep them chase." Poor Nunnes: lettuce on its own is not much of a diet. Like pastry, it provides a background for other livelier ingredients – such as walnut oil, olives, hard-cooked eggs, and anchovies.

LETTUCE, BACON, AND BLUE CHEESE SALAD
Serves 4

½lb (250g) smoked bacon
1 crisphead lettuce (such as 'Iceberg')
1 bunch watercress
1lb (500g) small tomatoes
2 avocados
4 tbsp lemon juice
8oz (250g) Gorgonzola cheese, sliced
4 tbsp olive oil
2 tbsp red wine vinegar
1 tsp coarse-grain mustard
2 tbsp honey

1 Grill the bacon until it is crisp and crumble it.

2 Wash the lettuce and watercress, then gently pat the leaves dry. Halve the tomatoes and mix with the bacon, lettuce, and watercress.

3 Peel and slice the avocados and dress them with lemon juice to prevent discoloration. Add them to the salad with the cheese.

4 Combine the remaining ingredients to make a dressing and pour it over the salad just before serving.

CULINARY NOTES

❧ Use the inner leaves of romaine lettuce as crunchy scoops for dips.

❧ Braise lettuce leaves with fresh young peas, some chopped onion, a pat of butter, and a little water for the French classic *petits pois à l'étuvée.*

❀ **SEMICOS
LETTUCE**
'Little Gem'

**BUTTERHEAD
LETTUCE**
'All the Year
Round'

**ROMAINE
(COS) LETTUCE**
'Parris Island Cos'

❀ **LOOSE-LEAF
LETTUCE**
'Lollo Rossa'

❀ **CRISPHEAD
LETTUCE**
'Iceberg'

CUT-AND-COME-AGAIN

*This method of growing salad
leaves is ideal for a small garden.
Choose loose-leaf varieties and
start cropping when the plants are
3–6in (7–15cm) high, cutting
them just above the lowest leaves.
They will then resprout from the
remaining 1½in (3cm) of stem.*

OTHER SALAD LEAVES

WATERCRESS, SUMMER PURSLANE, CORN SALAD (MÂCHE), AND MUSTARD AND CRESS are all useful to add a tang to a salad bowl. In the garden, you can grow them as catch crops between other slower-growing vegetables. Since the seeds germinate fast – mustard and cress can be cut within two weeks of sowing – you can use them to make instant edgings or to "paint" patterns in a bed. Mark out a diamond trellis in the soil and sow along the lines of the pattern. Children like seeing their initials rise magically from the ground. Sharp-tasting summer purslane is best as a seedling cut-and-come-again crop. It needs a warm spot to grow well. Corn salad, or lamb's lettuce, is very hardy and is eaten as a cool-season substitute for lettuce. Watercress, too, is at its best in cool weather. It can be grown without running water, but will not be quite as succulent.

WATERCRESS

SUMMER PURSLANE

CORN SALAD

MUSTARD   **CRESS**

Cultivation

However smoothly you try to plan the production of these salad crops, sowings either catch up with each other or else dawdle like recalcitrant racehorses to widen the gap between themselves and the crop in front. Sow little but often.
SITE AND SOIL You would not want to give up your best ground to these crops. They must make do with what they are given. **Watercress,** however, will succeed only in a moist, shady bed and is happiest of all growing in a stream.
SOWING Sow small quantities of **mustard and cress** at weekly intervals for a continuous supply. It grows well on wads of damp newspaper, paper towels, or towels on a windowsill. You can sow it outside in furrows (see page 170), barely covering the seed with soil. Canola seed (*Brassica napus*) is often substituted for true mustard. If growing this crop inside, wait for 3 days before sprinkling the mustard or canola seed on top of the cress. Then they germinate together. Sow **corn salad** in late spring for a summer crop or in late summer for fall or winter. Sow seed thinly, just under ½in (1cm) deep, in a row if you want to thin or transplant seedlings later. Broadcast seed over a wide bed (see page 170) for a cut-and-come-again crop. Corn salad is slow to resprout, so it is often better transplanted to grow to maturity. Set out young plants 4in (10cm) apart, in rows that are 12in (30cm) apart.
Summer purslane can be sown outdoors in early summer. Broadcast the seed (see page 171) for a cut-and-come-again crop.
Watercress is best when it is grown from rooted cuttings (stems will readily produce roots in a jar of water). Make a narrow trench, 2in (5cm) deep, with a hoe and fill it with water until it is really soggy. Dribble sand in the trench about 1in (2cm) deep and then, using a dibber or stick, make small holes in it about 6in (15cm) apart. Drop the cuttings into the holes and water frequently.
THINNING Thin **corn salad**, if necessary, to about 4in (10cm) apart. **Summer purslane** will not need thinning if used as a seedling crop, nor will **mustard and cress,** nor **watercress** if planted at the spacing given above.
ROUTINE CARE Watering and weeding are all that is required.
YIELD AND HARVESTING Yield depends on the time of year and the stage at which you harvest the crop. You can gather individual leaves from **summer purslane**, **corn salad,** and **watercress**, or cut the whole plant. Snip **mustard and cress** with scissors.
PESTS AND DISEASES These crops are generally free of troubles.

Check specialty catalogs for cultivars.

CHARD & LEAF BEET
Beta vulgaris Cicla Group

RED-STEMMED CHARD HAS A DRAMATIC BEAUTY in the vegetable garden, but it needs to be well grown. If you can nurse it through the early stages without upsetting it, it will develop into a superb plant. Its glowing red stems are topped by luxuriant, crinkled foliage, either green or, in the variety 'Burgundy', deep purplish-ruby. The leaf stalks are broad and meaty, and you eat these and the leaves separately. Chard is used to magnificent effect in the vast potager at Villandry in France, where the ruby stems are set off against deep red roses and the blue spikes of *Salvia superba*. Leaf beet, or perpetual spinach as it is sometimes called, has a much smaller midrib. It is often used as a substitute for true spinach, a much trickier crop to grow, but the flavor is not as fine.

❀ **RED-STEMMED CHARD**

WHITE-STEMMED CHARD

LEAF BEET

Cultivation

Chard is a biennial and can usually be cropped over a long period before running to seed in its second season. Once through the ticklish early stages, it will survive quite well in drought conditions but, if checked in the first two or three months of its life, it will forget all about being a biennial and run straight to seed. Those people who consider themselves to be connoisseurs of chard claim that the steamed stalks, especially those of white-stemmed varieties, are as good as asparagus, but the taste is more watery and less concentrated. Leaf beet, sometimes called perpetual spinach or spinach beet, is also biennial and fairly tolerant of drought. This makes it a useful, if slightly coarse-flavored, substitute for true spinach, especially if it is grown on ground that does not retain moisture.

SITE AND SOIL Chard and leaf beet like fertile soil, rich in nitrogen. Add plenty of manure or compost. If it can be arranged in your planting timetable, they make good late crops after peas or beans.

SOWING Sow chard and leaf beet from late spring to midsummer, setting the seed no deeper than ¾in (1.5cm) in rows 15–18in (38–45cm) apart (see page 170). The plants should then crop through the winter in mild climates, until late spring of the following year, when they will start to run to seed. Both crops will run to seed in the same year if they are sown too early.

THINNING These grow into fairly large plants, so allow room for them to develop. Thin seedlings to at least 12in (30cm) apart in the row (see page 171).

ROUTINE CARE The early stages are by far the most critical, especially for chard. Keep young plants growing smoothly by providing sufficient water and plenty of liquid fertilizer. Mulch to conserve moisture.

YIELD AND HARVESTING Expect about 7lb (3.5kg) from a 10-ft (3-m) row. Pull, rather than cut, the stems as required. Be very careful not to take too many leaves from any one plant at a time. Otherwise the plant may not be able to recover.

PESTS AND DISEASES These are generally easily grown, trouble-free crops.

RECOMMENDED CULTIVARS

CHARD
'Lucullus': *white stems, dark green foliage.*
'Rhubarb Chard': *bright scarlet ribs.*
'Burgundy': *purplish-red stems.*
LEAF BEET
Also sometimes listed in catalogs as perpetual spinach. Named cultivars are not generally available.

SPRING			SUMMER			AUTUMN			WINTER		
Early	Mid	Late	Early	Mid	Late	Early	Mid	Late	Early	Mid	Late
		⚘	⚘	⚘	✄	✄	✄	✄	✄	✄	✄
✄	✄	✄									

CHICORY & ENDIVE
Cichorium intybus & C. endivia

THESE ARE DESIGNER VEGETABLES *par excellence*. You could fill a potager with combinations of this group, contrasting the smooth leaves of chicory with a shaggy endive, or playing with the marbled colors of the red chicories, often called radicchio. The names are muddling. In France, curly endive is called *chicorée frisée* and chicory, which looks like a small cream bomb, is called Belgian endive in much of North America. In growing terms, the major difference is that curly endive is an annual. Belgian endive is not and, in its second year, will produce sheaves of blue flowers.

❀ **RADICCHIO** 'Chioggia'

BELGIAN ENDIVE 'Witloof'

Cultivation

To blanch or not to blanch, that is the question. Blanching alleviates the bitterness that is a characteristic of both of these salad crops. With Belgian endive, of course, it is essential. With the other types of endive, such as the frizzy specimens, you can experiment. For example, you can try blanching hearts using a plate or saucer turned upside down, or blanch an entire plant by covering it up completely with an overturned bucket or flowerpot. The French use chic little caps, like berets, to blanch the hearts. An upturned plate does the same thing, though less stylishly.

SITE AND SOIL Both crops need fertile, well-drained soil, preferably in full sun.

SOWING Radicchio (red chicory) seeds can be sown in spring and summer, using early or late-maturing cultivars. Sow ½in (1cm) deep in rows 10–12in (25–30cm) apart. Sow Belgian (blanching) endive seeds in spring as thinly as possible, ½in (1cm) deep, in rows 12in (30cm) apart. The best time to sow curly endive is spring for summer harvest or summer for fall harvest. Sow ½in (1cm) deep in rows 10–15in (25–38cm) apart. Escarole seeds should be sown at the same depth and spacing. Sow in spring in cold climates or summer in warm climates.

THINNING Thin Belgian endive to 9in (23cm) apart and escarole to 10–12in (25–30cm). This spacing also suits most curly endives but the very large types need to be 12–15in (30–38cm) apart.

ROUTINE CARE Keep the plants weeded and well watered during the months between sowing and harvesting.

FORCING AND BLANCHING To force Belgian endive, lift the roots in fall, discarding any which are very thin. Trim the leaves 1in (2cm) above the neck, pack the roots flat in a box of sand, and store in a cool place until you need them. Take them out to force a few at a time. Trim off sideshoots and shorten the main roots to 6in (15cm). Pack the roots in moist soil. You can fit 3–6 in a 9-in (23-cm) flowerpot. Put another pot over the first and store at 60° F (15°C); chicons (the blanched heads) develop in about 3 weeks. In a cool cellar – not below 50°F (10°C) – forcing will take longer.

YIELD AND HARVESTING Expect about 6lb (3kg) of Belgian endive, or 10–15 heads of chicory or endive, from a 10-ft (3-m) row. Cut forced chicons when they are 5–6in (12–15cm) long. Treat chicory and endive like lettuce, picking a few leaves at a time. If you cut whole heads, leave 1in (2cm) or so of the neck, which will then resprout.

PESTS AND DISEASES Chicory and endive are robust vegetables and usually trouble-free, but they may rot in hot weather. Rot can also set in if you blanch the vegetables when the foliage is wet.

RECOMMENDED CULTIVARS

RADICCHIO/RED CHICORY
'Chioggia': *early, with red and white leaves.*
'Giulio': *slow bolting*
BELGIAN ENDIVE
'Witloof': *traditional cultivar for forcing.*
CURLY ENDIVE
'Green Curled': *pretty, frilly head.*
ESCAROLE
'Broad-leaved Batavian': *large leaves surround creamy heads.*

	SPRING			SUMMER			AUTUMN			WINTER		
	Early	Mid	Late	Early	Mid	Late	Early	Mid	Late	Early	Mid	Late
		⚘	⚘		⚘	⚘						
				✂	✂	✂	✂	✂				
		⚘	⚘						✂	✂		
		⚘	⚘		⚘	⚘						
						✂	✂	✂	✂			
		⚘	⚘		⚘	⚘						
						✂	✂	✂	✂			

☐ Radicchio/Red chicory   ☐ Curly endive
☐ Belgian endive   ☐ Escarole

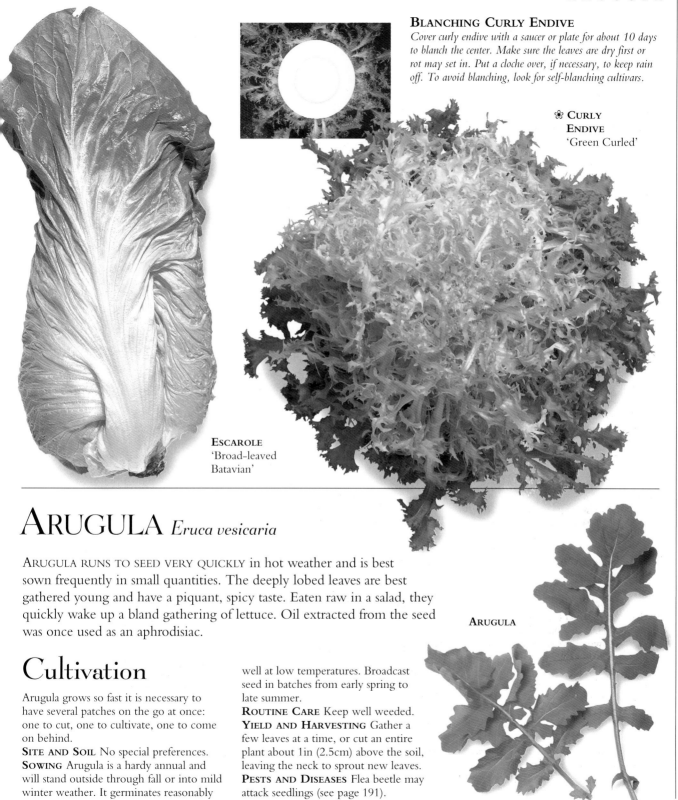

BLANCHING CURLY ENDIVE
Cover curly endive with a saucer or plate for about 10 days to blanch the center. Make sure the leaves are dry first or rot may set in. Put a cloche over, if necessary, to keep rain off. To avoid blanching, look for self-blanching cultivars.

❀ **CURLY ENDIVE** 'Green Curled'

ESCAROLE 'Broad-leaved Batavian'

ARUGULA

ARUGULA *Eruca vesicaria*

ARUGULA RUNS TO SEED VERY QUICKLY in hot weather and is best sown frequently in small quantities. The deeply lobed leaves are best gathered young and have a piquant, spicy taste. Eaten raw in a salad, they quickly wake up a bland gathering of lettuce. Oil extracted from the seed was once used as an aphrodisiac.

Cultivation

Arugula grows so fast it is necessary to have several patches on the go at once: one to cut, one to cultivate, one to come on behind.
SITE AND SOIL No special preferences.
SOWING Arugula is a hardy annual and will stand outside through fall or into mild winter weather. It germinates reasonably well at low temperatures. Broadcast seed in batches from early spring to late summer.
ROUTINE CARE Keep well weeded.
YIELD AND HARVESTING Gather a few leaves at a time, or cut an entire plant about 1in (2.5cm) above the soil, leaving the neck to sprout new leaves.
PESTS AND DISEASES Flea beetle may attack seedlings (see page 191).

FRUITING & FLOWERING VEGETABLES

EXCEPT FOR CAULIFLOWER AND BROCCOLI, this group of plants hates frost. In cold areas, they cannot go out until early summer, but once planted, they grow rapidly and peak in a rich harvest of golds, greens, and oranges in autumn. Zucchini, squash, and pumpkins can be used to great effect trailing over the ground between upright blocks of sweet corn or securely tied staked tomatoes. In this respect, they are natural companions, one needing vertical space, and the other horizontal. Squashes can be striped, spotted, shiny pewter gray, or as vivid as a setting sun. This family alone could make a splendidly decorative summer bed.

PUMPKIN HARVEST

Each large enough to serve as Cinderella's coach, these pumpkins are being cured in the sun before being stored. Enormous cultivars such as these are stunning to look at and extremely showy, but cooks may find the smaller types more practical in the kitchen.

PLANT SCULPTURE

A whole avenue of globe artichokes is planted in this narrow border. Spectacular plants at their peak, with sculpted, arching foliage, they leave little room for other plants around them. In a smaller space, use a single plant as a centerpiece for a potager or herb garden.

GLOSSY EGGPLANT

Few plants can boast of fruit as glossily polished as the eggplant. In very cool areas it succeeds best in a greenhouse border. Elsewhere, you can grow eggplants in containers. Group them with pots of hot peppers and trailing cascades of cherry tomatoes.

FLOWERING SQUASH

The trailing stems of pumpkins and squashes can easily be trained over arches or supports like this wigwam of bamboo stakes. Use cultivars with smallish fruit. The extraordinary shapes and colors of many of the squashes will make a spectacular end to the season.

CREAM OF THE CAULIFLOWERS

The smooth curds of unblemished cauliflower have the strange texture of an underwater sponge, the heart protected by great, contrasting leaves of green. But cauliflower is not an easy crop to grow well and, like many other brassicas, needs a long growing period before it comes to fruition.

CAULIFLOWERS
Brassica oleracea Botrytis Group

IF YOU CAN GROW A GOOD CAULIFLOWER, you can award yourself maximum merit stars. They are not easy vegetables to bring to crisp perfection and will produce only small, misshapen heads if their growth is checked in any way. Cauliflowers are generally creamy white, the heads surrounded by a crisp green frill of leaves, but there are also lime green and purple varieties. Cauliflowers grow best in mild temperatures that hover around 60°F (15°C). Identify when you enjoy this temperature and grow your plants then. If this time is brief, grow early cultivars or less picky, later maturing purple- or green-headed varieties.

CREAM CAULIFLOWER

Cultivation

In cool climates, you can grow cauliflower for summer or fall harvesting. In mild climates, you can overwinter cultivars for harvest in spring. If you have only a short period of cool weather, grow quick-maturing cultivars such as 'Snow Crown'. Later-maturing fall cultivars such as 'Dok Elgon' need cool fall temperatures to develop a nice head. Mini-cauliflowers are useful for filling small beds in a potager.

SITE AND SOIL Cauliflowers like a more alkaline soil than other brassicas. Acid soils, even if limed, may not produce worthwhile crops. They need deeply dug, fertile soil with enough moisture for them to grow smoothly and productively.

SOWING Start seedlings indoors 4–6 weeks before the last spring frost or ideal planting date (see page 168). Where seasons are long and mild, or when mini-cauliflowers are used, sow seeds outdoors, ½in (1cm) deep (see page 170).

TRANSPLANTING Transplant vigorous young seedlings outdoors when spring weather becomes mild and the threat of frost has passed. Disturb the roots as little as possible (see page 171). You can plant late-maturing cultivars a little later than early-maturing cultivars. Allow at least 24in (60cm) between plants in the row, and space the rows 24in (60cm) apart. Mini-cauliflowers can be planted closer together – 6in (15cm) apart each way.

ROUTINE CARE Water frequently throughout the growing season and keep them well weeded. Mulch to conserve moisture in the soil.

YIELD AND HARVESTING You will get about 6 cauliflowers from a 10-ft (3-m) row, but the sizes may vary greatly. Cut while the heads are still firm before the florets start to grow away from the core.

PESTS AND DISEASES As with cabbages, cabbage maggots and clubroot are the worst problem (see pages 157, 191, and 193). If necessary, protect from birds with nets, and pick caterpillars off the plants as you spot them.

RECOMMENDED CULTIVARS

WHITE-HEADED
'Alpha': *sow midspring for a late summer crop.* **'Dok Elgon'**: *well-packed, round heads; ready in autumn if sown late spring.*
'Snow Crown': *early-producing, medium-sized heads in spring or fall.*
PURPLE-HEADED
'Rosalind': *deep purple, but turns green when cooked. Fairly fast-maturing and may be ready to cut by late summer.* **'Violet Queen'**: *early and productive.*
GREEN-HEADED
'Alverda': *late-maturing, sweet, mild heads.*
MINI-CAULIFLOWERS
'Bambi': *produces small heads in about 85 days from seed.*

GREEN CAULIFLOWER

SPRING			SUMMER			AUTUMN			WINTER		
Early	Mid	Late	Early	Mid	Late	Early	Mid	Late	Early	Mid	Late
🌱	♧										
	➡		✂	✂	✂						

BROCCOLI
Brassica oleracea Italica Group

THE COLORS OF BROCCOLI are similar to those of the cauliflower family: lime green, white, and purple. The most common broccoli has one heavy, central head. The prettiest are the 'Romanesco' types. Less common sprouting broccolis have masses of small florets, produced over a long season from fall into winter, or even spring in mild climates. Like Brussels sprouts and kale, they are a welcome late-season harvest. The name is Italian, but it is likely that these vegetables arrived from the eastern Mediterranean some time during the 17th century. Philip Miller, who wrote one of the first gardening dictionaries in 1724, called broccoli "Italian asparagus"; if you eat the first of the crop with some hollandaise sauce on the side, it is hard to decide which is the more ambrosial.

HEADING BROCCOLI

SPROUTING BROCCOLI

Cultivation

In character these plants are very different. Heading broccoli goes in for the one big extrovert gesture, while sprouting broccoli twitters into life with a shower of possibilities but has the greater staying power. You can get a similar performance from heading broccoli if you let sideshoots resprout after harvesting the main head.

SITE AND SOIL Broccoli copes with less luscious soil than cauliflower, although the best crops come from well-dug, well-fed ground. Both sprouting and heading broccoli thrive in cool, well-drained sites but tolerate some heat.

SOWING Start broccoli seedlings indoors (see page 168), 4–6 weeks before transplanting. In areas with long growing seasons or when growing sprouting broccoli, you can sow seed directly into the garden (see page 170), putting 2 or 3 seeds at "stations" 6in (15cm) apart, to avoid the need for transplanting. Keep the rows 12in (30cm) apart and sow seed ½in (1cm) deep.

THINNING AND TRANSPLANTING Thin sprouting broccoli to leave one strong plant at each station (see page 171). Transplant broccoli seedlings when the weather becomes mild in spring and again in summer for a fall harvest. Set the plants 24in (60cm) apart in every direction.

ROUTINE CARE Make sure that plants are never short of water.

YIELD AND HARVESTING Expect 6–8lb (3–4kg) from a 10-ft (3-m) row. Broccoli heads are ready from summer to autumn; sprouting broccoli is ready about 70 days after planting.

PESTS AND DISEASES As with cabbages, they may suffer from cabbage maggots and clubroot (see pages 57, 191, and 193). Green caterpillars are well camouflaged on broccoli heads. Soak the broccoli in salty water before cooking it. Spray plants with Bt to prevent future problems.

RECOMMENDED CULTIVARS

HEADING BROCCOLI
'Premium crop': *large, early heads.*
'Romanesco': *handsome lime-green heads.*
SPROUTING BROCCOLI
'Purple Sprouting': *the hardiest type, producing a succession of tender shoots.*
'White Sprouting': *the white equivalent, but less prolific.*

SPRING			SUMMER			AUTUMN			WINTER		
Early	Mid	Late	Early	Mid	Late	Early	Mid	Late	Early	Mid	Late
🌱	🌱		🌱								
		➡	➡	✂	✂	✂					
🌱	🌱										
				✂	✂	✂	✂				

☐ Heading broccoli	☐ Sprouting broccoli

DECORATIVE BROCCOLI
With its cone-shaped clusters of tiny flowers grouped in a geometric dome, 'Romanesco' is the most striking of all these varieties. It is ready to be harvested in the autumn.

ZUCCHINI *Cucurbita pepo*

YOUNG ZUCCHINI ARE DELICIOUS RAW or sautéed, but they have the frightening capacity to metamorphose into monsters if you go away on vacation at the wrong time. Zucchini have heroic status among gardeners who are also showmen – look for giant zucchini (marrows) at county fairs, where there is often a competition to find the heaviest one of the year. Zucchini are best grown from hybrid bush cultivars and are easy to manage in a confined space. You can use vigorous trailing varieties to camouflage a compost pile, or even a chainlink fence. The great golden flowers that open before the zucchini swell glow richly among the sober foliage; yellow-fruited varieties make an even greater impact.

Cultivation

Zucchini are thirsty beasts, so any device you can think of to conserve water will be a great advantage. You can build a shallow wall of soil in a circle about 24in (60cm) wide around each plant. When you water, it stays where you want it. Mulching is also very beneficial: it suppresses weeds as well as conserving moisture.

SITE AND SOIL Rich, moisture-retentive soil will give the best results. Plants can cope with very light shade if necessary.

SOWING Zucchini seeds need warmth and will not germinate at temperatures lower than 56°F (13°C). Sow inside, 4 weeks before the last spring frost, putting one seed to a 3in (7cm) pot (see page 168). Let them grow in the pot until frost-free weather, when after hardening off, the plants can be set outside. Or be patient and sow direct outside in late spring or early summer, setting the seed 1in (2cm) deep and 3–4ft (1–1.2m) apart each way. Floating row covers, or even jam jars turned upside down and placed over the plants, will act as miniature greenhouses, protecting the plants from pests and keeping the site extra warm.

TRANSPLANTING If you have sown seed inside, set the plants out when they have 3 or 4 true leaves, and danger of frost has passed. Use care not to disturb the roots. Leave plenty of room for plants to develop. Bush varieties of zucchini will need 3–4ft (1–1.2m) each way. Trailing varieties should have slightly more.

ROUTINE CARE Zucchini must be fed and well watered. There are two critical periods: when the plants are first set out and when they are flowering and forming fruit. Once they have become established, their huge leaves will smother all competition from weeds. However, they will also smother other crops. Do not put less competitive plants too close.

YIELD AND HARVESTING Expect about 16 zucchini from each plant. If you want a monster zucchini, pick off all fruits except one. Picking the fruit regularly will keep the plants cropping.

PESTS AND DISEASES Cover young plants with floating row covers to keep off cucumber beetles, squash vine borers, and squash bugs (see page 191). Cucumber beetles may spread bacterial wilt, which can kill a thriving plant.

RECOMMENDED CULTIVARS

ZUCCHINI

'Black Magic': *dark firm fruit on compact plants.* **'Cocozellé'**: *dark green fruit with paler stripes.* **'Condor'**: *dark green cylindrical zucchini with highly glossy fruit.* **'Gold Rush'**: *not as heavy a cropper as green cultivars but a beautiful addition in a decorative planting.* **'Roly Poly Hybrid'**: *pale green, round fruits, very good flavor.* **'Scallopini'**: *rounded, dark green; prolific.* **'Zahra'** *("Lebanese zucchini"): light green, white spotted fruit; compact plants.*

	SPRING			SUMMER			AUTUMN			WINTER		
	Early	Mid	Late	Early	Mid	Late	Early	Mid	Late	Early	Mid	Late
	🌱	⚘	⚘									
			➡	➡	✂	✂	✂	✂				

IN THE KITCHEN

Ratatouille is one of the classics of the kitchen and, as with all classic dishes, there are many variations. This is my own favorite.

RATATOUILLE
Serves 4

1 large eggplant, cubed
salt
3 tbsp olive oil
2 onions, sliced
2 cloves garlic, crushed
1lb (500g) tomatoes, peeled and quartered
3 zucchini, chopped
1 green pepper, seeded and chopped
2 tbsp mixed fresh herbs (preferably including thyme and basil), finely chopped
2 tbsp tomato paste

1 Sprinkle the eggplant with salt in a colander and leave for half an hour so that the bitter juices drain away.

2 Heat the olive oil in a large pan and sauté the onion and garlic until slightly colored. Rinse the eggplant cubes, pat dry, and add them to the onion mixture, cooking gently for 5 minutes.

3 Add the tomatoes, zucchini, pepper, and herbs, and cook for 15 minutes, stirring occasionally. Stir in the tomato paste, let it heat through, and check the seasoning.

CULINARY NOTES

❧ For the most intense flavor, pick zucchini when they are little bigger than a finger. Slice lengthwise and broil them.

❧ If you can bear to sacrifice the zucchini to come, pick the flowers just as they are fully open and use as tiny packages to stuff with a rice and meat filling, well flavored with herbs. Bake with a covering of homemade tomato sauce.

✿ **ZUCCHINI**
FLOWERS

✿ **ZUCCHINI**
'Condor'

MARROW
'Tiger'

✿ **ZUCCHINI**
'Gold Rush'

PUMPKINS & SQUASH
Cucurbita maxima, C. moschata & C. pepo

"SQUASH NEVER FAIL TO REACH MATURITY. You can spray them with acid, beat them with sticks, and burn them; they love it," wrote the American humorist S. J. Perelman. So, secure in the knowledge that you will have to work hard to stop them from growing, you can think instead about which of the staggering variety of pumpkins and squash you would like to have in the garden. The smaller ones can be grown over fences and strongly built arches, or winding through the tall stems of corn. There are two main kinds: summer squash, which are eaten when small and tender, and winter squash and pumpkins, which need to mature until their shell hardens in order to store successfully through the winter.

Cultivation

In essence, you raise pumpkins and squash in the same way as zucchini, which are members of the same family, the cucurbits. They are no hardier, and the plants cannot be set out in the open until all danger of frost has passed.

SITE AND SOIL Choose an open, sunny site in ground that is rich and well fed but also well drained. Pumpkins and squash grow most happily where the soil is slightly acid to neutral.

SOWING Sow indoors from midspring on, pressing the seeds on edge 1in (2cm) deep into individual 3-in (7-cm) pots of peat-based mix. Cover with clear plastic and keep at a temperature of 70°F (21°C) until the seeds have germinated (see page 168). An alternative for areas with long growing seasons is direct sowing.

TRANSPLANTING In early summer, once the soil has warmed up, set the hardened-off plants out (see page 169), raising up ridges of soil in a circle around them to retain water. Set them at least 4ft (1.2m) apart, and far away from less robust crops which they may smother. Corn, with its upright growth, will not be bothered by the territorial habits of the squash.

ROUTINE CARE These are hungry and thirsty plants. Food is best supplied by incorporating plenty of compost or manure into the ground before planting. Drink must be lavishly provided. The smothering foliage of pumpkins and squash will take care of any weeds.

YIELD AND HARVESTING The yield depends entirely on the type of pumpkin or squash that you are growing. The little pancake-shaped squash should be cut when they are just 3in (7cm) across. Cut the summer squash as you need them. Leave the winter squash and pumpkins until the skins are hard and the fruit sounds hollow when tapped. Then store them in a frost-free, cool area.

PESTS AND DISEASES Pumpkins and squash may be attacked by several pests (see page 191).

RECOMMENDED CULTIVARS

SUMMER SQUASH
'Spaghetti Squash': *spaghetti strands of flesh in fruit that ripens to straw yellow.*
'Sunburst': *yellow, pancake-shaped squash.*
'White Patty Pan': *pale, scallop-edged fruit.*
PUMPKINS
'Autumn Gold': *smaller, more manageable fruit than the giant, record-breaking varieties.*
WINTER SQUASH
'Buttercup': *firm, sweet flesh in a gray-green skin.* **'Butternut'**: *creamy fruit, bred to mature early in cooler climates.* **'Little Gem'**: *apple-sized fruit which ripen from green to gold.* **'Red Kuri'**: *big, teardrop-shaped, orange fruit.* **'Turk's Turban'**: *intricately shaped and marked with orange, red, green and cream.*

	SPRING			SUMMER			AUTUMN			WINTER		
	Early	Mid	Late	Early	Mid	Late	Early	Mid	Late	Early	Mid	Late
		🌱	🌱	🌱								
				➡	➡	✂	✂					

IN THE KITCHEN

For this soup you need one beautiful, unblemished example to use as a natural soup tureen. Do not be too ambitious with size – a monster may buckle under its own weight. And be sure you choose one that will fit in the oven.

PUMPKIN OR SQUASH SOUP
Serves 4

1 pumpkin or winter squash, ideally about 8in (20cm) high and wide
2 tbsp softened butter
salt and black pepper
1 medium onion, finely sliced
¼ cup (60g) long-grain rice
3½ cups (900ml) good chicken stock
freshly grated nutmeg or ground cumin
to garnish: 6 slices of bacon, cooked until crisp, and 3 tbsp crumbled Mozzarella cheese

1 Cut a lid from the stalk end of the pumpkin or squash and scoop out the seeds (see below). Rub butter around the flesh inside and season. Place the onion and the rice inside.

2 Bring the stock to the boil in a saucepan. Put the pumpkin or squash in a big roasting pan, pour the stock into the pumpkin, and put on the lid. Bake for 2 hours at 375°F (190°C).

3 Remove the pumpkin or squash from the oven, take off the lid, and scrape some of the softened flesh from the walls into the soup and mix it in.

4 Correct seasoning and add either nutmeg or cumin to taste. Garnish with the bacon and Mozzarella and serve.

CULINARY NOTES
❧ Do not waste the seeds when you prepare pumpkins for cooking. Spread them on a baking sheet, sprinkle lightly with salt, and bake in the oven for 20 minutes at 375°F (190°C).

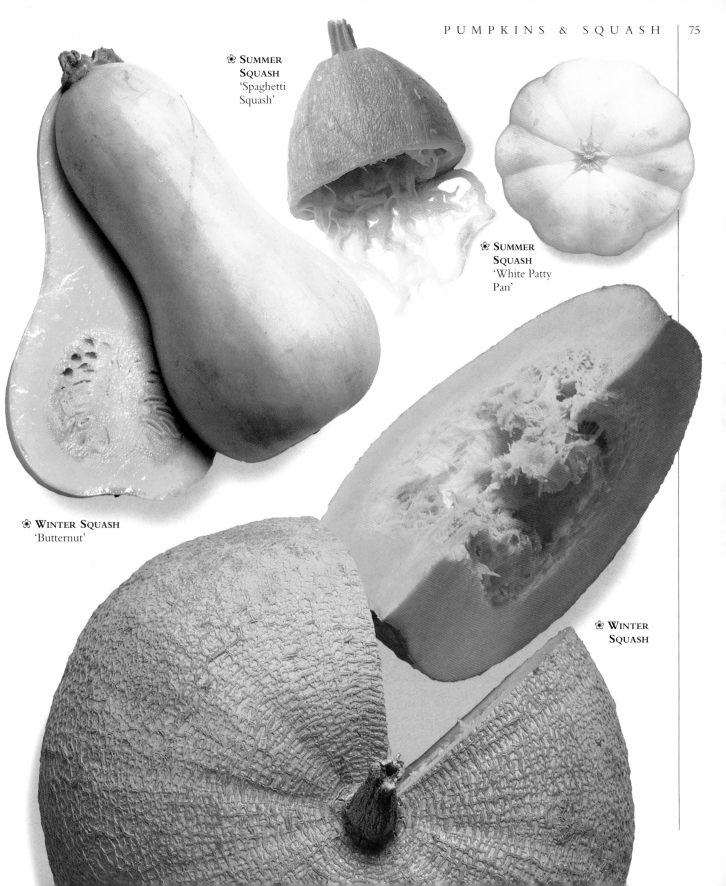

❀ **SUMMER SQUASH** 'Spaghetti Squash'

❀ **SUMMER SQUASH** 'White Patty Pan'

❀ **WINTER SQUASH** 'Butternut'

❀ **WINTER SQUASH**

EGGPLANTS, SWEET & HOT PEPPERS
Solanum melongena & Capsicum sp.

NOTHING LOOKS QUITE SO UNREAL in a vegetable garden as a waxy eggplant, smooth, glossy, and enigmatic. The standard type is deep purple, almost black, but the white-skinned kind is more likely to have given the eggplant its common name. There are also pretty striped varieties – maroon or purple flecked and streaked with cream – that are grown in France and Italy. Set the dark lustrous fruit of eggplants close to the brilliant red of the sweet peppers or the hot peppers. All three crops do well in a warm, frost-free sunny spots but are unlikely to succeed outside in very cold areas. In cool climates, start with quick-cropping early cultivars. In late spring you can buy young plants which saves the bother of raising them from seed. Plant them in your garden – they need no complicated staking – or keep them on your patio in mellow clay pots.

EGGPLANT
'Black Beauty'

Cultivation

Eggplants and peppers, which are related to tomatoes, need much the same growing conditions. Eggplants, however, are a little more touchy, being highly susceptible to soil-borne wilt diseases and fond of warm, near-tropical weather. In cool climates with short summers, try Oriental eggplants, which fruit early and prolifically despite slightly cool weather. If wilts become a problem, you can grow eggplants in pots on your patio; peppers also make handsome potted plants.

SITE AND SOIL In cool climates, you can give eggplants and peppers a boost by warming the soil with black plastic before planting and by situating them beside a heat-catching south-facing wall. In order to minimize problems with diseases, choose a site that has not been used recently to grow tomatoes, peppers, or eggplants.

SOWING Sow seed in trays or pots indoors (see page 168), ½ –1in (1–2cm) deep. Germinate at about 70°F (21°C) in early spring. For eggplants and peppers, you need to maintain a growing temperature for the seedlings of 65–70°F (18–21°C).

TRANSPLANTING Transplant the seedlings when they are about 2in (5cm) high, putting each in a separate 3-in (7-cm) pot to grow on. Harden off the seedlings (see page 169) and plant them in their permanent positions once the weather is frost-free and the soil is warm. In cool climates, it helps to prewarm the soil with plastic mulch. Space them about 18in (45cm) apart. Alternatively move them into larger pots, setting each plant in a pot at least 9in (23cm) wide.

ROUTINE CARE Keep the plants well watered, particularly when the fruits have begun to set. Tomato fertilizer is a good booster for plants growing in containers.

YIELD AND HARVESTING Expect about 4 large eggplants, more small Oriental eggplants. Small-fruited peppers will also produce more than large – 20 or more hot peppers on a plant. Green peppers will ripen and turn red if they get enough warmth and you leave them until early autumn. As hot peppers mature and turn red, they also get hotter.

PESTS AND DISEASES Cover young eggplant seedlings with floating row covers to keep off flea beetles (see page 191). Look for disease-resistant pepper cultivars to encourage reliable crops.

RECOMMENDED CULTIVARS

CLASSIC EGGPLANT
'Black Beauty': *well-flavored, pear-shaped fruit, early to ripen.*
ORIENTAL EGGPLANT
'Orient Express': *early and prolific with long, thin fruit.*

PEPPERS
'Bell Boy': *thick-walled, bulbous-shaped fruit.*
Gypsy': *high-yielding, wedge-shaped peppers.*
HOT PEPPERS
'Yellow Cayenne Hybrid': *relatively large hot pepper, suitable for drying, good in containers.*
'Jalapeño': *smooth, bullet-shaped fruit*
'Super Cayenne Hybrid': *hot and prolific.*

HOT PEPPER
'Jalapeño'

HOT PEPPER
'Super
Cayenne
Hybrid'

HOT PEPPER

**SWEET
PEPPER**
'Bell Boy'

CUCUMBERS
Cucumis sativus

THERE ARE TWO KINDS OF CUCUMBER, beauty (slicers) and the beast (picklers). Dark, glossy slicers are delicious in salads; lighter, lilliputian picklers stay firm and crunchy as pickles. Cucumbers, like melons, used to be one of the crops that old-fashioned gardeners of the Victorian age minded about to an extraordinary degree. A kinked cucumber was a sign of moral slackness, so gardeners put long glass tubes over newly set fruits to ensure that they grew as straight as rulers.

Cultivation

Modern cucumbers include a great variety of improved cultivars of both pickling and slicing cucumbers. You can grow cultivars that contain no bitter compounds, which makes for great eating and is less attractive to pesky cucumber beetles. You can buy super-high-yielding vines that produce only female flowers or that produce fruit without pollination. This allows you to grow them under floating row covers.
SITE AND SOIL Cucumbers like a very rich soil, enriched with manure or compost. They lap up water faster than camels and must never be allowed to dry out. In sheltered sites, they will grow in dappled shade. The compact variety 'Salad Bush Hybrid' does well in pots.
SOWING Sow seed indoors 4 weeks before the last spring frost, 1in (2cm) deep, in individual 3-in (7-cm) pots (see page 168). Cover with clear plastic until it germinates. Keep plants growing well, repotting if necessary, to put outside after the last frost. Seed can also be sown directly outside in early summer, covering it with jam jars for protection. Set seed no deeper than 1in (2cm), 24in (60cm) apart.
TRANSPLANTING Harden off indoor-raised plants (see page 169) and set out in early summer at least 24in (60cm) apart.
ROUTINE CARE Water frequently – lack of water is the most usual reason for fruit failing to develop.

CUCUMBER
'Salad Bush Hybrid'

YIELD AND HARVESTING A slicing cucumber may produce about 10 fruits, a pickling cucumber probably twice as many. Pick regularly.
PESTS AND DISEASES Cover seedlings with floating row covers to keep off cucumber beetles (see page 191) that carry bacterial wilt. Avoid diseases by planting disease-resistant cultivars.

**BURPLESS
CUCUMBER**
'Orient
Express'

RECOMMENDED CULTIVARS

PICKLING
'County Fair': *mostly female vines, extra productive, resists bacterial wilt.*
ORIENTAL
'Orient Express': *long, slender, gourmet fruit.*
SLICER
'Jazzer': *bitter-free fruit that needs no pollination.* **'Salad Bush Hybrid'**: *compact vines for small gardens.*

SPRING			SUMMER			AUTUMN			WINTER		
Early	Mid	Late	Early	Mid	Late	Early	Mid	Late	Early	Mid	Late
🌱	🌱										
		➡	➡		✂	✂	✂				

SPRING			SUMMER			AUTUMN			WINTER		
Early	Mid	Late	Early	Mid	Late	Early	Mid	Late	Early	Mid	Late
🌱	🌱	🌱									
			➡	✂	✂	✂	✂				

SWEET CORN *Zea mays*

TALL SHEAVES OF SWEET CORN provide an authentic hint of harvest in the late summer garden. It is a stately plant and an anciently cultivated one: husks found in caves in Mexico and Peru suggest that people were growing and eating it by 3500BC. Breeders have been working hard to make it as happy in cool northern climates as it is in its Latin American home, so while a traditional variety might take over 80 days to reach maturity, a modern cultivar will ripen in under 60. Early sweet corn, however, isn't always as flavorful as later sweet corn. Interplant it with low-growing cucumbers to make the best use of limited space.

Cultivation

Pollination is the key to fat, well-filled cobs, and since sweet corn is wind-pollinated, it is best planted in blocks rather than rows. The pollen from the male tassels at the top of the plant then has the best possible chance of reaching the silky tassels of the female flowers. New "supersweet" cultivars have been bred for extra sweetness but are slightly tender. They must be grown on their own to avoid cross-pollination with unimproved varieties, which would make them lose some of their sweetness.

SITE AND SOIL Sweet corn needs a warm site in full sun and grows best on deep, well-drained, fertile, and slightly acid soils.

SOWING Climate dictates how you should proceed. In warm areas, sow seed directly into the soil after the last spring frost, about 1in (2cm) deep (see page 170), in a block pattern. Set a few seeds together at each growing point, about 14in (35cm) apart, and thin out weaker seedlings after germination. Seed will not germinate in soil temperatures below 55°F (12°C), but you can use a floating row cover (see page 166) to warm up the ground beforehand or set jam jars over the seeds to act as miniature greenhouses. In areas with a short growing season, sow seed in gentle heat – 65–70°F (18–21°C) – indoors in midspring, setting it no more than 1in (2cm) deep in individual 3-in (7-cm) pots (see page 168). Make sure that seedlings are hardened off before transplanting (see page 169).

TRANSPLANTING Set out the plants when all danger of frost has passed, spacing them in a block about 14in (35cm) apart in each direction. For baby corn, it is essential to use a cultivar that has been bred to mature early and also to set the plants no more than 6in (15cm) apart.

ROUTINE CARE Little water will be needed until the cobs start to swell. Sweet corn is usually sturdily self-supporting, but in windy areas you may need to hill up the soil around the base of the plants when they are 12in (30cm) high (see page 167) in order to give them extra support.

YIELD AND HARVESTING Expect no more than 1 or 2 ears from each plant. Do not leave them toughening on the stem. Pick them when the silky tassels begin to turn brown and the juice that oozes from the kernels, if pressed, is milky (see below right). Use as quickly as possible after picking. Sugar in the kernels turns rapidly to starch once they are picked, though the conversion process is slower in new "supersweet" cultivars.

PESTS AND DISEASES Raccoons will feed on corn when it is nearly ripe. Corn earworms and European corn borers will eat the kernels in the husk.

RECOMMENDED CULTIVARS

'Tuxedo': *a yellow "supersweet" cultivar with long cobs.* **'Early Sunglow'**: *good for maturing early in cooler climates with shorter summers.*

❀ **SWEET CORN** 'Tuxedo'

SPRING			SUMMER			AUTUMN			WINTER		
Early	Mid	Late	Early	Mid	Late	Early	Mid	Late	Early	Mid	Late
🌱	🌿	🌿									
➡	➡		✂	✂	✂						

TESTING FOR RIPENESS
Once the creamy tassel has turned brown, turn back the husks and press one of the kernels with your nail. A milky liquid will ooze out when the corn is ripe; if underripe, the juice is watery; if overripe, it looks thick and starchy.

GLOBE ARTICHOKES & CARDOONS
Cynara scolymus & C. cardunculus

A GLOBE ARTICHOKE has the right dramatic credentials for being a star of the kitchen garden. With its jagged, grayish-green leaves and showy, fat flower buds – the edible part – it looks as though it has been sculpted by one of the builders of the Parthenon. Unfortunately, it is an all-or-nothing plant. It looks stunning from late spring to mid-autumn, when it will spread four feet in all directions, but once it is reduced to nothing by the first frosts, it is a big nothing. Cardoons are equally handsome, but it is the fleshy leaf bases, tied up and blanched, that you eat, not the flower.

❦ GLOBE ARTICHOKE

❦ CARDOON

Cultivation

Seed-raised plants are very variable, so globe artichokes are generally grown from rooted offsets, propagated from types which are known to have good flower heads. If you leave the buds too long before picking, they open into spectacular great thistleheads of bluish purple. These dry well for winter flower arrangements. Cardoons are also best raised from offsets. They are generally available from mail order specialists of vegetables or ornamentals. They have smaller, more prickly flower heads which, like artichokes, look superb dried.

SITE AND SOIL In the great artichoke-growing areas of coastal California, the soil is light and the climate mild. A combination of heavy soils and cold winters is likely to be too much for them. In very hot areas, artichokes will tolerate shade but elsewhere they should have sun, as should cardoons. In cool climates look for quick-cropping artichoke cultivars that can be grown as annuals.

PLANTING Young offsets of both artichokes and cardoons should be planted shallowly, with only as much of the base below ground as is needed to keep them upright. New offsets quickly develop a sustaining root system. Set them out in late spring, about 4ft (1.2m) apart each way, and keep them well watered until they are established.

ROUTINE CARE Offsets may produce small flower heads late in the season of their first year. For perennial plants, pick these off both artichokes and cardoons to encourage the plants to develop more sideshoots. Where winters are hard, protect established plants by packing them with straw. Mulch thickly with well-rotted manure in spring. Plants are not long-lived. After 3–4 years replace old ones with new offsets that will have been produced (see page 172). Begin blanching cardoons in spring (see below). Blanching generally takes about 3 weeks.

YIELD AND HARVESTING Expect about 10 artichokes from an established plant, fewer from an annual. Cut the terminal "king" bud first, with 2in (5cm) of stem attached. The head should be large but the scales not yet opening away from the center. While the artichokes are still young, the inside of the stem is very succulent. Simply peel back the stringy outside and nibble out the innards.

PESTS AND DISEASES Artichokes and cardoons are relatively disease free, though aphids can be a problem (see page 190). Cold, wet winters may rot the plants.

RECOMMENDED CULTIVARS

GLOBE ARTICHOKES
'Green Globe': *flat, rounded head with blunt-ended scales.* **'Vert de Laon'**: *one of the best for flavor.*
CARDOONS
'Blanc Ameliore': *a French selection with great flavor.* **'Gigante'**: *an Italian favorite for blanching.* **'Violetto'**: *early-producing cultivar to use as an annual.*

BLANCHING CARDOONS
Start to blanch cardoons in late spring when the leaves are about 18in (45cm) high. Tie them in a bundle with soft string. Wrap them in newspaper, and then in black plastic.

TOMATOES *Lycopersicon esculentum*

FOR THE DECORATIVE VEGETABLE GARDEN, outdoor tomatoes, either of the staked-up cordon or bush type, will be your first choice. They are simplicity itself to manage and the flavor of the new cultivars, especially when buffed up by hours of sunshine, is outstanding. Once planted in tubs, grow bags, or even hanging baskets, the bush varieties can be left to their own devices. The cordon types, trained up tall stakes, make good centerpieces for decorative designs, especially if you contrast a yellow-fruited cultivar like 'Taxi' with the stunning red-and-gold 'Tigerella'.

Cultivation

Grow determinate-type tomatoes, compact plants which ripen all at once. Or grow indeterminate types which get to be lanky and produce fruit over a long period of time.

SITE AND SOIL Find a sunny site with fertile, well-drained, well-manured soil that has not been used to grow peppers, tomatoes, eggplants, or potatoes the previous season. This reduces disease problems.

SOWING Start seeds indoors 6–8 weeks before the last spring frost. Scatter seed thinly on the surface of a 5-in (12-cm) pot of seed-starting mix and cover lightly with more mix or vermiculite (see page 168). Cover with plastic wrap to retain moisture during germination, and keep at 70°F (21°C). When the seedlings develop their first true leaves, transplant them into individual 3-in (7-cm) pots (see page 169).

TRANSPLANTING First, plants must be thoroughly hardened off (see page 169). When planting, set the lower portion of the stem underground. Roots will form along the submerged stem and encourage better growth. Set staked tomato plants 15–18in (38–45cm) apart. Caged plants must be placed 24–48in (60–120cm) apart.

ROUTINE CARE Caged tomatoes need little attention, but indeterminate varieties need to be staked and tied in. Sideshoots ("suckers") must be nipped out regularly (see opposite). Encourage earlier fruiting on indeterminate types, by pinching off the tip of the main stems in early summer. Overwatering and overfeeding have a detrimental effect on flavor, and irregular watering is the most common cause of blossom end rot (see page 192). Mulching helps to discourage this problem. In open ground, no extra feeding should be necessary, but plants in containers, especially hanging baskets, need plenty to eat and drink.

YIELD AND HARVESTING Expect 4–8lb (2–4kg) of fruit per plant. For the best flavor, leave the tomatoes to ripen fully on the plant. In fall, or any time frost threatens, cover plants with clear plastic or a cloche (see page 185). This will encourage the tomatoes to continue to ripen despite cool weather conditions.

PESTS AND DISEASES Tomatoes are susceptible to *Verticillium* and *Fusarium* wilts, nematodes, and mosaic virus (see pages 192–94). Avoid by planting disease-resistant cultivars and rotating crops.

RECOMMENDED CULTIVARS

RED TOMATOES
'Celebrity': *nice tomatoes, good disease resistance on a determinate plant.*
'Gardener's Delight': *small but exceptionally sweet fruits.*
'Oregon Spring': *an extra-early determinate tomato that fruits even in cool weather.*
'Roma': *heavy-cropping plum tomato (bush).*
'Super Beefsteak': *large, meaty fruit on disease-resistant plant.*
SPECIALTY TOMATOES
'Taxi': *sweet yellow fruit on determinate vines.*
'Tigerella': *distinctive fruit striped red and yellow; early and well-flavored.*

SPRING			SUMMER			AUTUMN			WINTER		
Early	Mid	Late	Early	Mid	Late	Early	Mid	Late	Early	Mid	Late
🌱	🌱	🌱	➡	✂	✂	✂	✂				

IN THE KITCHEN

Tomatoes are one of the few crops that you can scarcely have too much of. They freeze well and, although the texture of the fruit disintegrates in the process, the flavor remains very good. The easiest way is to bag them as they are. They stay whole and separate, and the skin slips off readily when held under running water.

STUFFED TOMATOES
Serves 4

4 large beefsteak tomatoes
salt and black pepper
4 slices bacon
1 cup (125g) mushrooms, finely chopped
handful of parsley, finely chopped
4 eggs
2 tbsp (30g) butter
4 slices of bread for toasting

1 Preheat the oven to 350°F (180°C). Cut the tops off the tomatoes and scoop out the seeds and flesh. Season the insides with salt and pepper.

2 Fry the bacon until crisp, then crumble and set aside. Brown the mushrooms in the bacon fat, then mix them with the bacon and parsley.

3 Spoon the mixture into the tomatoes and break an egg into the top of each one. Dot with butter and bake in the oven for 15 minutes or until the eggs are set. Serve with toast.

CULINARY NOTES

🌿 Tomatoes will sit happily on the plant for 2 weeks or more. They are certainly better there than in the refrigerator.

🌿 Homegrown tomatoes make superb salads. Sprinkle with finely chopped basil or chives, dress with vinaigrette, toss with black olives and feta cheese, and enjoy.

TOMATO 'Celebrity'

TOMATO 'Gardener's Delight'

TOMATO 'Taxi'

TOMATO 'Roma'

TOMATO 'Sweet Million'

TOMATO 'Tigerella'

PINCHING OUT SHOOTS
Pinch out sideshoots ("suckers") as they develop in the axils of staked types to prevent excess growth.

LATE SUMMER PINCH
Nip out the top of staked plants to stop more flowers from forming, encouraging existing fruit to ripen.

TOMATO 'Super Beefsteak'

PODDED VEGETABLES

THE SCRAMBLING HABIT OF SOME peas and beans can be used to good effect in the decorative kitchen garden, whether over a tunnel made from twiggy branches or up a tripod. Scarlet runner beans hold on by twining; the exploratory tendrils of peas grasp any useful prop as tightly as a baby's fist. All the podded vegetables are attractive in bloom, but not all are as showy as the scarlet runner bean with its blazing red flowers. The broad bean, though a beefy-looking plant, has delicate flowers marked with black on white. Bean pods may be purple, green, cream, yellow, or striped. There is a wonderful strain of snap beans (look for the cultivars 'Rob Roy' and 'Rob Splash') with cream pods that are streaked with bright pink or purple.

INTO THE TUNNEL

Two different scarlet runner beans, 'Painted Lady' and 'White Achievement', have been trained over this tunnel straddling a path. A border of tall purple alliums, the striped rose 'Ferdinand Pichard', and catmints crowd the space at their feet.

SWEET BEANS

Rows of broad beans and peas, scrambling up a support of chicken wire, are backed by decorative sweet peas. For scent these are unparalleled, but if you bend your nose to the more humble broad bean, you will find that this has sweet-smelling flowers, too.

THE COLOR PURPLE

The dark purple that suffuses the foliage of this climbing snap bean is intensified in the pods and flowers. The color disappears when it is cooked, but you can use it to great effect with dark red dahlias such as 'Bishop of Llandaff' and clumps of bronze fennel.

BEANS WITH A PAST

The scarlet runner bean 'Painted Lady', with its red and white flowers, was grown in kitchen gardens 150 years ago. It is a decorative climber and produces a heavy crop of tasty beans. Grow it over an arch with white-flowered 'White Achievement' and clematis.

SOCIABLE CLIMBERS

Red-flowered scarlet runner beans are combined with pink, white, and purple sweet peas on this tripod that is nearly matched in height by the tall flowering stems of red orach, Atriplex hortensis 'Rubra'. The orach is a fast-growing annual that self-seeds itself vigorously.

PEAS *Pisum sativum*

EARLY VISITORS TO TROY, where Heinrich Schliemann excavated Priam's fabled palace, were said to have been fed on peas from the great king's larder. One huge storage jar contained more than 400lb (180kg), which had remained perfectly preserved for 3,000 years. More recently, there has been a revolution in peas as the 'Sugar Snap' and its offspring have entered our gardens. Snap peas have tender edible pods and sweet juicy peas inside. They far out-yield shelling peas (eaten without the pod) and snow peas, (eaten in the pod before the seeds swell). Now you can find many types of peas in low-growing bush types, which can be used to make low, informal hedges around plots. Tall varieties, such as 'Sugar Snap', will scramble up a trellis or fence to 5ft (1.5m). 'Alderman', a shelling pea from the Victorian era, is another tall type worth growing for its fine flavor.

Cultivation

Start peas when the weather becomes mild in spring. If planted too early, the seeds may rot or remain dormant. From spring onward, you can then sow more, at 3–4 week intervals until early summer.

SITE AND SOIL Peas positively like cool weather but will tolerate temperatures up to about 80°F (27°C). Soil should be fertile and well dug. Provided there is plenty of moisture, they do not mind some shade.

SOWING Sow seed 1½–2in (3–5cm) deep and 2–3in (5–7cm) apart. If growing a straight row, perhaps as a pea hedge, dig out a wide trench (see page 170) about 2in (5cm) deep and the width of a spade. Sow the seed about 2in (5cm) apart. Cover with soil and tread down. Protect from birds using wire netting.

ROUTINE CARE Provide some form of support for tall cultivars, either a trellis or branched sticks. Semi-leafless peas, in which many of the leaves have been modified into tendrils, need less staking (see opposite). If you have used wire netting to protect seed, you can draw this up and bend it into a V-shaped ridge to support low-growing cultivars rising through it. In a potager, try growing peas in combination with broad beans, which will support the crop.

YIELD AND HARVESTING Expect 10lb (5kg) from a 10-ft (3-m) row. Pick peas regularly to encourage more to form. Pick snow peas while the peas are visible only as tiny swellings. Harvest snap peas before the peas reach full size. When the crop has finished, chop off the stems, leaving the roots in the ground. Their nitrogen-bearing nodules will help enrich the soil.

PESTS AND DISEASES Birds and mice are the most serious pests.

RECOMMENDED CULTIVARS

SHELLING PEAS
'Alderman' ('Tall Telephone'): *popular, late-producing pea.* 'Daybreak': *compact, extra-early, great for spring crops.* 'Novella': *leafless, self-supporting pea.*

SNOW PEAS
'Oregon Sugar Pod': *fine flavor, grows to more than 3ft (1m) tall.*

SNAP PEAS
'Sugar Ann': *compact, self-supporting vines with early pea pods.* 'Sugar Snap': *fleshy pods, long season.*

SPRING			SUMMER			AUTUMN			WINTER		
Early	Mid	Late	Early	Mid	Late	Early	Mid	Late	Early	Mid	Late
	🌱	🌱	🌱	🌱							
				✂	✂	✂	✂				
	🌱	🌱	🌱	🌱							
				✂	✂	✂	✂				
	🌱	🌱		🌱							
				✂	✂	✂	✂				

☐ Shelling peas   ☐ Snap peas   ☐ Snow peas

IN THE KITCHEN

If only a few peas are available, use them as a first course, braised in the French way with some shredded lettuce leaves, finely chopped carrot, and scallion. If you have plenty, try combining them with other vegetables.

PEAS AND CUCUMBER
Serves 4
1 cucumber, peeled
2–3lb (1–1.5kg) peas, shelled
4 tbsp (60g) butter
sprig of mint, chopped
salt and black pepper
1 tsp sugar

1 Cut the cucumber into 1½in (3cm) chunks, then into matchsticks. Place in a colander, sprinkle with salt, and let drain.
2 Bring ½in (1cm) water to a boil and add the cucumber, peas, butter, and mint. Season with salt, pepper, and sugar and cook for about 5 minutes, until just tender.

PEAS SPICED WITH CUMIN
1½tsp whole cumin seeds
2 dried hot red peppers
3 tbsp vegetable oil
1 medium (175g) onion, chopped
2 medium (175g) carrots, diced
1 cup (175g) peas, shelled
2 medium (175g) cooked potatoes, diced
salt
½tsp sugar
1 scallion, finely sliced

1 Fry the cumin and peppers in the oil for a few seconds, then add the onions and cook until soft. Add the carrots and peas and cook for another 5 minutes, until tender.
2 Add the potatoes, sugar, and salt, and cook for a few minutes until the potato is heated through. Remove the peppers before serving and garnish with the scallion.

SUPPORTING PEAS

1 *Once the seedlings grow tendrils, push branched sticks firmly into the soil. Position them 4in (10cm) apart, outside of the peas.*

2 *The tendrils twine around the sticks as the peas grow. Make sure the sticks are long enough if they are to support a tall cultivar.*

SNOW PEAS

SHELLING PEAS

SNAP PEAS

SEMI-LEAFLESS PEAS

Peas of this kind need little staking. The tendrils wind around their neighbors instead of sticks and the whole mass becomes virtually self-supporting – group therapy in the vegetable garden.

SCARLET RUNNER BEANS *Phaseolus coccineus*

IN THE WILD, scarlet runner beans grow in the Mexican mountains together with dahlias, begonias, and lobelias. There is no reason why you should not make your own beans feel comfortably at home by providing similar companions. The hummingbirds that pollinate the flowers in Mexico will be in short supply in most gardens. Fortunately, bumblebees have learned the trick of opening the petals and provide an efficient pod-setting service. Use scarlet runner beans scrambling up a taut net to make a quick summer screen in the garden. They will soon grow up to 10ft (3m). Grow them up tripods in a flower border, or use them to disguise an arbor, where they can twine happily among clematis, late summer nasturtiums, or flame-colored trumpet vine.

❦ SCARLET RUNNER BEANS

Cultivation

Scarlet runner beans, with their scarlet flowers and red and black seeds, are decorative in any garden but are reluctant to produce pods in hot weather. They will not set fruit where temperatures reach 90°F (32°C), at least not until cooler weather arrives. It helps to keep the roots sufficiently moist. Avoid using insecticides that harm bumblebees, which pollinate scarlet runner bean flowers.

SITE AND SOIL Start thinking about the site 6 months before you sow, and dig masses of well-rotted manure or compost into the soil. Scarlet runner beans are deep-rooted, and their roots like to feel the journey has been worthwhile. Some shade is beneficial, provided the ground is fertile.

SOWING Do not be in a hurry to sow directly into the ground outside, since the soil temperature must be at least 50°F (10°C) for the seeds to germinate, which is usually not until the very end of spring (see page 170). Warm the soil up quickly by covering it with black plastic. Remove the plastic after the last spring frost and plant. Sprinkle some nitrogen-fixing bacteria into the furrow before planting: available as dark granules from garden centers, it captures nitrogen for legumes and helps them to fertilize themselves.

TRANSPLANTING Scarlet runner beans are tender, so do not transplant indoor-sown beans while there is any danger of frost. Set out plants 6in (15cm) apart (see page 169) or space them regularly around the base of

a wigwam, a row of poles or netting, or some other support that they can climb.

ROUTINE CARE Water liberally, especially as the plants come into flower. Mulching will help to conserve moisture and keep down weeds. In mild climates, give the plant a chance to resprout in spring. It may return from a fleshy bulb.

YIELD AND HARVESTING Expect about 2lb (1kg) of beans from each plant. Pick the pods before the beans have started to swell inside. If you leave mature pods, the plants will not produce more.

PESTS AND DISEASES Diseases are uncommon, but flowers may not set in high temperatures. Water attentively.

RECOMMENDED CULTIVARS

'Scarlet Runner': *the classic with red flowers producing red and black speckled seeds.*
'White Dutch Runner': *bears white flowers and produces tasty white seeds.*

SPRING			SUMMER			AUTUMN			WINTER		
Early	Mid	Late	Early	Mid	Late	Early	Mid	Late	Early	Mid	Late
	♧		♧								
		➡		✂	✂	✂	✂				

MAKING THE MOST OF BEANS

Grow scarlet runner beans up tripods or wigwams to make a superb feature in the vegetable patch or the flower border. When first taken to Europe in the 17th century, the plants were grown for ornament instead of food.

SNAP & DRIED BEANS
Phaseolus vulgaris

FRENCH SNAP BEANS ARE NOT REALLY FRENCH. Like scarlet runner beans, they are American beans and were taken to Europe by the Spanish conquistadores. These beans, wrote the early herbalist John Gerard, "boiled together before they be ripe, and buttered, and so eaten with their cods, are exceeding delicate meat, and do not ingender wind as the other pulses do." Snap beans may climb or grow as bushes. They may have flat or round pods. They may be green, purple, yellow, or wonderfully speckled as in the old Dutch variety 'Dragon Tongue', which has cream pods flecked with purple. The beans of some types can be eaten either green in a succulent young pod or allowed to mature and then dried.

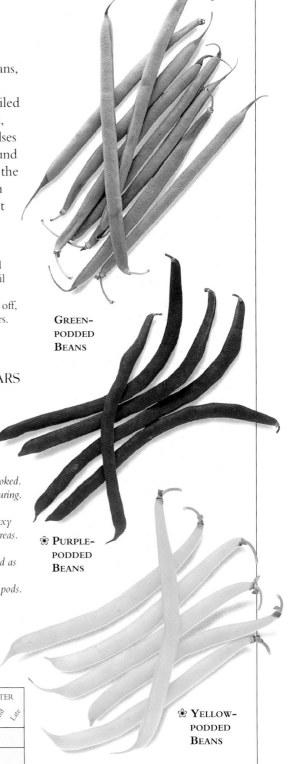

GREEN-PODDED BEANS

❀ **PURPLE-PODDED BEANS**

❀ **YELLOW-PODDED BEANS**

Cultivation

By nature, these are fast-growing annuals, so it is a waste of seed to sow it in cold, dank ground. The climbing types will need stakes or other support, but the compact bush varieties that crop in the garden or in pots need no extra support.
SITE AND SOIL Beans like rich, light soil, which can be neutral or slightly acid. They do best in a sunny position.
SOWING Sow beans outside once the last spring frost passes and the soil temperature is over 60°F (15°C). The cultivar 'Provider' does tolerate cool soils. Replant bush beans every 2 to 3 weeks until midsummer for an extended harvest). Set seed 1½in (3cm) deep, in staggered rows, so that plants grow about 9in (23cm) apart in the rows. They will germinate in 1–2 weeks.
TRANSPLANTING The shock to the system holds back transplants, and plants set out from seed sown indoors may crop no sooner than a later sowing outside. Water the transplants well (see page 171).
ROUTINE CARE Hill up soil around the stems of young plants as they grow to give them extra support (see page 167). Provide support for climbers and short twigged sticks to prop up bush varieties, which tend to get top-heavy when laden with beans. Keep the soil moist throughout the growing period, especially when the plants come into flower.
YIELD AND HARVESTING Expect 8lb (4kg) of beans from a 10-ft (3-m) row. For fresh beans, pick the pods frequently while they are still succulent. For dry shelled beans, leave the pods on the plant until the end of the season. Hang the stems under cover until the pods have dried off, shell the beans, and store in airtight jars.
PESTS AND DISEASES As for scarlet runner beans (see opposite).

RECOMMENDED CULTIVARS

GREEN-PODDED
'Provider': *tender beans on disease- and sprawl-resistant plants; germinates well even in cooler soils.*
PURPLE-PODDED
'Purple Queen': *unparalleled flavor; the glossy purple beans turn green when cooked.*
'Purple Teepee': *productive; quick maturing.*
YELLOW-PODDED
'Kinghorn Wax': *stringless, round, waxy beans.* **'Rocquencourt'**: *good in cold areas.*
CLIMBING
'Blue Lake': *excellent flavor; can be used as a dry shell bean.*
'Kentucky Wonder': *bears tasty long pods.*
DRY SHELL
'Rattlesnake': *tan seeds with brown mottling; drought-resistant.* **'Pinto'**: *tan seeds cherished for refried beans.*
'Navy': *small white beans that stay firm when cooked.*

SPRING			SUMMER			AUTUMN			WINTER		
Early	Mid	Late	Early	Mid	Late	Early	Mid	Late	Early	Mid	Late
	⚘	⚘	⚘								
		➡	✂	✂	✂	✂					

BROAD BEANS *Vicia faba*

BEFORE POTATOES, beans such as broad beans had long provided the staple carbohydrate for those living in the cooler parts of Europe. Although they have never been as popular in North America, broad beans are a nice change from more traditional fare. Broad beans are useful in a decorative vegetable garden because they grow well during cool seasons and can then be cleared away to make room for another vegetable, such as ornamental kale or broccoli. Both would benefit from the nodules of nitrogen left in the soil by the beans' root systems. The plants themselves can be tall or short, depending on cultivar. All have glaucous foliage and fragrant black-and-white-lipped flowers.

❧ LONG-PODDED BROAD BEANS

❧ SHORT-PODDED BROAD BEANS

Cultivation

Broad beans are the hardiest of the whole bean family and in mild climates can survive a winter outside, if mice, slugs, and birds will let them. Many gardeners use broad beans as a winter cover crop. Sown in fall, they fix nitrogen all winter, then in spring are worked into the soil to add organic matter. In cold climates, it is better to wait until spring to plant.

SITE AND SOIL Deep, heavy soils produce the best crops, but the ground must not be waterlogged. Broad beans do best on a soil that is neutral or very slightly acid (pH6–6.5). Do not grow them in the same place 2 years running, or you run the risk of encouraging a buildup of diseases in the soil. To encourage maximum nitrogen fixation, you can sprinkle nitrogen-fixing bacteria into the planting furrow before covering up the seeds. Nitrogen-fixing bacteria are available in small packets at most garden centers or mail-order vegetable seed companies.

SOWING The seeds are large and can be planted with a trowel or hoe. Set them about 1½ in (3cm) deep, at intervals of 9in (23cm), in rows that are also 9in (23cm) apart (see page 170). The beans germinate well at low temperatures, but overwintering crops will succeed better under a floating row cover (see page 166) or cloches. Sow a few extra seeds at the end of the row to fill in any holes.

ROUTINE CARE This is an easy crop, and the plants are so vigorous they deter all but the most pernicious weeds. Support is needed for the tall forms. Posts at either end of a row with strings stretched between help keep the plants on their feet. Dwarf cultivars can be propped up with short lengths of branched twigs. In hot weather, the plants may stagnate and refuse to set pods. Give them light shade, and plenty of moisture until the temperature cools.

YIELD AND HARVESTING Expect about 20lb (9kg) of beans from a 10-ft (3-m) row, less if you eat them when they are at their best, before the skins have become leathery and when the scar on the bean's edge is still white or green. Broad beans can also be picked and eaten whole. Pick them when they are no bigger than your little finger.

PESTS AND DISEASES The worst pests are aphids (see page 190), which cluster on the growing tips from midsummer. Nip out the shoot together with its colony of aphids. If you sow in winter or early spring, the plant will be advanced enough by midsummer to take this treatment.

RECOMMENDED CULTIVARS

'Aquadulce': *early, hardy, white-seeded old variety, growing to 3ft (1m) tall.* **'Broad Windsor'**: *plants reach 4ft (1.2m) tall and are hardy to several degrees below freezing.* **'Express'**: *matures in 10 weeks in good conditions; hardy.* **'Imperial Green Longpod'**: *pods grow to 15in (38cm) long.* **'Loreta'**: *extra-large seeds with some heat tolerance.* **'Sweet Lorane'**: *extra cold-hardy with good flavor.*

SPRING			SUMMER			AUTUMN			WINTER		
Early	Mid	Late	Early	Mid	Late	Early	Mid	Late	Early	Mid	Late
							⚘	⚘			
⚘	⚘		✂	✂	✂	✂					

LIMA BEANS & SOUTHERN PEAS
Phaseolus lunatus & Vigna unguiculata

THE LIMA BEAN IS AS ANCIENT AS THE BROAD BEAN, cultivated by the Mayans in Yucatan and growing in the wild from Guatemala to Peru. It grows well in warm southern climates, but northern gardeners can do well with bush limas that tolerate cool soil. This also applies to the southern pea, which goes by many other names including crowder, blackeye bean, and cowpea. This is a decorative vegetable, producing pods that are variously stippled with cream, green, pink, and purple. The beans inside are equally diverse: some have pink blotches; crowders are greenish but turn khaki when cooked; and blackeyes are cream with a distinct black notch.

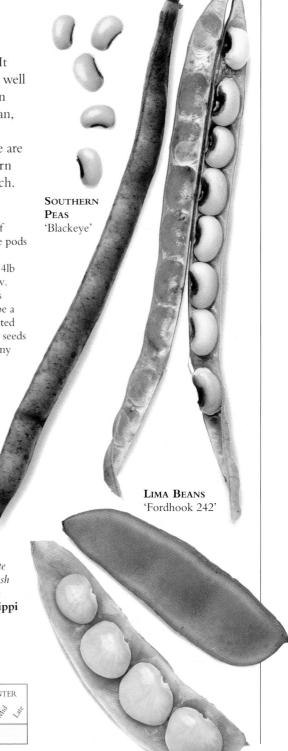

SOUTHERN PEAS 'Blackeye'

LIMA BEANS 'Fordhook 242'

Cultivation

Both lima beans and southern peas can be grown as bushes or climbers, depending on the cultivar, and both can be eaten fresh or dried. Southern peas will mature in 60–70 days from planting, but the seeds need a temperature of about 70°F (21°C) to germinate and grow. They succeed in areas where shelling peas would frazzle. The climbing varieties of lima bean need a growing season of about 80 days, the bush types a slightly shorter time. The soil needs to reach a temperature of 65°F (18°C) before the seeds will germinate.

SITE AND SOIL In the South, southern peas and lima beans are grown in sandy loam, which gives good drainage. On heavier soils, they will do best on raised beds. The soil should have a pH of 6–6.5. More acid soils can be limed (see page 160) but you will need to do this at least 3 months before sowing.

SOWING Sow in late spring, 2 weeks after the last expected frost. Set the seeds about 1in (2cm) deep and 4in (10cm) apart in rows about 3ft (1m) apart (see page 170). Climbing types need stakes or some other support. Make successional sowings from early to midsummer.

ROUTINE CARE Watering increases eventual yield, but if water is scarce save it for the time when the plants are in flower. This is when they will need it most, if the beans are to set well and swell. Don't apply extra nitrogen to southern peas or they may refuse to set fruit.

YIELD AND HARVESTING For fresh beans, pick the pods when they are bulging, but not showing any signs of drying out. For dried beans, leave the pods on the stem to dry and then shell the beans into a container. Expect about 4lb (2kg) of beans from a 10-ft (3-m) row.

PESTS AND DISEASES Insects such as cowpea curculio (see page 191) can be a problem. Viruses are quickly transmitted to plants by visiting aphids. Buy only seeds that are certified virus-free, and kill any aphids with insecticidal soap.

RECOMMENDED CULTIVARS

LIMA BEANS
'Fordhook 242': *reliable bush variety, white seeds.* **'Geneva'**: *bush baby-lima for cool regions.* **'King of the Garden'**: *strong-growing climber, large pods, whitish-green seeds.*

SOUTHERN PEAS
'Blackeye': *high-yielding, wilt-reisistant.* **'Calico Crowder'**: *vine with red-splotched white peas.* **'Knuckle Purple Hull'**: *old bush variety, prone to virus but producing large brownish beans in purple pods.* **'Mississippi Silver'**: *early-producing, easy to shell, tolerates heat and humidity.* **'Zipper Cream'**: *bush type with long pale pods that are easy to shell.*

SPRING			SUMMER			AUTUMN			WINTER		
Early	Mid	Late	Early	Mid	Late	Early	Mid	Late	Early	Mid	Late
		🌱	🌱	🌱	✂	✂	✂	✂			

STEM, BULB & ROOT VEGETABLES

THIS GROUP IS LARGELY composed of vegetables whose important edible parts are hidden underground. What you see is not what you eat. Among the bulb, stem, and root vegetables, your greatest allies in arranging decorative groups will be onions, leeks, fennel, kohlrabi, carrots, beets, and parsnips. Asparagus is very ornamental when the spears are allowed to grow up into fine clouds of foliage, but you need a lot of space for a proper asparagus bed, and it cannot be moved. Put some plants in the herbaceous border instead, or grow it among roses for an instant boutonniere. Rhubarb is a handsome plant, but it also ties up ground on a permanent basis. The stars are onions and leeks, whose foliage contrasts well with carrots and lettuce.

GOURMET ASPARAGUS

A fashionably gaunt scarecrow spreads its protective arms over an asparagus patch that is in danger of being swamped by nasturtiums. Flowers such as this can be sown directly into the ground and soon spread to make a highly colorful, weed-suppressing carpet.

POTATOES AND ROSES

Potatoes do not have great decorative merit, but they are an important crop in this traditional kitchen garden where they have been surrounded by roses. Low floribundas and hybrid teas grow in the side border, while the central path is swagged with climbers.

CURIOUS KOHLRABI

The swollen stem of a kohlrabi rests on the earth like a strange egg from which a baby dinosaur might suddenly emerge. In themselves, kohlrabi are not especially decorative vegetables, but their curious form of construction makes them a good choice for a potager.

BRIGHTER BEETS

Pot marigolds provide bright strokes of color in a patch of beets. They are useful, too, attracting hoverflies, which devour aphids faster than any other predator in the garden. Companion planting can be a visual delight as well as having practical advantages.

FEATHERED FENNEL

A thick swath of cornflowers fences in a rectangular patch of feathery Florence fennel, cool as a pool of water. Tall Verbena bonariensis, *with its lean, wiry stems, would be equally at home here, or you could introduce purple-leaved beets and columbines.*

ONIONS *Allium cepa*

"KITCHEN GARDEN GODS," SAID JUVENAL, the Roman satirist, about the pungent family of onions. It is true. There are few savory dishes that do not require a hint of onion, though when they first swept into Europe, the onion tribe were considered luxury items, useful to flavor a rich man's meat. In the garden, the tubular, blue-green leaves contrast well with the feathery foliage of carrots. There is also a practical reason for combining these two crops. The scent of the onions is said to mask the smell of carrots and so deter the carrot rust fly from laying its eggs.

SCALLION
'Evergreen Long White Bunching'

RED-SKINNED ONION
'Giant Red Hamburger'

YELLOW-SKINNED ONION
'Sweet Sandwich Hybrid'

Cultivation

The first task is to choose between seed, nursery seedlings, or sets (small, immature bulbs). Sets and nursery seedlings, though more expensive, have advantages. You skip stage one of the growing process and move swiftly on to stage two. There are disadvantages, however. The range of cultivars is limited, and large sets are more likely to bolt (run to flower). To ensure good bulb production, grow long-day onions in northern climates during spring and summer. In southern climates, grow short-day onions in fall and winter.

SITE AND SOIL Well-drained, fertile soil that has been well manured the previous autumn is ideal. The site should be sunny so that bulbs will ripen satisfactorily.

SOWING Sow seed in pots indoors in midwinter (see page 168), then transplant the seedlings into 6-packs to grow on. Sets can be planted outdoors in spring. Push them gently into the soil so that the tops just show above the surface. Set them 4in (10cm) apart in rows 10in (25cm) apart. Scallions can be sown directly outdoors in spring for summer harvest and in summer for fall harvest.

TRANSPLANTING After hardening off (see page 169), seed-grown onions will be ready to plant out in spring, spaced as above. Plant at the same depth as they have been growing in their 6-packs.

ROUTINE CARE Onions hate competition from weeds, especially in the first half of the growing season. They are not hungry for nitrogen, nor particularly thirsty.

YIELD AND HARVESTING Expect 7lb (3.5kg) from a 10-ft (3-m) row. They will be ready to pull up when the foliage starts to wither. Thorough drying is essential if onions are to be stored through the winter (see page 186). Use any with thick necks immediately because they will not keep.

PESTS AND DISEASES Onion maggot (see page 190) is a bad pest, laying its eggs in young bulbs which the maggots then eat. Cover plantings with floating row covers to prevent attack. Parsley, planted in rows between the onions, is a traditional deterrent. Look for disease-resistant cultivars to avoid other diseases.

RECOMMENDED CULTIVARS

YELLOW-SKINNED
'Granex' *(short-day): sweet and mild, stores only briefly.*
'Sweet Sandwich' *(long-day): grows sweeter with storage.*
RED-SKINNED
'Giant Red Hamburger' *(long-day): a lovely slicer.*
SCALLIONS
'Evergreen Long White Bunching': *fine, fresh flavor.*

SPRING			SUMMER			AUTUMN			WINTER		
Early	Mid	Late	Early	Mid	Late	Early	Mid	Late	Early	Mid	Late
										🌱	🌱
🌱	➡			✂	✂						
	🌿			✂	✂						
	🌿	🌿		🌿	🌿						
		✂	✂			✂	✂				

☐ Onions from seed   ☐ Onion sets

☐ Scallions

IN THE KITCHEN

The onion is perhaps the most often-used vegetable in the kitchen, though it too rarely has a chance to star on its own. This soup warms the coldest winter day. Treat it as a main course rather than an appetizer.

FRENCH ONION SOUP
Serves 6

4tbsp (60g) butter
1 tbsp olive oil
1½ lb (750g) onions, thinly sliced
½ cup (60g) flour
8 cups (2 liters) good beef stock
¾ cup (150ml) dry white wine
salt and black pepper
6 thick slices country bread
1 clove garlic, halved
2 tbsp grated raw onion
6oz (175g) grated Gruyère

1 Heat the butter and oil in a large, heavy-bottomed pan and gently sauté the onions for 15 minutes. Stir in the flour and cook for another 2–3 minutes. Gradually add the stock and wine, stirring to prevent lumps, and simmer for 45 minutes. Season to taste.
2 Rub the slices of bread with the garlic and bake them in the oven until crisp and dry.
3 Pour the soup into ovenproof bowls or one large bowl. Stir in the raw onion and float the bread on top. Sprinkle the cheese on the bread. Brown under the broiler.

CULINARY NOTES

❧ For less of a meal, omit the bread and cheese and add 2 tablespoons of flamed brandy heating it in a ladle and putting a lighted match to it to quickly burn off the alcohol.
❧ For more of a meal, ladle into individual bowls and add a very lightly poached egg to each. Add the bread and cheese and brown.

GARLIC & SHALLOTS
Allium sativum & A. cepa Aggregatum Group

GARLIC HAS LONG BEEN SUPPOSED to have magical properties. A single whiff is considered enough to scare off even the most bloodthirsty vampire. Shallots, though, have a more prosaic reputation. Nobody carries them in their pocket on a dark winter's night. In the garden, both are equally easy to grow, and their upright foliage, like that of onions, provides welcome contrast to the rounded shapes of lettuce.

Cultivation

Shallots, which grow in small bunches, can be harvested earlier than onions. This characteristic is useful in a small plot where the space can then be used for a later crop. Garlic needs a dormant period of cold, 32–50°F (0–10°C), lasting 1–2 months, to develop a good head. If you plant it in autumn, this will occur naturally during winter. Garlic leaves grow best in cool conditions. When foliage growth stops, the underground bulb begins to swell, usually in early summer.
SITE AND SOIL Light, well-drained soil suits garlic; shallots can cope with something heavier. Both need an open situation and fertile soil, though it need not be heavily manured.
SOWING Plant shallots like onion sets (see opposite) in spring in cool climates or in fall in warm climates. Plant garlic in autumn. Heads of garlic should be broken up into individual cloves before planting. Set both 6in (15cm) apart, in rows 12in (30cm) apart.
ROUTINE CARE Weeding is the only imperative.
YIELD AND HARVESTING Expect about 20 heads of garlic and 7lb (3.5kg) of shallots from a 10-ft (3-m) row. Harvest shallots, which grow in small clusters, in the same way as onions. Garlic should be lifted as soon as the foliage turns yellow.

SHALLOTS

GARLIC
'Italian Purple Skin'

PESTS AND DISEASES They are generally trouble-free, but may sometimes suffer the same problems as onions (see left).

RECOMMENDED CULTIVARS

GARLIC
'Italian Purple Skin': *lovely color and great flavor.*
SHALLOTS
'Atlas': *a pink shallot.*
'French Shallots': *large bulbs available in sets.*

	SPRING			SUMMER			AUTUMN			WINTER		
	Early	Mid	Late	Early	Mid	Late	Early	Mid	Late	Early	Mid	Late
								❧				
					✂							
								❧				
❧				✂	✂							

☐ Garlic   ☐ Shallots

LEEKS *Allium porrum*

THE ONLY GOOD THING known about the Roman emperor Nero is that he liked a bowl of leek soup as often as he could fit one in. Was vichyssoise born in the steamy cookhouses of first-century Rome? Leeks are easy to grow, and the steel-blue ribbons of foliage look surprisingly good set among tall waving heads of purple verbena. Leek plants will furnish the ground from midsummer until spring and need little attention. Edge your leek bed with violas. Plant rows of leeks to pierce through a bright blanket of yellow pansies. You could even paint a patch with alternate stripes of blue-gray and gold using leeks and pot marigolds.

Cultivation

If you are lucky, some other grower will take on the responsibility of raising young plants and you can buy bundles to set out in summer. If not, take heart. Leeks are not difficult to raise from seed.

SITE AND SOIL Leeks need rich, well-drained ground that has been liberally fed with manure or compost. Dig thoroughly before planting. The soil needs to be loose enough to enable you to make deep holes when setting out young plants if they are to develop long, well-blanched stems.

SOWING There are early and late varieties, the early ones tending to be tall, thin, and less cold hardy, the late ones squat and fat. Sow leek seeds in pots or 6-packs indoors in late winter, 12 weeks before spring planting time.

TRANSPLANTING Transplant seedlings outdoors in spring when they are about 8–9in (20–23cm) tall. Using a dibber or stick, make holes 6in (15cm) deep, 6in (15cm) apart in rows that are 12in (30cm) apart. Drop a leek into each hole and fill up with water to wash soil over the roots. Traditionally, leaves and roots were shortened before transplanting, but this is not necessary.

ROUTINE CARE Little attention will be needed. Water them in dry weather. You can leave extra-hardy late leeks in the ground into fall or even winter. Mulch them thickly with straw for protection.

YIELD AND HARVESTING Expect 10lb (5kg) from a 10-ft (3-m) row. Leeks can be lifted as needed, although they are extremely difficult to extract from the soil when the ground is frozen. In these conditions, the stem snaps, leaving the best part of the vegetable in the soil. Where this is likely to be a problem, lift a supply before the soil freezes and trim the leaves (generally called flags). Wrap the leeks in newspaper and store them in a cool place.

PESTS AND DISEASES Leeks can get diseases similar to onions (see page 190), and rust can be a big problem (see page 194): it shows as orange spots on the leaves. Rotate leeks to prevent a buildup of diseases in any particular spot, and avoid growing them in sites recently used for onions, shallots, or garlic.

RECOMMENDED CULTIVARS

'Laura': *extra hardy, late leek.* **'King Richard'**: *tall, early leek.* **'Titan'**: *sweet, mild, late leek.*

SPRING			SUMMER			AUTUMN			WINTER		
Early	Mid	Late	Early	Mid	Late	Early	Mid	Late	Early	Mid	Late
											🪴
🌱	➡	➡									
						✂	✂	✂	✂	✂	

❀ **LEEK** 'King Richard'

IN THE KITCHEN

Leeks, gentler in taste than other members of the onion family, make superb soups. Sliced and sautéed briefly in butter, they also combine with bacon to make an excellent filling for a tart. This one can be eaten hot or cold but is best somewhere between the two.

LEEK TART
Serves 6 as an appetizer, 4 as a main course

For the shortcrust pastry
6 tbsp (90g) butter
1½ cups (175g) all-purpose flour
pinch of salt
a little cold water
For the filling
6 tbsp (90g) butter
1lb (500g) leeks, washed, trimmed, and finely sliced
salt and black pepper
4 thick slices (125g) of bacon
2 eggs
¾ cup (175ml) milk or light cream, or a mixture of the two

1 Make the pastry: mix the flour and salt, then rub in the butter to form fine crumbs. Bind with water, form a ball, and let rest for 30 minutes.

2 To make the filling, melt the butter and sauté the leeks gently for 3–4 minutes. Season with pepper and allow to cool. Fry the bacon and cut into small pieces.

3 Line a 9-in (23-cm) greased flan dish with pastry, weight it, and bake in a hot oven (400°F/200°C) for about 10 minutes, until the pastry is lightly cooked.

4 Mix the bacon and leeks and pack into the tart. Beat the eggs with the milk or cream. Add a little salt and pour over the top.

5 Bake in a cooler oven (350°F/180°C) for about 30 minutes until the egg mixture sets.

FLORENCE FENNEL
Foeniculum vulgare **var.** *dulce*

WITH ITS FINE FEATHERY FOLIAGE and neatly layered bulb, Florence fennel is a very decorative vegetable but, like a highly bred horse, it tends to bolt if faced with anything it does not understand. It is a recent addition to North American gardens but is widely grown in Mediterranean countries where, well watered, it grows unchecked to produce a succulent crop. In chillier climates, this plant may leap into flower without ever forming an edible bulb.

Cultivation

For the biggest bulbs, time the planting of Florence fennel carefully to prevent it from bolting. In cool climates, sow in spring after the danger of the last frost has passed. In warm climates, sow in late summer for harvesting in winter. Fennel will withstand light frost, but is not generally hardy. Fennel's aniseed flavor is strongest if you slice the bulb finely and use it raw in a salad. Sautéed, the flavor is gentler, excellent when mixed with tomato and sprinkled with cheese to make a bubbling gratin.

SITE AND SOIL Light, sandy soil is best, though the bulbs must never dry out.

SOWING Scatter the seed thinly outside (see page 170), ½in (1cm) deep in rows 12in (30cm) apart, watering first if the soil is dry. Allow 15 weeks between sowing and harvesting.

THINNING Thinning is a much better option than transplanting, since fennel rarely recovers from the shock and bolts into flower instead of swelling to form a bulb. Thin to leave about 12in (30cm) between the plants.

ROUTINE CARE Fennel must never be starved or thirsty. Keep the plants growing smoothly by watering and fertilizing regularly. Mulch to conserve moisture and keep down weeds. Once the bulbs start to swell, hill soil up around them to keep plants stable and to blanch the stems (see page 167).

🌱 **FLORENCE FENNEL** 'Zefa Fino'

YIELD AND HARVESTING Expect approximately 9 bulbs of fennel from a 10-ft (3-m) row. Cut the bulbs just below ground level about 3 weeks after hilling them up. The stump may throw up some feathery shoots which you can use in exactly the same way as the fennel herb.

PESTS AND DISEASES The vagaries of climate have a far greater effect on fennel than any pest or disease.

RECOMMENDED CULTIVARS

'Finocchio': *the classic old world cultivar.*
'Mammoth': *has extra-large bulbs.*
'Zefa Fino': *strong resistance to bolting, ideal for cool climates.*

SPRING			SUMMER			AUTUMN			WINTER		
Early	Mid	Late	Early	Mid	Late	Early	Mid	Late	Early	Mid	Late
	🌱	🌱	🌱	✂	✂	✂					

CELERIAC & KOHLRABI

Apium graveolens var. *rapaceum* &
Brassica oleracea Gongylodes Group

GREEN
KOHLRABI

PURPLE
KOHLRABI

CELERIAC

THE BULBOUS, EDIBLE PARTS of celeriac and kohlrabi are not roots, such as a carrot has, but swollen parts of the lower stem. Though homegrown celeriac rarely swells to the impressive size of store-bought specimens, it has crisp, cut foliage that you can use to good effect in a decorative kitchen garden. It is a rugged vegetable. Horizontal roots cover the manically uneven surface, and lifting requires a crane rather than a shovel. Kohlrabi is one of the cabbage family, and its smooth globes of purple or whitish green can also look very attractive in the kitchen garden. It is more tolerant of drought than most brassicas.

Cultivation

The most critical time in raising celeriac is immediately after having set out the plants. Keep them growing as smoothly as possible, watering if necessary. They have a long growing season. Kohlrabi, in contrast, may be ready to pull only 7 or 8 weeks after sowing and is more tolerant of drought than most brassicas. Eat it when it is no larger than a tennis ball because it can quickly turn woody.

SITE AND SOIL By nature, celeriac is a plant of marshland and likes rich, damp soil. Kohlrabi can take drier conditions and does best in fertile, light, sandy soil.

SOWING Sow celeriac in a pot inside in early spring (see page 168). Germination takes about 3 weeks. When the seedlings are large enough to handle, transplant them out into individual 3-in (7-cm) pots. You can also sow seeds in 6-pack trays: set several seeds in each one, thinning out the weakest seedlings. Sow kohlrabi, little and often, outdoors in its growing position (see page 170), ½ in (1cm) deep, in rows 12in (30cm) apart.

TRANSPLANTING By the time of planting out, the celeriac seedlings should be about 3in (7cm) tall and hardened off (see page 169). Set them 12–16in (30–40cm) apart. The point where the leaves join the root should be level with the soil surface. Thin kohlrabi as it develops, leaving the plants about 6–9in (15–23cm) apart.

ROUTINE CARE Water celeriac liberally, and mulch to conserve moisture. Pull off any leaves that start to splay out from the globe, and do not allow secondary growing points to develop. Kohlrabi needs little attention except weeding.

YIELD AND HARVESTING You should get 8–10 celeriac and 15–20 kohlrabi from a 10-ft (3-m) row. Both can be left in the ground into fall or even winter in warm climates.

PESTS AND DISEASES Celeriac may suffer the same problems as celery (see opposite). Clubroot is the most likely disease to attack kohlrabi, but crops may also be spoiled by flea beetle or cabbage maggots (see pages 191–93).

RECOMMENDED CULTIVARS

CELERIAC
'Brilliant': *a newer cultivar that resists developing hollow hearts.* **'Prague'**: *a classic grown in America since 1871.*

KOHLRABI
'Grand Duke Hybrid': *green skinned, tender white flesh and disease tolerant.*
'Purple Vienna': *purple type with some resistance to frost.*

SPRING			SUMMER			AUTUMN			WINTER		
Early	Mid	Late	Early	Mid	Late	Early	Mid	Late	Early	Mid	Late
🌱											
	➡					✂	✂				
⚘	⚘		⚘	⚘							
	✂	✂		✂	✂						
☐ Celeriac					☐ Kohlrabi						

IN THE KITCHEN

If you grow a modern variety of celeriac such as 'Brilliant', you escape the rigamarole of using lemon juice to stop the flesh from turning brown as you prepare it for cooking.

GRATIN OF CELERIAC
Serves 4

1 large or 2 small celeriac
6 tbsp freshly grated Parmesan cheese
2 tbsp (30g) butter
approx. 2 tbsp (30g) breadcrumbs
For the tomato sauce
4 thick slices (125g) bacon or Italian coppa, chopped
1 large onion, finely chopped
3 large cloves garlic, finely chopped
3 tbsp olive oil
1 large carrot, diced
2lb (1kg) tomatoes, peeled and chopped
½ cup (150ml) dry white wine
salt and black pepper
dried oregano, to taste
about 8 fresh basil leaves, chopped

1 Preheat the oven. Bake the gratin at any temperature between 325–375°F (160–190°C), depending on how soon you want to eat or what else you are cooking.

2 Make the tomato sauce by softening the bacon, onion, and garlic in the oil. Add the carrot, tomatoes, and wine and cook over high heat for 15 minutes, then add seasoning and herbs to taste.

3 Peel the celeriac, cut it into chunks, and cook it in boiling salted water until just tender.

4 Drain and arrange the celeriac in layers in a gratin dish, adding some grated Parmesan and a few dabs of butter between each layer.

5 Pour over the tomato sauce, then top with breadcrumbs and some more Parmesan and butter. Bake until the sauce is bubbling and the top golden and crunchy.

CELERY *Apium graveolens*

WILD CELERY IS A MARSH PLANT, growing widely in Europe and Asia. Its extreme pungency is tolerable if you are taking it as a medicine, the way it was first used, but not if you want to eat it for pleasure. Hundreds of years of cultivation have turned wild celery into the succulent kind we now crunch noisily. You can grow traditional green varieties with long, pale stems and a good flavor, or try self-blanching golden types. There are even unusual and extra-hardy old-fashioned pink or red cultivars.

SELF-BLANCHING CELERY

Cultivation

Good celery is rated by the size and succulence of its leaf stalks. To achieve this end, plants have to grow fast with an endless supply of water at hand. The foliage is fresh and green and the leaves pleasantly cut. They contrast well with the solid foliage of cabbages or the ribbonlike leaves of leeks. Green and self-blanching cultivars are ready by late summer.
SITE AND SOIL Deep, well-drained ground is a necessity. Work plenty of organic matter into the soil. The pH needs to be between 6.5 and 7.5.
SOWING Seed may take a long time to germinate or fail completely if too warm. Aim for about 70°F (21°C) and sow the seed indoors, in a pot, on the surface of a peat-based mix without covering it: the seeds need light to germinate. Transplant seedlings into individual pots as soon as possible (see pages 168–69).
TRANSPLANTING When the seedlings have 5 or 6 true leaves, harden them off and transplant them to their growing quarters (see page 169). Plant red and non-self blanching types in a trench 4in (10cm) deep. Wait until a week before the last spring frost date to minimize the danger of bolting. Space the plants 12–18in (30–45cm) apart. Self-blanching and green kinds can be planted in a block, 6–11in (15–28cm) apart, depending on the size of plant you want to grow.
ROUTINE CARE Water generously during the whole growing period, and mulch to conserve moisture. On infertile soils, a liquid fertilizer given a month or so after transplanting may be beneficial. Start blanching celery when the plants are about 12in (30cm) high, first by filling in the trench and then by hilling up more soil around them.
YIELD AND HARVESTING Expect 14lb (6kg) of celery from a 10-ft (3-m) row.
PESTS AND DISEASE Slugs like to feast on the stems. Aphids can spread diseases. Spray with insecticidal soap if necessary.

RECOMMENDED CULTIVARS

OLD-FASHIONED CELERY
'Pink': *turns pink with frost.*
SELF-BLANCHING CELERY
'Golden Self-Blanching': *early.*
GREEN CELERY
'Par-cel': *vigorous.*
'Ventura': *improved heat tolerance.*

SPRING			SUMMER			AUTUMN			WINTER		
Early	Mid	Late	Early	Mid	Late	Early	Mid	Late	Early	Mid	Late
🌱	➡			✂	✂						

ASPARAGUS
Asparagus officinalis

❀ ASPARAGUS

AS A CROP, ASPARAGUS IS QUITE DIFFICULT to fit into a decorative kitchen garden. You need at least 30 roots to be able to pick a decent meal at any one time and the bed, once made, should remain undisturbed for 20 years. But on the other hand, few vegetables are so ambrosial, and asparagus is expensive to buy. It also deteriorates fast. Steam asparagus as soon as you pick it, boiling water on the stove even before you cut the spears. Left to itself, it produces both male and female plants: female ones carry small red berries among the ferny foliage that grows up when you finish cutting the spears in early summer. You can now buy "all-male" asparagus that produces fatter spears.

Cultivation

Make a good rich home for your asparagus by digging in plenty of well-rotted manure. Time spent making a good, rich home for your asparagus will be amply repaid by the crop. Any perennial weeds must be eradicated before you start. Traditional asparagus beds are 4ft (1.2m) wide, giving room for 2 rows of plants and allowing for easy weeding and cutting. Leave 3ft (1m) between beds.

SITE AND SOIL Asparagus grows best in well-drained, nutrient-rich sandy soils. Incorporate coarse sand as well as well-rotted manure if the soil is heavy. On really heavy soil, make a deep bed (see page 166) so that water drains away from the roots. If they are permanently soggy, they rot. Acid soils will need to be limed (see page 161) to achieve a pH of 6.5–7.5.

PLANTING Asparagus can be raised from seed – the cheapest method – but is usually sold ready-grown as bare roots, which may be from 1–3 years old. The younger roots transplant more easily, although you will have to wait longer before picking a decent crop. If you plant 1-year-old roots, you can start cutting lightly in the second year after planting. Plant them in early spring, about 18in (45cm) apart in rows that are also 18in (45cm) apart. Soak the roots in water for a few hours before planting.

ROUTINE CARE Asparagus must be kept free of weeds at all times. In some European countries, white asparagus is preferred to green, so the shoots are blanched by covering them with soil. Mulch the beds thickly with manure or compost in late winter. Cut down the foliage only when it has turned yellow in autumn.

YIELD AND HARVESTING Expect 8–10 spears from each root, once established. When the spears are 5–7in (12–18cm) high, cut them just beneath the surface of the soil using a sharp knife. The cutting season should last no more than 6–8 weeks, ending in early summer. Cut asparagus sparingly in the second season; in cold climates, wait until the third season to harvest lightly.

PESTS AND DISEASES Slugs can inflict great damage (see page 192). The asparagus beetle lays its black eggs on the emerging shoots. Both larvae and adult beetles feed on the foliage (see page 191). Control by spraying with rotenone. Avoid rust and *Fusarium* wilt (see page 194) by planting disease-resistant cultivars. Destroy plants infected with crown rot.

RECOMMENDED CULTIVARS

'Jersey Knight': *mostly male plants, so highly productive; disease tolerant.*
'UC 157': *grows in warm climates with mild winters.*

PLANTING ASPARAGUS ROOTS
Dig a trench 12in (30cm) wide and 8in (20cm) deep with a ridge down the middle. Plant the asparagus with the roots draped either side of the ridge. Roots should be 4in (10cm) below the surface when the trench is filled in.

IN THE KITCHEN

Given the shortness of the season, there is little time to tire of asparagus simply steamed and served with butter or, for a special occasion, hollandaise or cream sauce. Steam it by standing the spears upright so that the heads are out of the water. Put a domed cap of foil over the pan instead of a lid.

HOLLANDAISE SAUCE
Serves 4 as an appetizer

2 tbsp white wine vinegar
4 tbsp water
4 black peppercorns, crushed
4 egg yolks
¾ cup (175g) butter, melted
salt and black pepper
juice of 1 lemon, or to taste

1 Place the white wine vinegar, water, and peppercorns in a pan and boil to reduce by a third. Strain into a basin set on top of a pan of hot water (or use a double boiler).

2 Over a gentle heat, whisk the egg yolks into the mixture until it begins to thicken. Add the butter in a slow stream, whisking continuously.

3 Season with salt, pepper, and lemon juice and serve promptly, while the sauce is still warm.

CREAM SAUCE
Serves 4 as an appetizer

1¼ cups (300ml) light cream
2 tbsp mixed, chopped, fresh herbs
(try using tarragon, chives, and parsley)
salt, black pepper, and cayenne

1 Gently heat the cream, stir in the herbs, and season to taste with the salt, black pepper, and cayenne.

2 Serve warm. If you prefer, this sauce is also good served slightly chilled as a dressing for cold asparagus. Do not heat the cream.

RHUBARB
Rheum × cultorum

RHUBARB IS A MISFIT. It is a vegetable that wants to be a fruit, and nobody quite knows in which category to put it. The stalks of culinary rhubarb are green, pink, or red. They can be made to grow longer and yield more if covered with a bucket or basket. Unfortunately, culinary rhubarb is not as showy as its ornamental cousin *Rheum palmatum,* which is so striking you could grow it as a centerpiece if you have room.

Cultivation

Like asparagus, rhubarb, once settled, does not like to be moved and will tie up ground for a long time. But you can pick it from spring until early summer, and it is little trouble if planted in the right place.
SITE AND SOIL Rhubarb will grow on any kind of soil, including an acid one, providing it is well fed and well drained. The site needs to be open, away from shade cast by overhanging trees. Dig in plenty of manure before planting.
PLANTING Rhubarb can be grown from seed, but is usually planted as a dormant bare-root plant or potted nursery plant. You must start with certified virus-free stock. Plant bare-root stock in fall or spring, setting the plants 3ft (1m) apart. The buds should be covered by no more than 1in (2cm) of soil. Plant potted rhubarb into summer or early fall.
ROUTINE CARE The best plants are those that can be kept damp in summer and dry in winter. Water liberally, if necessary, and mulch around the stems with manure or grass cuttings to retain moisture. Tall stems of cream flowers are produced on mature plants. These are decorative but normally reduce plant vigor, so remove them before they grow large. About every 5 years, plants need dividing (see page 172). The most vigorous offshoots are generally those that have formed around the edges of a clump.

RHUBARB

FORCING Forcing lengthens the stems of rhubarb and brings it into production several weeks earlier. To force a plant, cover the crown with straw in late winter, and then put an upturned bucket, bushel basket, or a specially made terracotta cloche over the whole thing. Leave the protective cover on for about 4 weeks, or until the stems are long enough. Remove the cover when you have pulled the first stems.
YIELD AND HARVESTING Expect 5lb (2.5kg) of stalks from an established plant. Pull the stems upward and outward rather than cutting them, always leaving at least 4. Do not pull stems after midsummer so that the plant has a chance to replenish itself.
PESTS AND DISEASES Watch for rhubarb curculio that tunnels into the stalks. It can be controlled using rotenone. Watch carefully for crown rot and viruses.

RECOMMENDED CULTIVARS

'Cherry Red': *bright red, sweet stalks.*
'Giant Cherry': *suitable for climates with mild winters.*
'Valentine': *old, reliable cultivar.*
'Victoria': *old, reliable cultivar.*

CARROTS *Daucus carota*

MODERN CARROTS ARE ALL DESCENDED from purple and yellow types that came from Arabia in the 14th century. Selection by 17th-century Dutch growers produced the forerunners of the varieties we grow today. For decades, breeders have been in pursuit of the perfect carrot, but, unfortunately, the carrot rust fly, *Psila rosae*, whose larvae greedily attack the roots, has had the same objective. In the garden, the ferny, upright foliage contrasts well with the rounded shapes of lettuce or with strappy garlic leaves. Intercropping carrots with onions or annual flowers such as love-in-a-mist may discourage attack by carrot rust fly.

Cultivation

By growing your own carrots, you can be assured of having sweet, tender carrots – not cardboard supermarket carrots. You can choose: baby carrots, quick-growing, and tolerant of heavy soils; thick carrots, with plenty of meat; or long, sweet carrots. Plant carrots every two weeks during spring and summer, into fall in warm climates, to have fresh carrots available most of the time.

SITE AND SOIL The ideal soil is light and friable, well drained, and deep so roots can swell without constraint. In heavy soil, leaves tend to grow at the expense of roots, which are sometimes deformed.

SOWING Sow seed as thinly as possible (see page 170), ½in (1cm) deep, in rows 6in (15cm) apart. Seed germinates poorly in crusty soil. Cover the seed with a blend of loose sand and peat, or interplant with radishes, which come up first and loosen the soil surface.

THINNING Thinning carrots is a bad idea. It releases a smell that the carrot rust fly finds utterly irresistible, and the little crevices left in the soil provide ready-made entry holes for the adults to lay their eggs. Sow sparsely instead.

ROUTINE CARE Weed carefully while the seedlings are small. Do not overwater.

YIELD AND HARVESTING Expect 8–10lb (4–5kg) from a 10-ft (3-m) row. On light soils, leave carrots in the ground and pull them as required. On heavy soils, lift and store in boxes of sand (see page 187).

PESTS AND DISEASES Carrot rust fly is the most persistent nuisance because the larvae burrow deep into the roots (see page 190). Some cultivars have a far greater resistance to it than others. This seems to be associated with the level of phenolic acids contained in the roots. The fly's larvae need these acids to further their own development, so they avoid carrots with a low level of this particular fix.

RECOMMENDED CULTIVARS

BABY CARROTS
'Parmex': *tiny globe-shaped roots, very sweet and ideal for growing in containers.*
'Short 'n' Sweet': *cylindrical carrots that grow to 4in (10cm) in length despite heavy soil.*
'Thumbelina': *extra-early, globe-shaped carrots that tolerate heavy soil.*
MEDIUM-SIZED CARROTS
'Chantenay Royal': *stump-rooted, ready late autumn and winter, excellent flavor.*
'Fly Away': *a new cultivar with pleasant roots, made that much better by their resistance to carrot rust fly larvae.* **'Nantes Express'**: *ready by early summer, excellent quality.*
LONG CARROTS
'Artist': *extra-sweet roots, high in vitamin A and best when grown for fall harvest.* **'Blaze'**: *smooth and bright with disease tolerance; good for cold storage.* **'Camberley'**: *tapered roots 7–9in (18–23cm) long, overwinters well on heavy soils.* **'Ingot'**: *long stump root, excellent flavor, and high concentrations of carotene and vitamin C.*

	SPRING			SUMMER			AUTUMN			WINTER		
	Early	Mid	Late	Early	Mid	Late	Early	Mid	Late	Early	Mid	Late
	⚘	⚘	⚘	⚘	⚘	⚘						
			✂	✂	✂	✂	✂	✂	✂	✂	✂	✂

✿ **CARROTS**
'Nantes Express'

✿ **BABY CARROTS**
'Parmex'

IN THE KITCHEN

Home-grown carrots have a much sweeter flavor than supermarket carrots. Do not overcook them. If you steam them, you may feel that they need nothing more than to be finished off with some melted butter and finely chopped parsley.

CARROTS WITH CREAM SAUCE
Serves 4

¾–1lb (375–500g) carrots, scrubbed and cut into chunks
½ pint (300ml) chicken stock
½–1 tsp puréed garlic (see below)
½ cup (150ml) light cream
1 tbsp chopped chervil

1 Simmer the carrots in the chicken stock for about 8 minutes, or until just tender.

2 Stir in puréed garlic (see below) to taste. The sauce should be quite thick. Add the cream and sprinkle with chervil to serve.

CULINARY NOTES

❧ This recipe calls for puréed garlic. A small supply is very easy to make. Cover several heads of peeled cloves with boiling water, and blanch them for 2–3 minutes. Drain the water and repeat the blanching process twice more using fresh water, until the cloves are very soft. Then purée them. The purée will keep for several weeks in the fridge, covered with olive oil.
❧ Hot steamed carrots are delicious sprinkled with crumbled blue cheese and broiled until brown.
❧ If you like them raw, try Madhur Jaffrey's Indian Gujerati carrot salad: heap grated carrots on to a large dish and sprinkle with lemon juice to taste. Heat together 2 tablespoons of oil and 1 of mustard seeds. When the seeds start to pop, pour the mixture over the carrots.

BEETS *Beta vulgaris* subsp. *vulgaris*

YOU CAN USE SHINING beet leaves to telling effect among the lacy foliage of carrots or coriander. They also look sumptuous with pot marigolds. For the greatest impact, choose a variety like 'Sweetheart' with ruby-tinted leaves. Beets are easy to grow but have had problems shedding their captured-in-a-can image. Try cooking fresh beets with butter and orange juice.

Cultivation

There are many "novelty" beets that are worth experimenting with: yellow and white forms and a very pretty old cultivar called 'Chioggia', which has dark flesh marked with concentric white rings. Unfortunately the contrast fades when the beet is cooked.

SITE AND SOIL The best soil is rich, light, and fertile, but not recently manured.

SOWING Start sowing in midspring. To stop plants from running to seed, choose a bolt-resistant cultivar for early sowings, and sow as thinly as possible, ¾in (1.5cm) deep, in rows 8in (20cm) apart, or 12in (30cm) for later sowings (see page 170). Seed contains a natural germination inhibitor, so it may help to soak it for half an hour first. The seed is usually gathered in small clusters, but monogerm varieties produce only one plant from each seed and so reduce the need for thinning.

THINNING Thin as soon as the seedlings start to touch each other, leaving them about 6in (15cm) apart.

ROUTINE CARE Mulch around the crop to conserve moisture, and keep weeded.

YIELD AND HARVESTING Expect 10–18lb (5–8kg) from a 10-ft (3-m) row. Use before the roots are too big. Beets can be stored in boxes of sand through the winter, but twist off the foliage first (see page 187).

PESTS AND DISEASES Beets are generally free from pests and diseases.

❀ **LONG BEETS** 'Forono'

❀ **ROUND BEET** 'Monogram'

RECOMMENDED CULTIVARS

ROUND BEET
'**Bikores**': *bolt-resistant.* '**Boltardy**': *can be sown earlier than other cultivars.* '**Burpee Golden**': *sweet, mild, golden roots.* '**Detroit Dark Red**': *tasty and tender.* '**Monogram**': *monogerm variety.*
LONG BEET
'**Forono**': *slow to go woody; good flavor.*
BABY BEET
'**Little Ball**': *pick early while still small.*

SPRING			SUMMER			AUTUMN			WINTER		
Early	Mid	Late	Early	Mid	Late	Early	Mid	Late	Early	Mid	Late
🌱	🌱	🌱	🌱								
		✂	✂	✂	✂	✂					

POTATOES *Solanum tuberosum*

DIGGING POTATOES IS ALWAYS AN ADVENTURE. The vines, stems, and leaves give no indication of the extent of the treasure buried underneath. Sometimes the potatoes cluster together as neatly as a clutch of goose eggs. At other times you dig wildly down a row to find that bugs or blight have beaten you to the prize. There are three types: early, midseason, and late, which you lift in their appropriate seasons from midsummer until autumn. Even their best friends would not call potatoes decorative, but what they lack in looks they make up for in comfort. A baked potato, or thick potato and leek soup, makes even the deepest winter doldrum more bearable. In North America, thanks to connoisseurs who have rescued old varieties from the edge of oblivion, many more kinds of potato are now available than there were 10 years ago. Try a few different novelties each year.

Cultivation

Early potatoes mature in about 14–16 weeks, midseason in 16–17 weeks, and late potatoes in 18–20 weeks. The heaviest crops come from the later liftings. Choose a succession of varieties, bearing in mind that, in a small garden, early potatoes are the most valuable. You can grow potatoes in pots, but you should not try to fit more than 2 plants in a container less than 12in (30cm) wide and deep.

SITE AND SOIL Although they prefer slightly acid ground (pH 5–6), potatoes grow in a wide range of soils, doing best in moisture-retentive ground. Dig in plenty of compost the autumn before planting, and rotate crops to try to stop pests from building up in the soil.

SOWING Before planting, potatoes are usually presprouted. Do this by setting them in a single layer in trays or boxes indoors, the end with the most "eyes" uppermost, so that shoots start to grow. This generally takes about 6 weeks. Do not plant early potatoes until 2 weeks before the last frost is expected. Set them about 4–5in (10–12cm) deep and 12in (30cm) apart in rows 24in (60cm) apart (see opposite). Late types should be set at slightly wider spacings, 15in (38cm) apart in rows 30in (75cm) apart. You can also use a no-dig method, laying the potatoes in shallow depressions on top of the soil and then mulching them thickly with compost, grass cuttings, or leaf mold. It sounds lazy, but it works.

ROUTINE CARE Mound soil up to prevent greening of any tubers that push their way up to the soil surface (see opposite). With the no-dig method, add more mulch as necessary. For high yields, water thoroughly once every 2 weeks.

YIELD AND HARVESTING Expect 14–23lb (6–10kg) from a 10-ft (3-m) row. The earliest crops can be lifted when the flowers on the vine begin to open, the latest when the vine has died down. To prevent them from turning green, keep potatoes in cool storage in the dark.

PESTS AND DISEASES Colorado potato beetle is the worst pest (see page 191). Blight can be a problem in cool, damp summers (see page 193). Where it is prevalent, choose blight-resistant cultivars.

RECOMMENDED CULTIVARS

EARLY POTATOES
'Onaway': *a great long-storing potato with white flesh and light brown skin, resistant to scab and late blight.* **'Yukon Gold'**: *one of the earliest of long-storing yellow-fleshed potatoes; virus-resistant.*
MIDSEASON POTATOES
'Frontier Russet': *new baking potato with disease resistance.*
LATE POTATOES
'Kennebec': *classic large baker with tan skin and white flesh.* **'Desirée'**: *oval and red-skinned, good for french fries and baking.*
HEIRLOOM POTATOES
'Lady Finger': *old-fashioned with slim, yellow tubers and delicious flavor.*

IN THE KITCHEN

To taste potatoes at their best, you need to choose the right kind for the right dish. Some, like 'Desirée', mash well. Others, like 'Kennebec', bake beautifully, while knobbly, old-fashioned 'Lady Finger' is supreme in salads. No one potato does everything equally well.

ONION, BACON, AND POTATO HOTPOT
Serves 4

(The proportions of the three main ingredients can be varied to taste.)
a little butter
1lb (500g) onions, thinly sliced
8 oz (250g) bacon, diced
1½ lbs (750g) potatoes, thinly sliced
For the sauce
4 tbsp (60g) butter
⅔ cup (60g) all-purpose flour
2½ cups (600ml) milk
1 cup (125g) aged Cheddar cheese, grated
salt and black pepper, optional

1 Preheat the oven to 375°F (190°C). (Use a slightly lower temperature if the dish you are using is shallow and wide rather than deep.)

2 Butter a deep ovenproof dish (with a lid, if possible), and put in the onion, bacon, and potato in layers, finishing with a potato layer.

3 Make the sauce by combining the butter and flour in a saucepan over a low heat. Slowly add the milk, stirring all the time to avoid lumps. Stir in the cheese until melted. Season if necessary, then pour the sauce over the layers of potato, onion, and bacon.

4 Cover the dish (with foil if there is no lid) and bake for about 1 hour, or until the potatoes are cooked. Uncover the dish for the final 10 minutes so that the top becomes nicely crisp and brown.

PLANTING AND HILLING UP

1 *Make a furrow 4–5in (10–12cm) deep. Set the potatoes in it so that the ends with the most sprouts are pointing upward. Cover with soil. Do not plant early potatoes too soon (see opposite), since the foliage is easily frosted.*

2 *Hill up the soil around the stems with a hoe when the foliage is about 12in (30cm) high. This stops tubers near the surface from working their way up through the soil and turning green. Green potatoes are poisonous.*

EARLY POTATO 'Onaway'

MIDSEASON POTATO 'Frontier Russet'

HEIRLOOM POTATO 'Lady Finger'

EARLY POTATO 'Yukon Gold'

TURNIPS & RUTABAGAS

Brassica rapa rapa & Brassica napus napobrassica

IT HAS USUALLY BEEN THE turnip's misfortune to be lumped together with the rutabaga, a much less malleable vegetable. The rutabaga is large with yellow flesh and seems to smack more of the farmyard than the dinner table, however you cook it. The turnip, especially since the spread of the small, summer-maturing Japanese types, is far more succulent, though less hardy and less high-yielding. There are two important rules to bear in mind with turnips: never let them get too big, and never eat them when they are too old. Neither vegetable is very decorative, but if you grow your own turnips, you can enjoy the added bonus of cooking and eating the young green tops of the plant.

Cultivation

The early-maturing types of turnip deteriorate quickly. Sow small batches of seed every 3 weeks. A cultivar such as 'Tokyo Cross' may be ready to harvest after only 6 weeks. Hardy autumn types take about 12 weeks to mature.

SITE AND SOIL Neither crop will thrive in an acid soil (the ideal pH is about 7). Use ground that has been well manured for a previous crop and is cool and friable. In cool climates, summer sowings of turnip can be made in light shade, provided the soil is moist.

SOWING Start sowing turnips in mid-spring for spring and summer crops and from mid- to late summer for fall and winter crops. Sow seed as thinly as possible in furrows about ¾ in (1.5cm) deep in rows 12–15in (30–38cm) apart (see page 170). Start sowing rutabagas in midspring. They will need the same depth but a wider spacing of 15–18in (38–45cm) between the rows.

THINNING Turnips grow fast, so thin them while the seedlings are still small (see page 171). Thin spring and summer plants to 4in (10cm) apart. Thin fall and winter plants to 6in (15cm) apart. Rutabagas will need 10in (25cm) in order to develop.

ROUTINE CARE Water, if necessary, in dry periods. Shade during hot weather.

HARVESTING AND YIELD Expect 14lb (6kg) of turnips and 30lb (14kg) of rutabagas from a 10-ft (3-m) row. Early sowings of turnips should be pulled when the roots are no bigger than a golf ball.

Scratch away some soil from the top of the roots if you want to check the size. Summer-sown long-keeping varieties can be left in the ground until needed, as can rutabagas. Any roots not used by midwinter should be lifted and stored in a cool, frost-free place (see page 187).

PESTS AND DISEASES Turnips and rutabagas are members of the cabbage family, so seedlings may be attacked by flea beetle and root maggots (see page 191).

RECOMMENDED CULTIVARS

TURNIPS

'De Milan': *a spring crop with rose shoulders and white bottom.* '**Milan White Forcing**': *early crops of flattish roots.* '**Tokyo Cross**': *fast-maturing, with small, white-fleshed roots. May bolt if sown before midsummer.*

RUTABAGAS

'**Marian**': *globe-shaped, yellow-fleshed roots, resistant to mildew.*

	SPRING			SUMMER			AUTUMN			WINTER		
	Early	Mid	Late	Early	Mid	Late	Early	Mid	Late	Early	Mid	Late
		⚘	⚘	⚘	⚘							
		✂	✂					✂	✂	✂		
		⚘	⚘	⚘			✂	✂	✂	✂		
☐ Turnips						☐ Rutabagas						

RED-TOPPED TURNIP

WHITE TURNIPS

RUTABAGA

PARSNIPS *Pastinaca sativa*

NOBODY WRITES POEMS ABOUT PARSNIPS, nor do you find chefs fussing over them in restaurants. Zucchini have all the fun, primped out in a hundred ways. The English food writer, Jane Grigson, first pointed out that the Russian word for parsnip was *pasternak*. Would we feel the same way about *Dr. Zhivago* if we knew it had been written by Boris Parsnip? Yet before the advent of the potato, the unfairly neglected parsnip was highly valued for its sweetness, its hardiness, and its ability to overwinter in the ground.

Cultivation

Cold intensifies the flavor of parsnips and converts some of their starch into sugar, so they are sweeter in cold winters than they are in mild ones.

SITE AND SOIL Grow parsnips in an open situation on soil that is deep and light with a pH around 6.5. Acid soils make the roots more prone to canker. Recently manured ground has traditionally been avoided for this crop since it was thought to promote forking in the root, but research has not borne this out. On shallow soil, use a short, bulbous variety such as 'Avonresister'.

SOWING Seed must be fresh and kept moist to germinate. Even under good conditions, germination can take 3 weeks. Sow seed about ½in (1cm) deep in rows 12in (30cm) apart (see page 170). If the soil is cold, germination will be slow and erratic. You can warm it up a month before sowing with sheets of plastic. Crops sown later seem to be less prone to canker.

THINNING Thin the seedlings once they are well established. For large roots leave 6in (15cm) between plants; for smaller ones, leave 3in (7cm).

ROUTINE CARE Parsnips tend to split if watered after a prolonged dry spell. Water regularly, or not at all.

HARVESTING AND YIELD Expect 8lb (4kg) of parsnips from a 10-ft (3-m) row. Lift from mid-autumn onward if the ground is not frozen. Where winters are severe, laying straw over the crop makes lifting easier.

PARSNIPS

PESTS AND DISEASES Canker is the main enemy, showing as reddish brown or black patches on the roots (see page 194). There is no effective remedy. Choose a resistant variety such as 'Cobham Improved Marrow', and sow later rather than earlier.

RECOMMENDED CULTIVARS

'All American': *tender flesh, long keeper.*
'Andover': *US-bred, long narrow roots, good resistance to canker.* **'Avonresister'**: *short-rooted, canker-resistant, good on shallow soil.*
'Cobham Improved Marrow': *long shape, smooth skin, good canker resistance.*
'Tender and True': *traditional cultivar, very long roots with little hard core.*

SPRING			SUMMER			AUTUMN			WINTER		
Early	Mid	Late	Early	Mid	Late	Early	Mid	Late	Early	Mid	Late
♧	♧	♧					✄	✄	✄	✄	✄

IN THE KITCHEN

Although they are traditionally baked with a roast, parsnips have many other roles to play in the kitchen. They make delicious purées and, having a rich sweetness themselves, combine particularly well with tart fruit, such as apples.

PARSNIP AND APPLE BAKE
Serves 6

3lb (1.5kg) parsnips, peeled and cubed
a little butter, for greasing
2 large cooking apples, peeled, cored, and thinly sliced
juice of a lemon
4 tsp brown sugar

1 Cook the parsnips in boiling water, drain, and purée them in a food processor or blender. Spread half the purée in a buttered gratin dish, then cover it with half of the apple slices.

2 Repeat the process, arranging the second batch of apple slices neatly on top of the parsnips. Sprinkle the lemon juice and sugar over the top.

3 Bake in a moderate oven 350°F (180°C) for 30–40 minutes until the apples have softened.

CULINARY NOTES

⚘ Try glazing parsnips with melted butter mixed with a little fresh orange juice to serve as an accompaniment to a meal.

⚘ You can make parsnip chips to eat as a snack or a side dish. Parboil them first, slice thinly, and deep-fry the slices in hot oil.

⚘ If you intend to roast parsnips in the traditional way, tucked around a roast, parboil the prepared roots for a couple of minutes before putting them in the roasting pan. This will make them both succulent and crisp.

RADISHES *Raphanus sativus*

THE RADISH IS TAKEN MORE SERIOUSLY in China and Japan than it is in other places. Chinese chefs carve huge 'China Rose' radishes into intricate flowers, and Japanese gardeners cultivate long white daikon radishes, a single root of which can weigh 33lb (15kg). The typical American red globe radish is the size of a large marble, though there is a bigger black Spanish winter radish. None is decorative when growing, but they are good in salads, and the globe radishes are extremely useful for growing as a catch crop.

Cultivation

Different types of radishes need different sowing times. Start with the small globe types, such as 'Easter Egg', in early spring. Since these will be ready to harvest within a few weeks, you can grow them between other slower-maturing vegetables, such as parsnips. Delay sowing daikon types until after the longest day of summer or they will bolt, as will winter radishes. These are best sown toward late summer or even later in warm climates.

SITE AND SOIL Radishes grow best in a light, sandy soil in an open situation. Summer crops will tolerate partial shade.

SOWING Little and often is the key with globe radishes. Sow short rows, ½in (1cm) deep and 6in (15cm) apart, every other week (see page 170). Encourage rapid germination and growth by watering the seed bed if necessary in dry weather. Sow daikon and winter types ½in (1cm) deep in rows 8–10in (20–25cm) apart, watering the seed bed first if the ground is dry.

THINNING Thin globe radishes to leave about 1in (2cm) between plants. Leave at least 6in (15cm) between daikon and winter types.

ROUTINE CARE This is an easy, carefree crop, requiring no feeding but some watering. Excessive watering makes leaves grow at the expense of the roots.

YIELD AND HARVESTING Expect about 30 globe radishes and 10lb (5kg) winter radishes from a 3-ft (1-m) row. Globe radishes should mature within a month and need to be eaten as quickly as possible before they get tough or pithy. If you let them run to flower, the plants produce small, hot seedpods that can be steamed, stir-fried, or made into a spicy relish.

Daikon and winter radishes can take up to 3 months to produce a crop.

PESTS AND DISEASES Flea beetle may leave seedlings peppered with small holes (see page 191). Cover the beds with floating row covers to prevent damage by cabbage maggots (see page 191).

RECOMMENDED CULTIVARS

GLOBE RADISHES
'Cherry Belle': *smooth, round roots, bright red color.* **'Easter Egg'**: *multicolored roots in red, purple, and white.* **'French Breakfast'**: *classic cylindrical root, mild and sweet.*

DAIKON RADISHES
'April Cross': *roots more than 12in (30cm) long, standing well through winter.* **'Mino Early'**: *popular and mild.*

WINTER RADISHES
'Black Spanish': *old variety that can be round or long-rooted.* **'China Rose'**: *long red roots, white flesh.*

PODS
'Münchner Bier': *good winter roots and by far the best pods, crunchy and succulent.* **'Rat's Tail'**: *has pods reaching up to 12in (30cm) long.*

	SPRING			SUMMER			AUTUMN			WINTER		
	Early	Mid	Late	Early	Mid	Late	Early	Mid	Late	Early	Mid	Late
					⚘							
								✂	✂			
	⚘	⚘	⚘									
				✂	✂		⚘	⚘				
								✂	✂			

☐ Daikon/winter radishes   ☐ Globe radishes

GLOBE RADISH 'Cherry Belle'

WINTER RADISH 'Black Spanish'

DAIKON RADISH 'April Cross'

JERUSALEM ARTICHOKES *Helianthus tuberosus*

MOST PEOPLE KNOW ONE THING about Jerusalem artichokes, and that was described by the 17th-century botanist John Goodyer. "In my judgment," he wrote, "which way soever they be drest and eaten they stirre and cause a filthie loathsome wind within the bodie." Being tall, however, they make useful summer screens, and some cultivars bear large yellow daisy flowers.

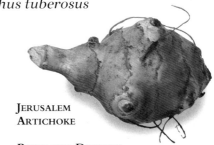

JERUSALEM ARTICHOKE

Cultivation

Jerusalem artichokes can grow to 10ft (3m) high, and as well as making a good screen will filter wind on an exposed site.
SITE AND SOIL No plant could be less fussy, but the best tubers come from plants grown in rich, cool soil, where they will spread rapidly and become invasive.

PLANTING Plant tubers 4–6in (10–15cm) deep and 12in (30cm) apart in spring.
ROUTINE CARE The top growth dies back in late autumn. Cut the withered stalks to within 3in (7cm) of the ground.
YIELD AND HARVESTING Each plant should yield about 3lb (1.5kg) of tubers. Lift as needed in winter, but by spring clear completely to prevent rampant spread.

PESTS AND DISEASES
Maggots, gophers, and mice are the pests that are most likely to munch on the tubers under the ground.

RECOMMENDED CULTIVARS

'Dwarf Sunray': *small and free-flowering.*
'Fuseau': *long, relatively smooth tubers.*

SALSIFY & SCORZONERA
Tragopogon porrifolius & Scorzonera hispanica

THESE TWO VEGETABLES GROW in a similar fashion, producing long, thin, horseradish-like roots that are tricky to prepare. It is easiest to skin them after cooking, like new potatoes. Salsify is a biennial and produces conical flower buds that are delicious picked just before they open and used in omelettes. Salsify produces a white root, but scorzonera's is black and the foliage is less glaucous. It is a perennial. Its name comes from the Spanish word for viper, for the root was once used to cure snake bites.

SCORZONERA

SALSIFY

Cultivation

If you can persuade the roots to swell thicker than your little finger, you will be doing well. You also need to prevent the roots from forking, which they will if the ground has been too recently manured. The flowers of mature plants are very decorative (salsify's are pinkish purple, scorzonera's are bright yellow). As the plants age, the roots become woody.
SITE AND SOIL Both need deep, light, friable soil and prefer an open, sunny site.
SOWING Sow seed thinly in midspring, ½in (1cm) deep, in rows that are at least 6in (15cm) apart (see page 170).
THINNING Thin to 4in (10cm) apart.
ROUTINE CARE Neither is troublesome, provided seed is sown in suitable soil.

YIELD AND HARVESTING You should get at least 20 roots (about 4lb/2kg) from a 10-ft (3-m) row. They can be left in the soil until needed. If the ground is likely to freeze, lift the roots, trim the tops, and keep them in a cool root cellar in moist sand, wrapped in newspaper.
PESTS AND DISEASES White blister may appear on the foliage as glistening white pustules.

RECOMMENDED CULTIVARS

SALSIFY
'Sandwich Island': *long, sweet roots.*
SCORZONERA
'Russian Giant': *black skin, delicate flavor.*

SPRING			SUMMER			AUTUMN			WINTER		
Early	Mid	Late	Early	Mid	Late	Early	Mid	Late	Early	Mid	Late
⚘						✂	✂	✂	✂		

HERBS & EDIBLE FLOWERS

YOU ARE AS LIKELY TO FIND THYME in a rock garden as in an herb garden, or to use sage to bolster an herbaceous planting of misty blue, as you are to pen it off in a kitchen garden. The decorative possibilities of herbs were recognized long ago: pyramids of bay to flank a front door, or feathery stands of fennel to bring variety to a foliage border. Collecting herbs together in one place has an academic kind of charm, but you may find that you can create better plant groups by combining them with annual flowers or perennials. Set your chives free to edge a rosebed, or let them fraternize in a windowbox with ivy and feverfew. Be careful about liberating rampant herbs: *Mentha* × *gentilis* 'Variegata' is the only mint that will not try to overrun its neighbors.

TIME FOR BASIL

Basil is one of the most rewarding of all herbs to grow, either outside in beds or indoors in pots perched on a windowsill. Most common is the plain green basil, but there are types with luxuriant purple leaves. Others, such as Greek basil, grow as neatly as topiary.

BORDER OF FENNEL

Both green and bronze-leaved types of fennel have an important part to play in this cleverly thought-out herbaceous border. Seen here in late spring, the fennels' flat heads of yellow flowers will later reinforce the color of the golden hops climbing the backdrop of the hedge.

INTRICATE SAGE

'Tricolor' is the most complex of all sage cultivars. The green leaves have white edges, and the new growth is flushed with pink and purple. It grows more weakly than other types and is not reliably hardy. Plant it in full sun, where it can make a low, informal hedge.

CHEERFUL CHIVES

Chives, often used as edging, combine here with frilly lettuce to fill the boxwood-edged bed of a potager. The purple flowers echo the tone set by the dark-leaved lettuce. If chives are trimmed back when they begin to look scruffy, they will quickly sprout again.

BORAGE BLUES

Although the foliage is somewhat coarse, the fine hairs on the stems and flowerheads give borage a shimmering quality, especially when seen against the light. In mixed plantings use it with foxgloves, or grow it in its own bed in a formal fashion and allow it to self-seed with abandon.

ANNUAL & BIENNIAL HERBS

THESE HERBS NEED TO BE SOWN each spring, so use their relative impermanence to advantage by growing them in different places every year where they can bring variety to the decorative kitchen garden. The plan for an herb garden on pages 48–49 mixes annual with perennial herbs in a formal design, but you can also grow annual herbs in rows among vegetables to add color and contrast to a productive plot. You could also fill an open corner with some of the sun-lovers, broadcasting the seed in irregular patches to produce a carefree, random effect.

DILL
Anethum graveolens
Dill is grown for the aniseed flavor of its leaves and seeds, the seeds having the stronger taste. Like fennel, it has threadlike leaves and flat heads of yellow flowers from mid- to late summer. 'Dukat' is the best strain for leaves, 'Bouquet' for seed.
CULTIVATION Height 3ft (1m). Broadcast seed or sow in shallow furrows in a sunny spot (see page 170), spring to midsummer. Harvest a few leaves before the plants flower, when the foliage diminishes. Then let the plant flower and produce seeds. Cut heads as the seeds turn brown, and shake them upside down over a sheet of paper. Pick out insects and stray bits of stem before storing in an airtight jar.

ANGELICA
Angelica archangelica
A statuesque biennial producing umbels of pale green flowers on tall, stout stems. *Angelica gigas* has dramatic purple stems.
CULTIVATION Height 6ft (1.8m). Thrives in moist soil, in sun or partial shade. It will self-seed enthusiastically. If you do not have a self-sowing plant, try sowing fresh seed outside in fall, or buy nursery seedlings.

CHERVIL
Anthriscus cerefolium
Fresh chervil is a revelation to anyone who knows only the dried kind. It grows fast; useful quantities of its ferny leaves can be picked only 6 weeks after sowing.
CULTIVATION Height 12in (30cm). Prefers light shade. Sow in rows or broadcast seed (see page 170) every 2 weeks in small batches from early spring until late summer. Grow outdoors in a mild climate. Kept at 45°F (8°C), it will give fresh supplies of leaves all winter.

BORAGE
Borago officinalis
Borage is easy to please and bees love it. The brilliant blue flowers can be sprinkled on salads, while the cucumber-flavored leaves can be used in fruit punch.
CULTIVATION Height 24in (60cm). Prefers a sunny site and well-drained soil. Sow in spring in rows 12in (30cm) apart (see page 170). Thin to 12in (30cm) apart.

POT MARIGOLD
Calendula officinalis
An enthusiastic self-seeder with bright orange flowers that continue throughout summer. Use the petals instead of saffron to flavor and color rice, or sprinkle them fresh on top of a green salad.
CULTIVATION Height 18in (45cm). Likes sun. Broadcast seed in early spring (see page 171), covering with ¼in (5mm) of soil. Thin to 6in (15cm) between plants.

CILANTRO/CORIANDER
Coriandrum sativum
The first leaves (cilantro) resemble flat-leaved parsley, but as the plant shoots up, the leaves become wispy and develop a different taste. The seeds (coriander) and cilantro, both difficult to get in sufficient quantity, are what you need for cooking. Some strains are better for producing cilantro, others for coriander.
CULTIVATION Height 3ft (1m). Prefers sun. Seed germinates quickly. For a constant supply of cilantro, sow in rows or broadcast seed every 2 weeks in small batches from early spring (see page 170). You can also sow quite thickly in a large pot indoors and snip off foliage as needed. Coriander is ready to harvest in summer, but you need to be quick since the seeds drop as soon as they are ripe.

BASIL
Ocimum basilicum
One of the most rewarding herbs to grow, smelling of heat and summer vacations. It can be raised very successfully on a windowsill indoors (see page 42) and picked until late winter. Grown outside, its season is shorter, for it is tender and should not be sown until late spring or early summer. For fat, bushy plants, pinch out the tops once they are established. This will force new growth to sprout from the leaf junctions. If you grow Greek basil, the plants will naturally be fat and bushy. 'Dark Opal' is a very decorative variety with large purple leaves. There are many others. All are good.
CULTIVATION Height 12–18in (30–45cm). Needs warmth and sun. Sow seed indoors, from early spring, in pots or 6-pack trays and transplant into individual pots or containers (see page 168) to keep on the windowsill. Outside, sow seed ½in (1cm) deep in rows 15in (38cm) apart (see page 170). Thin seedlings to 12in (30cm) apart. Use a floating row cover (see page 166) for extra protection in the early stages.

PARSLEY
Petroselinum crispum
One of the most useful of all culinary herbs. You need two types: the curled kind for decorative effect, to grow among pot marigolds and red lettuce, and the flat-leaved French kind for the finest flavor.
CULTIVATION Height 12–18in (30–45cm). Grow in fertile, well-drained soil in sun or partial shade. Sow seed thinly in rows 10in (25cm) apart from early spring to early summer (see page 170). Thin gradually until plants are 9in (23cm) apart. Cut down in early autumn, and water to encourage fresh growth.

NASTURTIUM
Tropaeolum majus
The colorful flowers make pretty edgings in a potager but are edible, too, and can be strewn over salads. The peppery leaves are excellent in salads or sandwiches, while the seeds can be used as a substitute for capers.
CULTIVATION Height 9–12in (23–30cm). Best in sun. Sow in situ in midspring, setting seed ½in (1cm) deep (see page 170).

DILL

ANGELICA

CHERVIL

BORAGE

POT
MARIGOLD

BASIL

PURPLE-
LEAVED
BASIL

CILANTRO

FLAT-
LEAVED
PARSLEY

CURLED
PARSLEY

NASTURTIUM

PERENNIAL HERBS

ALTHOUGH SOME OF THESE PLANTS reach an impressive height by summer, in winter they disappear from view. In a herb garden, mix them with some of the evergreen herbs (see page 114). Several, notably garlic chives, fennel, mint, and sorrel, are thuggish in behavior, so your problem will be in controlling rather than growing them. Contain mint by planting it in a bottomless bucket sunk in the ground. Fennel spreads by enthusiastic self-seeding. Be prepared to cut off its head before it starts to shed its seed. If space is limited, chives should be your first choice in this group.

CHIVES
Allium schoenoprasum
Chives make neat edgings for paths, the delicately onion-flavored foliage topped with small, round heads of purple flowers from early to midsummer. They also do well in windowboxes if well watered. A dramatic variety 'Giant' is twice the normal size. Garlic chives, *Allium tuberosum*, have white starlike flowers in late summer (see pages 22–23), and the leaves taste mildly like garlic.
CULTIVATION Height 6–10in (15–25cm). Chives do best in moist, fertile soil. They can be raised from seed, but it is simpler to buy a clump and divide it with a sharp knife in early autumn to make more plants. Set these about 12in (30cm) apart.

HORSERADISH
Armoracia rusticana
The peppery-flavored taproot is grated to flavor sauces. Horseradish is difficult to get rid of once established, so grow it in a corner where it can be left undisturbed.
CULTIVATION Height 24in (60cm). Plant the bare roots in spring 12in (30cm) apart in a short row, with the top of the root about 2in (5cm) below the surface of the soil. Dig up roots as required.

FRENCH TARRAGON
Artemisia dracunculus
Tarragon spreads quickly by underground rhizomes, so you are unlikely to need more than one plant. The flavor of the leaves diminishes as plants get older. Renew them every 2–3 years.
CULTIVATION Height 18–24in (45–60cm). Plant in a sunny, sheltered site in light, well-drained soil in spring or autumn. Extend the growing season by planting a few rhizomes in a cold frame.

FENNEL
Foeniculum vulgare
Fennel gives sculptural height to a herb garden, especially the bronze-leaved variety, *Foeniculum vulgare* 'Rubrum'. The filigree foliage is topped by flat heads of golden flowers in midsummer.
CULTIVATION Height 5–8ft (1.5–2.5m). Plant in well-drained soil in spring or autumn. Cut down stems in autumn and be ruthless about discarding unwanted seedlings that emerge in the wrong place, or you will end up with a fennel forest.

LOVAGE
Levisticum officinale
A luxuriant plant, the leaves taste like celery with a dash of yeast. These are the most commonly used part, but you can also use the seeds to flavor soup. Lovage takes at least 3 years to reach full size.
CULTIVATION Height 6ft (1.8m). Plant in autumn in rich, moist soil in sun or partial shade. You can buy plants or raise them from seed, sowing in seed 6-pack trays indoors (see page 168) and later transplanting them to their final positions in the garden.

MINT
Mentha spp.
Mints are bullies, inclined to engulf their neighbors. Try to grow them together in one bed. *Mentha rotundifolia*, or applemint, with round, hairy leaves, is said to make the best mint sauce. Ginger mint (*Mentha × gentilis* 'Variegata') has gold-variegated leaves and makes excellent groundcover.
CULTIVATION Height 18in–3ft (45cm–1m). Mints like rich, moist soil and will grow happily in shade. If foliage becomes shabby in midsummer, shear it down to encourage fresh growth.

MARJORAM
Origanum spp.
Pot marjoram (*Origanum vulgare*) has purple-pink flowers, bliss for bees, but the flavor of the leaves is not as strong as that of sweet marjoram (*Origanum marjorana*). This has a smaller, neater, bushy habit, with grayish green leaves and white flowers. Both flower in summer, but sweet marjoram has a longer season. The herb can be used fresh or dried and brings a Mediterranean tang to the bland flavor of chicken. Like basil, marjoram has a natural affinity with tomatoes.
CULTIVATION Height 12–18in (30–45cm). Plant in late spring in well-drained soil in full sun. Cut bushes down by two-thirds in late autumn. Both types are reasonably hardy.

SORREL
Rumex spp.
Garden sorrel (*Rumex acetosa*) is a large-leaved plant, suspiciously like a dock. The leaves are sharp-tasting, getting more bitter as the season progresses. Use fresh in small quantities in salads, or cook to make a purée. Sorrel also makes good soup. French sorrel (*Rumex scutatus*) has prettier leaves, like little shields, that loll around on the ground.
CULTIVATION Height 9–12in (23–30cm). Sorrel succeeds in any well-drained ground in sun or partial shade. Raise it from seed (see page 170) or buy plants to set out in spring or autumn. Pinch out the flowering stems when they appear to force the plant to produce more leaves.

SWEET VIOLET
Viola odorata
The flowers, in shades of purple and white, are carried from late winter to midspring. They are often crystallized and used to decorate cakes, desserts, and ice cream. You can also scatter fresh violet petals on salads or use them to garnish a dish of fruit, tied in a little bunch with some of their own heart-shaped leaves.
CULTIVATION Height 7cm (3in). Plants of sweet violet are easy to establish in any fertile, moist soil. They will thrive in sun or partial shade, and clump up quickly by means of overground runners.

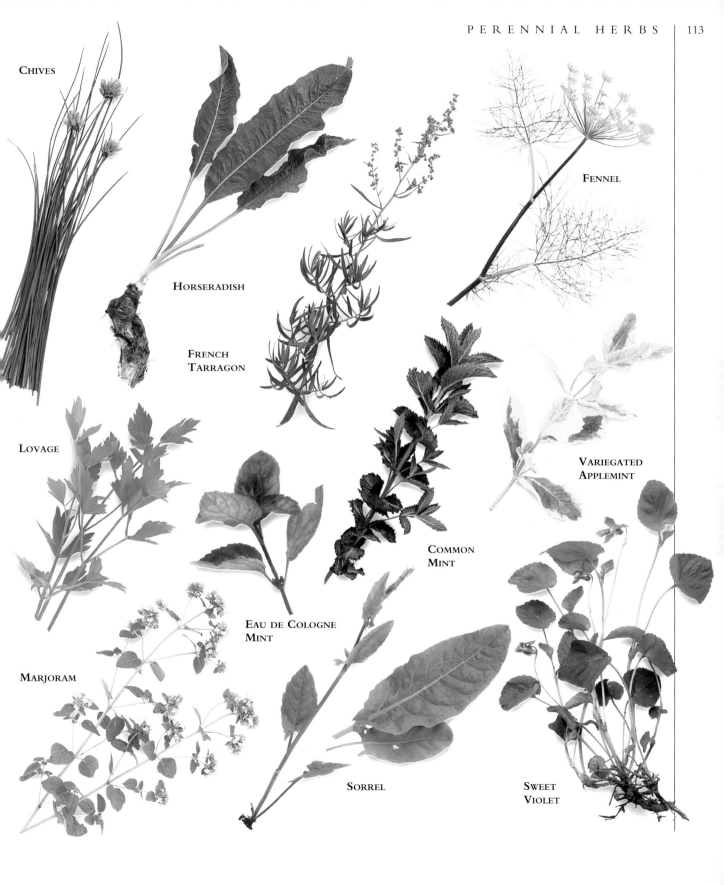

CHIVES

HORSERADISH

FENNEL

FRENCH
TARRAGON

LOVAGE

COMMON
MINT

VARIEGATED
APPLEMINT

EAU DE COLOGNE
MINT

MARJORAM

SORREL

SWEET
VIOLET

SHRUBBY PERENNIAL HERBS

THIS GROUP INCLUDES herbs with evergreen leaves and woody stems that range in size from miniature bushes to small trees. They are likely to be permanent fixtures in any planting, the built-in furniture of the garden room, so you need to think carefully about where you site them. All are sun lovers and some, such as thyme, rosemary, and sage, may rot off if they are planted in wet, badly drained ground. Bay can be clipped into splendid architectural shapes, but rosemary, too, lends itself to topiary treatment. Sage has the most handsome leaves, whether gray, purple, or variegated.

BAY
Laurus nobilis
Left to its own devices, the sweet bay makes a handsome tall tree as broad as it is high, the evergreen leaves joined in mid-spring by knobby little clusters of pale greenish white flowers. Trimmed into a geometric shape or grown as a mop-headed standard, it is the perfect plant for a formal herb garden or potager. The 17th-century herbalist Nicholas Culpeper said that "neither witch nor devil, thunder nor lightning, will hurt a man in the place where a bay tree is." Bay leaves may be used in fresh or dried forms for cooking; dried, they are an essential ingredient of *bouquets garnis*.
CULTIVATION Height 10–20ft (3–6m). Plant in midspring in a sunny, sheltered position. Bay is not dependably hardy but will grow well in a pot that can be moved inside where winters are harsh. Clip to shape if necessary during the summer. Bay can sometimes become infested with scale insects (see page 191).

ROSEMARY
Rosmarinus officinalis
Most rosemaries have greenish foliage and bluish flowers, both of which drift toward gray. The cultivar 'Miss Jessopp's Upright' is markedly taller and more upright in growth than the common kind and is useful, clipped as topiary, to give structure and height in a mixed planting. Prostrate rosemary, with bright blue flowers, has the opposite habit and can be planted to sprawl over a step or the edge of a raised bed, or hug a sloping bank. Rosemary can also be trained, fanlike, against a wall. If you want to train it into a more idiosyncratic freestanding shape, make a wire frame, tie in the growths, and trim regularly. Pillars and pyramids may need to be tied up, corset-like, with fine nylon line.
CULTIVATION Height 3ft (1m). Plant in spring in a sunny spot in well-drained soil, or in a large pot. Some cultivars are less hardy than the common type. Overgrown bushes can be cut back hard in midspring. This is also the time to trim any unwanted growth from plants that are being trained against a wall, to avoid missing out on the following year's flowers.

SAGE
Salvia officinalis
The variegated varieties of sage are just as useful in the kitchen as the ordinary plain green type. There is virtually no difference in flavor. 'Icterina' has rough-textured leaves of green and gold. 'Tricolor' is even showier, its leaves splashed in pink, white, and green. The deep purple leaves of 'Purpurea' look splendid combined with green-leaved herbs or orange pot marigolds. Sage is handsome enough to be used in an herbaceous border, especially when topped by its spikes of bright blue flowers.
CULTIVATION Height 18in–3ft (45cm–1m). Sages hate prolonged winter wet and may rot in heavy soils. Plant in spring in light, well-drained soil in a site that gets plenty of sun. Sages quickly become leggy but are easy to propagate from cuttings taken in summer. Pull off sideshoots about 3in (7cm) long with a "heel" attached, then line them out in a cold frame or poke them into pots of sand and peat-based mix. When the cuttings are rooted, nip out the tops to encourage bushy growth. Alternatively, try mound layering (see page 173). Neaten plants by clipping them during the summer. You can dry the leaf clippings and store them in airtight jars.

WINTER SAVORY
Satureja montana
Winter savory is a hardy, almost evergreen, dwarf subshrub, unlike its cousin summer savory, which is an annual. Summer savory has the better flavor of the two, but winter savory has, of course, a much longer season of use. The leaves are peppery in taste and are often used to flavor salami. Tiny, rather insignificant, whitish pink flowers appear in summer.
CULTIVATION Height 12in (30cm). Plant winter savory in spring in any fertile, well-drained soil in full sun. It will need replacing every 2–3 years since plants quickly become woody and intractable. Propagate plants by dividing them in spring or autumn. They can also be mound layered (see page 173).

THYME
Thymus spp.
The thyme clan contains various species with different habits of growth: some form tiny bushes; others are dense, spreading mats of foliage that put down roots as they travel. The creeping kinds, such as *Thymus serpyllum*, are excellent in paths and paving but are more difficult to manage in a mixed herb bed. This is the place for upright varieties such as *Thymus vulgaris*, the common thyme, with gray-green leaves and mauve flowers. The bushy cultivar 'Argenteus' has pretty silver-variegated leaves and pink flowers. *Thymus × citriodorus* smells like lemons; there is a variegated form, 'Silver Lemon Queen', with silver-splashed leaves. The cultivar 'Doone Valley' is a creeping thyme with green leaves variegated with gold.
CULTIVATION Height 10–12in (25–30cm). Dry, well-drained alkaline soil is best for all the thymes. Plant in spring, incorporating some grit into the soil to improve drainage where necessary. Trim frequently in spring and summer to stop plants from getting straggly. The harder they are cut, the more vigorously they grow. New plants are easily propagated by mound layering (see page 173). Like most of these herbs, wet winters and soggy ground are much more likely to cause problems than any pests or diseases.

BAY

ROSEMARY

PURPLE-
LEAVED
SAGE

COMMON
SAGE

COMMON
THYME

VARIEGATED
THYME
'Silver Lemon
Queen'

WINTER
SAVORY

IN THE KITCHEN

Some herbs have a long-established partnership with a particular fish, meat, or fowl: tarragon with chicken, or rosemary with lamb. But the cook with a ready supply of fresh herbs will want to experiment: sprinkle chopped mint on to strawberries, or add thyme to salads of mixed leaves and flowers. In this dish, tarragon (see page 112) is the essential catalyst.

BAKED EGGS WITH TARRAGON
Serves 4

a little butter
4 eggs
4 tbsp heavy cream
4 tbsp water
2 large sprigs of tarragon
salt, pepper

1 Butter 4 small ramekins and break an egg into each. Heat the cream gently in a small pan with the water and tarragon. Allow to reduce slightly, pressing the tarragon with a wooden spoon.

2 Take out the tarragon and pour the creamy mixture over the eggs, dividing it equally between the ramekins. Add a tiny pinch of salt and a flourish of freshly ground pepper on top.

3 Lower the ramekins into a pan with ½in (1cm) of boiling water in the bottom and cook the eggs gently (about 4–5 minutes) until the whites are just set. Serve decorated with a few leaves of fresh tarragon sprinkled on top.

CULINARY NOTES

❧ To make a savory bread, add chopped sage leaves and some sun-dried tomatoes or pitted black olives to the dough. Knead it, then let it rise, covered, in a warm place until it has doubled in bulk. Punch it back. Knead it again. Bake as usual.

FRUIT

WHILE MOST vegetables are temporary
residents in the garden, fruit, once planted,
will be with you for many years. Its presence
gives a comfortable sense of permanence and
continuity. Careful selection and breeding
has brought some fruit, such as apples and
peaches, a long way from their undomesticated
counterparts. Others, such as blackberries, still
have a whiff of the wild about them. Fruit
will set only if flowers have been properly
pollinated. Some trees are self-fertile, others
are not, so you must have different types
within reach to be sure of a crop. The
following pages explain how to achieve the
best results. Stars indicate the most decorative
varieties, especially when the trees or bushes
are trained in a formal style.

TREE FRUIT

These will be the longest-lived
elements of your kitchen garden.
The type of tree you buy – bush,
standard, cordon, fan, or espalier –
depends on where you want to put
it (see pages 174–75 for details of
the various styles). Bushes start
fruiting when very young and are
easy to pick, but they will never
have the satisfying shape of a full-
blown standard. Cordons trained
against wires make an excellent
screen. You need to study a
pruning handbook to keep them
in order, and they will not crop as
abundantly as a big tree, but this is
a good way of growing fruit in a
restricted space. Trees trained as
fans or espaliers are even more
elegant. You can create outdoor
rooms, walled around with trained
trees. Half-standards have a clear
stem of at least 4ft (1.2m), while
full standards go up to 6ft (1.8m)
before the branches start. Picking is
slightly more difficult, but the trees
are infinitely more pleasing to look
at than a dwarfed bush. All trees
can be grown as standards or half-
standards, although in cold areas,
peaches, nectarines, gages, and
apricots are most likely to succeed
as fans against a warm wall.

SOFT FRUIT

Soft fruit is too rarely trained into
decorative shapes, although you
can use a loganberry or tayberry to
make a summer screen, or let the
long growths of a blackberry to
wind decoratively in and out of a
hedge. Strawberries can be planted
as neat edgings to beds, and red
currants will make attractive double
cordons, shaped like wine glasses.
Gooseberries take on quite a
different character when grown as
round-headed standards.

VINE FRUIT

In a decorative kitchen garden,
you are as likely to plant a vine for
its foliage as its fruit, for the leaves
have great style and the wayward,
exuberant way that a vine grows
gives a sense of generosity in a
garden. In cooler climates, serious
grape fanciers will probably grow
their plants in a greenhouse,
training the rods and assiduously
thinning bunches of grapes as they
swell. Grown outside, the fruit may
not be flawless, but the foliage can
be allowed its head to a greater
extent. Other vine fruit such as
melons, kiwi, and passion fruit need
warmth to crop successfully.

TREE FRUIT

TRAINED FRUIT TREES give to the kitchen garden what clipped yew hedges and topiary give to a flower garden: good structure. With help, apples and pears can both be trained to make living screens between one part of the garden and another or to provide a fruitful backdrop for a border of old-fashioned flowers. Fruit trees pay rent twice a year, with spring blossoms and autumn harvest. Compared with a Japanese flowering cherry, this is rather generous. And trees such as apples and pears grow old gracefully, welcoming lichens and ferns to their capacious branches. In winter, they assume the gnarled, twisted shapes of avant-garde sculptures. In a small garden, a single tree, grown as a half-standard, may be used as a centerpiece in a lawn or splayed in a fan against a warm wall. When the tree itself is well established, use it as a prop for a rose or clematis.

BARE BONES

The supports on which this old espaliered apple were originally trained have long since rotted, but the tree, its structure fixed in youth, makes a strong feature in this kitchen garden. At this stage, it is easy to maintain and needs only a midsummer haircut.

SPRING PLUM

A warm brick wall protects the blossoms of this plum tree from frost in spring, and will later be equally useful in hastening the ripening of the fruit. This old tree has long since lost any pretension to being a formal fan, but nothing can stem its exuberant display.

WAIT FOR THE PEACH

The whitewashed wall of a greenhouse reflects sparkling light onto a peach tree, the unripe fruit thinned to regular spacings along the branches. A lean-to greenhouse on a south-facing wall provides ideal growing conditions for peaches, apricots, and nectarines.

ADD LEMON

Lemons are one of the easiest of the citrus family to grow in pots. Lined up in a row, they give a formal air to a garden, but they look equally attractive and inviting in an informal courtyard grouped in a display with pots of basil and lavender.

SCREEN OF PEARS

Pears, trained as espaliers, make a formal screen behind an asparagus bed, the long branches tied to sets of parallel wires. Pears are amenable creatures to train, easier in this respect than apples, which generally have a stiffer habit, making their limbs slightly trickier to manipulate.

APPLES *Malus sylvestris* var. *domestica*

NEXT TIME YOU SINK YOUR TEETH into a crunchy apple, spare a thought for Richard Cox, a retired brewer and besotted gardener who, in 1826, grew a seed into the wonderful 'Cox's Orange Pippin' that made him famous. The new apple would never have been known outside Mr. Cox's two acres in Buckinghamshire, England, without the help of the Duke of Devonshire's gardener, Joseph Paxton. When Paxton became the first president of the British Pomological Society in the middle of the 19th century, he promoted the new apple vigorously and, being a man of even more influence than his employer, sent 'Cox' graft wood all over the country. It is still one of the best known of all apples, although not the easiest to grow in your own garden. It is very prone to disease and needs regular doses of medicine to keep it on its feet. If you have no room for a freestanding tree, think of using espaliers or fans to make a decorative screen. They will never crop as heavily as a full-blown tree, but they make excellent garden dividers.

Cultivation

Apple cultivars are grafted on to rootstocks which largely determine the eventual size of the tree (see page 175). The question of the best rootstock is closely bound up with whether you want a semidwarf, dwarf, or full-sized tree. The trend now is to graft apples on to extremely dwarfing rootstocks such as M27, but a tree grafted on this is difficult to look after, since it needs very good soil and does not like sharing its patch with grass or other plants. MM106 is a good compromise, particularly for dwarfs and cordons.

SITE AND SOIL Apples like deep, well-drained ground that does not dry out. On hungry soil, dig in plenty of compost. Apple trees seldom succeed in coastal sites, where they may be damaged by salt-laden spray. Avoid planting on a windy site, or where trees may be set back by late frosts.

PLANTING Apples are best bought as bare-rooted trees and planted in early spring or fall in warm climates. This gives the roots time to become well established before the heat of summer in warm climates or the cold of winter in cool climates. Make a planting hole in which the roots can spread out, and stake with a short stake (see page 176).

POLLINATION Apple crops require cross-pollination (see page 177). This means that you must have more than one compatible variety in the vicinity. Any cultivar described as a triploid, including 'Bramley's Seedling', will not be a good pollinator. Trees must be in blossom at the same time if they are to cross-pollinate. You can also pollinate apples with some crabapples. Most good catalogs indicate which trees overlap in this respect, though late frosts can play havoc with the most carefully laid plans.

ROUTINE CARE During the first winter or two, firm the ground around young trees that may have been lifted by frost. Water well if the spring season is dry. In late spring, mulch thickly around the trees with compost or manure. If the tree is not thriving, try a dressing of ammonium sulfate, using 1oz/sq yd (30g/sq m). If fruit does not develop well, dress the soil in late winter with potassium sulfate at the same rate. Keep a circle around the base of the trunk, at least 4ft (1.2m) wide, clear of grass and weeds. Adjust ties on the stake as the stem swells. Thin fruit if necessary, as shown opposite.

PRUNING Specimen trees perform best if trained to the central leader system (see page 129). Trees trained as espaliers or fans need careful summer pruning (see pages 179) if they are to retain their geometric charm. Midsummer is the time to take off excess growth; that means anything you cannot train in as part of the basic shape. If you start pruning too early, the trees will start to sprout again and you may have to do the job a second time; if you do this job too late, the tree may suffer winter damage.

YIELD AND HARVESTING The earliest apples, such as 'Discovery', should be picked as soon as the stalk parts easily from the tree, and eaten immediately. 'Ellison's Orange' will keep 2 or 3 weeks if stored in a cool place. 'Egremont Russet', 'Freedom', 'Jonathan', and 'Liberty', which ripen in mid-autumn, will keep until early winter. Pick 'Ribston Pippin' in mid-autumn. It ripens in late autumn but can be kept until the new year. 'Orleans' and 'Wagener' should be left on the tree as long as possible before picking and storing. In good conditions they will keep until early spring (see page 187).

PESTS AND DISEASES Avoid disease where possible by choosing varieties that have some resistance. This means doing without 'Cox's Orange Pippin', 'Elstar', 'Fiesta', 'Gala', and 'Spartan', which are all prone to canker, which also attacks apples growing in poor, badly drained ground (see page 192). Use disease-resistant cultivars such as 'Freedom' or 'Liberty' to avoid scab (see page 194). Avoid using most dwarfing rootstocks, which make a tree fussier about its growing conditions.

RECOMMENDED CULTIVARS

DESSERT (IN ORDER OF RIPENING)
'Discovery': *fruits, flushed scarlet, form on tips of branches and spurs.* **'George Cave'**: *well-flavored apple, green with red flush.* **'Ellison's Orange'**: *clean, strongly-scented fruit.* **'Freedom'**: *disease-resistant, slightly tart red apple.* **'Jonathan'**: *classic red apple with juicy flesh.* **'Liberty'**: *the ultimate in disease-resistance with mostly red skin and light golden flesh.* **'Egremont Russet'**: *closely spurred so makes a good espalier.* **'Ribston Pippin'**: *superb flavor, prone to canker in poor soil.* **'Orleans'**: *prolific, hardy, golden fruit.* **'Wagener'**: *prolific, free from scab.*

COOKING
'Bramley's Seedling': *classic cooking apple, but not suitable for an espalier.*

❀ **DESSERT APPLE**
'Egremont Russet'

❀ **DESSERT APPLE**
'Orleans'

❀ **DESSERT APPLE**
'George Cave'

❀ **DESSERT APPLE**
'Gala'

❀ **DESSERT APPLE**
'Ribston Pippin'

APPLE THINNING

1 *If a tree has a very heavy crop, you will need to thin some of the apples. Wait until the tree has shed some fruit itself. This usually happens naturally in midsummer.*

2 *Remove any very small and misshapen fruit, leaving about 4–6in (10–15cm) between the remaining apples. They will then have room to develop and ripen.*

❀ **COOKING APPLE**
'Bramley's Seedling'

PEARS *Pyrus communis* var. *sativa* & *P. pyrifolia*

EUROPEAN PEARS ARE AS ORNAMENTAL as they are useful, but unfortunately it is harder to bring a pear to luscious perfection than it is an apple. The difficulty lies off rather than on the tree. A pear changes radically after it has been picked. Its flesh, still hard when the fruit is gathered, gradually softens in storage until it has the melting texture of butter. But the point of no return is quickly reached, and it is difficult to know when you have got there. European pears are like statesmen: the outside appearance gives little indication of what is going on underneath. In contrast, Asian pears (*Pyrus pyrifolia*) are round, crisp, and juicy; in fact, they are much like apples. You can harvest them fully ripe.

Cultivation

The wild pear, *Pyrus communis*, is a deep-rooted tree, able to make the best of poor soils. Most dwarf pears that you buy have been grafted on to quince rootstock (see page 175). This restricts the tree's size and brings it into fruit more quickly, but quince rootstock is shallow rooting and needs good soil. Pear trees usually grow to about 15–20ft (4.5–6m). You can grow pears as freestanding trees using central leader training (see page 129). Asian pears do well with open-center training (see page 126). You can also grow both types as espaliers. Fruiting will also depend on the effort you put into arranging a decent sex life for your pear (see page 177).

SITE AND SOIL Pears generally flower two weeks earlier than apples, so they are more prone to frost damage: choose a sheltered spot. They are tolerant of most well-drained soils.

PLANTING Plant in early spring in cool climates or in fall in warm climates. Full-sized trees will need 20ft (6m) between them; dwarfs will need 12ft (3.5m), and for espaliers allow 8–10ft (2.5m–3m).

POLLINATION Pears need cross-pollination from 2 or more compatible cultivars. Check nursery catalogs for suitable pollinator combinations. For small spaces, look for trees that have branches of pollinators grafted on.

ROUTINE CARE Mulch well in autumn and spring with manure or compost with some added potassium sulfate. If trees are growing in grass keep a circle of clear ground around them 4ft (1.2m) wide.

PRUNING When training young trees, weight the main side branches to make them more horizontal than upright. Trees growing as cordons or espaliers will need summer pruning (see page 179).

YIELD AND HARVESTING Harvest European pears before they are ripe, as soon as they will part from the tree. Summer pears are soon ready to eat. Late pears need to be stored for up to a month (see page 187), then ripened in warmth, a few at a time. Asian pears can be harvested when they taste sweet and juicy.

PESTS AND DISEASES Fireblight can attack soft new growth and spread through the tree, killing limbs or the entire tree (see page 193). Prevent infection by planting disease-resistant European cultivars, such as 'Moonglow' and 'Magness', or many Asian pears. If fireblight is a problem, spray with the antibiotic streptomycin when the weather is wet and temperatures exceed 60°F (15°C). Remove infected limbs in the winter, when the disease is dormant.

RECOMMENDED CULTIVARS

EUROPEAN PEARS (IN ORDER OF RIPENING)
'Moonglow': reliable and fireblight resistant. **'Bartlett'**: large, yellow fruit with classic flavor. **'Beurré Hardy'**: russet fruit, resistant to scab. **'Anjou'**: firm but sweet, short-necked fruit, moderate resistance to fireblight. **'Doyenné du Comice'**: superb flavor but unreliable cropping and susceptible to scab.
ASIAN PEARS
'Twentieth Century': tart, crisp, and juicy, an apple-shaped fruit with greenish yellow skin.

IN THE KITCHEN

For this recipe, you need pears of firm texture and pleasing shape. Use fruit with slight blemishes that may prevent their being stored successfully.

PEARS IN BURGUNDY
Serves 4

2lb (1kg) small pears
1 cup (250g) sugar
¼ tsp ground cinnamon
⅔ cup (150ml) water
⅔ cup (150ml) red Burgundy
whipped cream, to serve

1 Peel the pears, leaving the stalks intact. Do not core them. Stand them upright, stalk end up, in any pot or pan just large enough to hold them upright without crowding. Sprinkle with the sugar and cinnamon and add the water. Simmer on the stove, covered, for 10–15 minutes.

2 Add the wine and simmer, uncovered, for 10–15 minutes more, until tender. Using a slotted spoon, lift the pears into a serving dish and let cool.

3 Meanwhile, bring the liquid to a boil and let it simmer, uncovered, for 5–7 minutes, until it is reduced to a light syrup.

4 Pour the syrup over the pears and refrigerate the whole dish. Serve chilled, with whipped cream.

CULINARY NOTES

❧ The pear connoisseur will eat them uncooked, dwelling, as the Edwardian nurseryman Edward Bunyard did, on the texture and aroma of different varieties: "As it is in my view the duty of an apple to be crisp and crunchable," he wrote, "a pear should have such a texture as leads to silent consumption." A perfect 'Doyenné du Comice', he considered, should melt upon the palate "with the facility of an ice."

❀ **PEAR**
'Bartlett'

❀ **PEAR**
'Beurré Hardy'

❀ **PEAR**
'Anjou'

❀ **PEAR**
'Doyenné
du Comice'

PLUMS & PRUNES *Prunus domestica*

FEAST OR FAMINE SEEMS THE RULE WITH PLUMS, the famines caused chiefly by insatiable birds and badly timed frosts. But when the feasts come, you'll be glad you waited through the famines. You'll relish the sweet, melting flavor of European plums, the juicy goodness of round Japanese plums, the richness of prune plums, and the bountiful preserves you can make from 'Damson' plums. Planted as orchard trees, or as fans against a wall, the plum family is decorative in flower and fruit, though the blossoms are not as eyecatching as those of the apple or pear. If you look carefully through nursery catalogs you can find handsome weeping plums, like 'Weeping Santa Rosa', which has lovely cascading branches and delicious fruit. Choose full-sized or semidwarf plums for planting in grass where they will a make long-lived, attractive feature.

Cultivation

As with apples and pears, plums are grafted on to rootstocks that control their vigor (see page 175). 'St. Julien A' will produce a semivigorous tree; 'Pixy' reduces the eventual size of the tree by two thirds or a half, but the tree needs richer soil and more cosseting than a full-sized tree. In contrast 'Nemaguard' rootstock, which resists damage by some nematodes, requires well-drained soil. Where there is room for only one tree it should be a self-fertile cultivar, which crops well and regularly. Choose half-standards or standards for planting in grass. This way you will be able to mow under the trees without catching your hair in the branches, or bumping your head. If they are allowed to fruit heavily, some trees have a tendency to overcrop and will then want to rest the following year, like an enervated actor after a particularly stressful run of *Hamlet*.

SITE AND SOIL Choose plum cultivars that are appropriate for your climate. 'Stanley', for instance, needs a fairly long winter and flowers later as a consequence. It has a better chance of escaping late frosts than earlier bloomers. 'Methley', on the other hand, is early blooming, so the flowers can be damaged by frost in cold areas. In warm climates, it can produce the first ripe plums as early as June. To encourage later flowers in climates troubled by persistent frost, plant on the north side of a building or wall. Also avoid low-lying, frost-prone areas and provide the trees with shelter from the wind. European plums enjoy rich soils; Japanese plums prefer light, sandy soils.

PLANTING Plant in early spring in cool climates or in fall in warm climates (see page 176). Put full-sized trees 25ft (7.5m) apart; semidwarf 12ft (3.5m) apart. If you are planting in grass, keep a circle at least 4ft (1.2m) in diameter clear around the base. For fans, buy professionally trained trees. They will probably already have 6 or 8 long arms. Attach the corresponding number of bamboo stakes to the wall or support so that they are fanned out into a position to match the branches. Tie the branches to the stakes and keep tying them in as they grow.

POLLINATION Most European plums are self-fertile and do not need pollinators to set a crop, but even self-fertile plums crop more liberally if they are cross-pollinated by a different variety. Japanese plums generally require cross-pollination. To pollinate each other, plums obviously need to flower at the same time, so it is important to bear this timing in mind when you are choosing cultivars. Nursery catalogs will list compatible pollinators.

ROUTINE CARE Firm down any trees that have been lifted by frost in the first winter after planting. Mulch trees heavily every year with manure. If this is not available, top dress established trees with ammonium sulfate, at a rate of 2oz/sq yd (70g/sq m). Thin fruits if a tree overcrops, leaving no more than one fruit every 3–4in (7–10cm). The tree may shed some fruit itself, usually in early summer.

PRUNING Train freestanding European plums using central leader training (see page 129). Japanese plums do best with the open-center system (see page 126). Cut Japanese plums back more heavily each spring since they fruit on new wood. Espaliers require more attention to keep them in shape (see page 179). Shoots sprouting from the main framework should be nipped out in two stages. In midsummer, pinch back all sideshoots to leave about 6 leaves. These will be the shoots that bear fruit the next summer. When they have fruited, cut back these sideshoots by half, to about 3 leaves. Any shoots pointing forward or backward into the wall should be removed.

YIELD AND HARVESTING Expect about 30lb (14kg) of fruit from a 10-year-old fan-trained tree. A freestanding plum of the same age should provide about 50lb (23kg) of fruit. The fruit should be left on the tree until fully ripe.

PESTS AND DISEASES Knobbly and dark, black knot fungus can attack plum trees. Prune off affected limbs, including some healthy wood for good measure; spray with fungicides in spring to prevent spread. Plum curculio larvae (see page 192) may burrow into fruit, making it inedible. Use a preventative insecticide spray.

RECOMMENDED CULTIVARS

EUROPEAN PLUMS

'Methley': *early-producing and self-pollinating, produces sweet, reddish fruit and succeeds well in areas with short winters.*
'Stanley': *self-fertile, purple, prune-shaped plum with rich, sweet flesh.*

JAPANESE PLUMS

'Morris': *a Japanese plum for warm climates that produces large, reddish fruit. It has some resistance to brown rot.*
'Weeping Santa Rosa': *grown widely, a tart, red-skinned, Japanese plum for mild climates; this cultivar needs cross-pollination.*
'Shiro': *an extra-early, yellow, Japanese plum; needs cross-pollination.*

IN THE KITCHEN

PICKLED PRUNE PLUMS
Makes 8lb (4kg)

4lb (2kg) sugar
5 cups (1.25 liters) vinegar
1 tsp cloves, crushed
1 tsp ground allspice
1in (2cm) fresh ginger, crushed
1in (2cm) cinnamon stick, crushed
zest of half a lemon
8lb (4kg) prune plums, washed

1 Dissolve the sugar in the vinegar in a stockpot over a low heat. Tie spices and lemon zest in a muslin bag, then add to the pan.
2 Add fruit to the liquid and simmer until tender. Remove the spices and lift out the plums with a slotted spoon and pack neatly into sterilized jars, using your favorite canning method.
3 Bring the liquid to a boil and simmer until it becomes slightly thick and syrupy. Pour the syrup over the plums, so that they are well covered, and seal jars.

PLUM CHUTNEY
Makes 4½lb (2.25kg)

2lb (1kg) plums, washed, quartered, and pitted
1lb (500g) apples, peeled and chopped
1lb (500g) shallots, peeled and chopped
1lb (500g) raisins
1 cup (175g) brown sugar
1 tsp ground ginger
1 tsp ground allspice
¼ tsp each cayenne, ground cloves, dry mustard, and ground nutmeg
2 tbsp (30g) salt
2½ cups (600ml) vinegar

1 Bring all the ingredients slowly to a boil in a large, heavy pot. Simmer for 1–2 hours, or until the mixture has thickened considerably.
2 Using your favorite canning method, seal chutney in jars.

❀ **PLUM** 'Stanley'

❀ **PLUM** 'Victoria'

❀ **PLUM** 'Green Gage'

DAMSONS

❀ **GREENGAGE** 'Coe's Golden Drop'

PEACHES & NECTARINES
Prunus persica & Prunus persica var. *nectarina*

GROWING PEACHES AND NECTARINES is not easy, but the harvest delights make it worthwhile. By the time you have read all the gloomy predictions of leaf curl, canker, brown rot, and peachtree borers, you may want to give up all thought of growing your own and let the growers of California, Georgia, and southern Ontario take the strain. Forget peach problems that may never happen. Remember instead Mme. Recamier, siren, muse, and toast of the salons of 19th-century Paris. When she and all those around her thought she was on her deathbed, when for days she had refused all food however cunningly prepared, it was the smell and taste of a freshly picked peach that persuaded her she would, after all, prefer to live.

Cultivation

Peaches and nectarines need a sunny, frost-free spring to ensure pollination, a hot summer to ripen the fruit, and a cold resting season during the winter.

SITE AND SOIL Peaches grow in warm climates as well as cool climates. But they do need a site with well-drained, fertile soil and mild spring weather, free from late frosts. Select cultivars appropriate for your climate. An extra hardy, late bloomer for cool areas is 'Reliance'; 'Mid Pride' is an early bloomer for climates with short winters. For extra protection, avoid planting these trees in low frost pockets.

PLANTING Plant in spring in cold climates or in fall in warm climates (see page 176). Set full-sized, freestanding trees 20ft (6m) apart; dwarf trees 12ft (3.5m) apart. You can also grow peaches as espalier, or try genetic dwarf trees in big pots, providing protection during cold winter weather.

POLLINATION Peaches and nectarines are self-fertile, so you do not have to plant different varieties to ensure pollination. But where cultivars flower very early before there are any insects on the wing, you must do the pollinating yourself (see page 177).

ROUTINE CARE Mulch around trees each spring with a thick layer of manure. Refresh the soil of potted genetic dwarf peaches and nectarines in late winter, scooping off the top layer and replacing it with good garden soil mixed with bonemeal and potassium sulfate. For espaliered trees, thin shoots and fruits in spring and early summer as shown opposite. Water during dry weather.

PRUNING Train freestanding peaches using open-center systems, as follows. When young, cut back the main trunk and allow four side branches to grow in different directions to make a vase shape. Since fruit is borne on shoots produced the previous season, cut out half of the old wood annually so productive new wood can take its place. Once the fruit is picked, cut out the growth that bore it, and let new shoots arise.

YIELD AND HARVESTING Expect about 20lb (9kg) of peaches or nectarines from a mature trained espalier; freestanding trees will give much heavier crops. Pick fruit when the flesh around the stalk feels soft.

PESTS AND DISEASES Spray from the time the buds swell to prevent diseases. Use traps and sprays to deter pests such as Oriental fruit moths, borers, aphids, scale, tarnished plant bugs, and brown rot.

RECOMMENDED CULTIVARS

PEACHES (IN ORDER OF RIPENING)
'Red Haven': *an early, red-blushed fruit with yellow flesh.* **'Champion'**: *a favorite midseason, red-blushed fruit with white flesh.* **'Peregrine'**: *an old British peach that grows easily in cool areas and is well-flavored and juicy.* **'Belle of Georgia'**: *a delicious, late, white-fleshed peach.*
NECTARINES (IN ORDER OF RIPENING)
'Garden Beauty': *a genetic dwarf for pots.*
'Mericrest': *an extra-hardy tree with red skin and juicy yellow flesh .*

IN THE KITCHEN

Only when there is a glut of fruit will you want to cook a peach or nectarine or do anything other than sink your teeth straight into its luscious, succulent flesh. This recipe combines peaches with a piquant raspberry sauce.

POACHED PEACHES WITH A RASPBERRY SAUCE
Serves 4

4 ripe freestone peaches
½ cup (125g) superfine sugar
⅔ cup (150ml) water
1 cup (250g) raspberries

1 Skin the peaches by immersing them in boiling water for 1 minute. Drain, then carefully peel off the skin. Cut each fruit in half.

2 Combine the sugar and water in a saucepan over low heat, and stir continuously until the sugar has dissolved. Bring the syrup to a boil, add the peaches, and simmer gently for 5 minutes, until tender. Using a slotted spoon, transfer the peaches to a serving dish. Return the syrup to a boil and simmer until it is reduced by half.

3 Purée the raspberries by rubbing them through a sieve with a wooden spoon, gradually adding the peach syrup to the raspberry pulp to ease the process. You should be left with a fairly thin sauce. Spoon this over the peach halves, then chill before serving.

CULINARY NOTES

❧ Over the years we have been bludgeoned into believing that "fresh" can apply to any produce not pickled, dried, or canned. But the day you pick your first fresh peach or nectarine from your own tree and carry it inside for breakfast is the day you break faith with supermarket fruits in their cold, plastic beds.

❀ PEACHES

❀ NECTARINES

THINNING SHOOTS ON ESPALIERS

1 *The shoots of this branch have yet to be thinned. In spring, it is important to remove some of the foliage shoots on espaliered forms of both peaches and nectarines to give enough room for the fruit to swell and ripen.*

2 *Leaving 1 or 2 good shoots near the base of each branch to form the stems that will bear next year's crop, nip out all the others to give a shoot every 5–6in (12–15cm). Leave one shoot at the end to draw the sap along the branch.*

THINNING FRUIT
When the fruit is no bigger than a hazelnut, thin again. Remove any fruit that is awkwardly placed or facing into the wall, leaving a final gap of about 9in (23cm) between each.

APRICOTS *Prunus armeniaca*

THE PERFECT APRICOT IS NOT EASY TO FIND. Apricots flower so early that in many areas flowers are more likely to fail from frost damage than to survive and produce. When they are good, they are very, very good, but in cool climates they need the help of a warm wall if they are to ripen to perfection. Although they are not subject to leaf curl, apricot trees have a distressing habit of suddenly dying back. The strongest branches are often the first to go. This problem has been known ever since apricots were introduced into Britain during the reign of Henry VIII. The knowledgeable gardeners of Edwardian times thought that the trees should be root pruned, to curb the speed at which they grow. We now know the problem is caused by a disease, *Eutypa* dieback, which attacks through fresh pruning cuts in wet weather.

Cultivation

The apricot, which was carried by silk merchants westward from China into Armenia, needs cold winters and early springs to perform well. Then it needs a long, warm summer to ripen the fruit. You must plant a cultivar suited to your area.

SITE AND SOIL Choose a sunny, warm wall against which to train a fan-shaped tree; avoid low frost-prone areas for free-standing trees. The soil needs to be well drained, but not too well fed.

PLANTING Plant in early spring; fall in warm climates (see page 176). Space full-sized trees 25ft (7.5m) apart; dwarf trees 12–15ft (3.5–4.5m) apart. Allow 15ft (4.5m) between wall-trained, fan-shaped espaliers. Set trees about 12in (30cm) from the wall with the stems leaning back toward it. Tie the branches to stakes or wires stretched between vine eyes.

POLLINATION Apricots are self-fertile but blossom very early, often in late winter. Protect trees outside from frost with thermal blankets. If no insects are around, hand-pollinate the flowers with a fine camel-hair brush (see page 177).

ROUTINE CARE Water copiously in dry summers to help the fruit swell. Keep the soil around trees free of weeds, but do not disturb the roots by cultivating deeply. Thin the fruit at intervals during mid- and late spring, so that they are spaced roughly every 4in (10cm) along the branches.

PRUNING Train freestanding trees to one main trunk with well-spaced side branches emerging around it. Or try open-center systems (see page 126). If grown as an espalier, develop a fan shape (see page 179). Aim to build up a series of fruiting spurs about 6in (15cm) apart all the way along the branches of the fan by pinching back the lateral growths (these are the sideshoots springing from the main branches) in early summer, leaving about 3in (7cm) of each growth in place. Any shoots springing from these laterals should be pinched back, leaving just one leaf. Keep tying in the new growth on the ends of the main branches to maintain the fan shape.

YIELD AND HARVESTING Expect about 20lb (9kg) of fruit from a mature espalier, twice as much from a freestanding tree. Pick apricots carefully (their flesh bruises very easily) when the stem parts readily from the branch. They will keep for two weeks in a cool place.

PESTS AND DISEASES Dieback is the main problem; there is no cure. Avoid it by pruning in dry weather. Spray with light horticultural oils for aphids or mites.

RECOMMENDED CULTIVARS

(IN ORDER OF RIPENING)
'Moor Park': *popular variety with superb flavor; it is prone to suffer from dieback.* **'Alfred'**: *juicy, orange flesh, prone to biennial cropping.* **'Harglow'**: *extra hardy and disease-resistant.*

❦ **APRICOTS**

CHERRIES *Prunus avium & Prunus cerasus*

A SWEET CHERRY LEFT TO ITS OWN DEVICES will quickly make a large tree, and so is best in an orchard where it can spread its wings up to 27ft (9m) or more. Sour cherries are more petite, spreading up to 20ft (6m) across. Allow grass and wildflowers to grow uncut beneath mature trees (when young this can stunt them) for the kind of scene that drove the French Impressionists to their paintboxes. Cherries are extremely decorative when covered with blossoms. A sweet cherry tree can be trained as an espalier on a wall, but it needs to be a big wall, and you will have to fight to keep the tree under control. The best type for a home landscape is the sour cherry 'North Star', superb in pies. You can also drown the fruit in brandy, which makes a delicious topping for ice cream.

SWEET CHERRY
'Bing'

SWEET CHERRY
'Ranier'

Cultivation

Most cherries need to be cross-pollinated if they are to bear fruit. If there is not enough room for two cherry trees in your garden, plant the sweet cherry 'Stella' or the sour 'North Star' as both are self-fertile.

SITE AND SOIL Cherries fruit best where the climate is dry and reasonably warm, although sour cherries can cope with a cooler situation. It is not worth planting cherry trees in areas where late frosts may ruin the blossoms. The soil should be rich but well drained.

PLANTING Plant in early spring; in warm climates plant in the fall (see page 176). Set full-sized trees 25ft (7.5m) apart and espaliered trees 20ft (6m) apart. Plant sour cherry trees 20ft (6m) apart.

POLLINATION Sweet cherries generally need cross-pollination from compatible cultivars. Check nursery catalogs for suitable companions. If space is limited, get a tree with branches of pollinators grafted on it. Sour cherries tend to be self-fertile and do not require a second cultivar to be productive.

ROUTINE CARE Mulch with well-rotted manure in spring, and use scarers such as flash tape if birds attack the fruit. Keep trees that are trained against walls well watered during the summer.

PRUNING You can grow full-sized and semidwarf sweet cherry trees using modified central leader training. Allow a main trunk to grow and produce well-spaced side branches until the tree reaches

about head height. Then remove the main trunk and encourage a lateral side branch to take its place. Sour cherries grow best with the open-center system (see page 126). You can also train cherry trees into fan-shaped espaliers. Starting with a young tree, choose 6 flexible stems to spread and secure on a fan-shaped trellis. Cut out all other upright stems. Thin back old wood to encourage productive new shoots as necessary.

YIELD AND HARVESTING A mature freestanding cherry may provide 70lb (32kg) of fruit, and an espalier about 20lb (9kg). Sweet cherries are ready to pick in midsummer, sour cherries slightly later.

PESTS AND DISEASES Bacterial canker is a troublesome disease (see page 192) and is most likely when trees grow too fast due to overfeeding. Spores enter through wounds, so avoid damaging the bark and prune late in winter. Maggots of cherry fruit flies can riddle fruit. Hang sticky maggot traps in spring to catch egg-laying adults. When you find the first adult, begin spraying with an insecticide.

RECOMMENDED CULTIVARS

SWEET CHERRIES (IN ORDER OF RIPENING)
'Ranier': *handsome yellow fruit with a red blush.* **'Stella'**: *self-pollinating, sweet cherry.*
'Bing': *delicious, dark red fruit.*
'Windsor': *large, dark fruit.*
SOUR CHERRIES
'North Star': *hardy, compact tree; bright red fruit matures after many sweet cherries.*

SOUR CHERRY
'North Star'

CITRUS FRUIT *Citrus* spp.

CITRUS TREES, GROWING IN FANCY TERRACOTTA POTS or square wooden boxes, can be used like statues to decorate a garden, however small. Used as a centerpiece for a potager, or set like guardsmen at the side of a series of steps, they look grand and faintly unreal. The leaves are glossily evergreen, and the fruit hangs on the branches like decorations on a Christmas tree. They are not hardy and, wherever frost strikes, will need to be placed in a greenhouse or sunroom for the winter. But here, too, they are immensely decorative and the flowers, which begin to open in spring, scent the air for weeks. Some fruit takes a year to develop, so while the present season's flowers are opening, the previous season's fruit is maturing on the tree.

Cultivation

Growing in containers will be the only option for gardeners who do not share the climate of Florida, Texas, or the West Coast. Fortunately, citrus trees adapt well to pot culture, particularly the lemon-mandarin hybrid *Citrus* × *meyeri* 'Meyeri' (often called Meyer's lemon) and the calamondin, a mandarin-kumquat hybrid.

SITE AND SOIL All citrus need to be kept frost-free in winter. Fruiting is more likely to occur if the plants can be kept at about 50°F (10°C) during this time. Use an acidic potting mix (pH6–6.5, slightly lower for lemons) and make sure that the container has adequate drainage. Coarse grit blended with the mix will help.

PLANTING Trees may start their lives in small containers but must eventually be potted on into larger tubs. Winter is the best time for this job. When the trees are in their final homes, scrape off the top 2in (5cm) of soil each year in midspring and replace it with fresh soil.

POLLINATION Many citrus trees are parthenocarpic, which means they set fruit even when the flowers do not contain viable pollen. In other words, you need only one plant to be assured of a crop.

ROUTINE CARE Watering and feeding are of prime importance. Feeding should continue throughout the year, with a high-nitrogen formula used in summer to maintain growth. Winter feed should contain a combination of trace elements, particularly iron, magnesium, manganese, and zinc. Without these elements, trees will have yellowish foliage, growth will be stunted, and the fruit liable to drop off of

the trees in winter. Never allow the soil to dry out.

PRUNING Citrus trees do not need regular pruning. Trim new growth in early spring, if necessary, to keep the plants shapely.

YIELD AND HARVESTING Yield depends on the size and maturity of the tree. Expect 20 or 30 fruit from a well-grown specimen. Fruit can be harvested from late autumn through until early spring.

PESTS AND DISEASES In a greenhouse or sunroom, plants may suffer from aphids, spider mites, scale insects, and sooty mold (see pages 190–93).

RECOMMENDED CULTIVARS

SEVILLE ORANGES
Citrus aurantium: *bitter fruit on a spiny tree with slender, pointed leaves.*

SWEET ORANGES
Citrus sinensis 'Valencia': *great juicing orange with a long harvest period.*

OTHER CITRUS
Citrus reticulata 'Clementine': *bushy tree with mandarin fruit; cross-pollinate.*
× **Citrofortunella microcarpa**, *syn.* **C. mitis**, *or calamondin: mandarin-kumquat hybrid that flowers and fruits while still small.* **Citrus** × **meyeri 'Meyeri'**: *lemon-mandarin hybrid, slow growing and ideal in containers.*

GRAPEFRUIT
Citrus × **paradisi 'Golden Special'**: *well-branched tree with glossy, ovate leaves.*

LEMONS
Citrus limon 'Eureka': *open, spreading habit, excellent juicy fruit.*

LIMES
Citrus aurantiifolia 'Bearss': *compact tree, with seedless, exceptionally juicy fruit.*

IN THE KITCHEN

Many citrus recipes include the peel in some way, for the zest of the skin gives an extra-sharp kick to the taste of the dish. This orange dish is enhanced by the flavor and appearance of a sprinkling of finely cut strips of caramelized peel.

CARAMELIZED ORANGES
Serves 6

6 large oranges
1¼ cups (300ml) water
½ cup (125g) sugar

1 Finely peel away the zest of 1 orange with a vegetable peeler and cut into very fine strips, each about 1in (2cm) long.

2 Put the peel in a small pan with the water and sugar, bring to a boil. Simmer gently for about 30 minutes, until the liquid is syrupy.

3 Peel the remaining oranges, then cut all 6 fruit into thin rounds, taking out any seeds. Arrange the slices in a dish and pour over the syrup, with the strips of peel. Chill before serving.

CULINARY NOTES

🍃 The arrival of bitter Seville oranges or calamondins may inspire you into a brief orgy of making marmalade, for nothing else gives marmalade such a tang. But you can experiment with mixes of other citrus fruit to make conserves that, if not as sharp, are no less good to eat.

🍃 Lime, one of the best, is also the most difficult marmalade to make since the skins are so tough to cut. Easier to prepare is grapefruit marmalade. For each 2lb (1kg) of grapefruit, include 10oz (300g) lemons, to add enough pectin to set it. A three-fruit marmalade using 2 grapefruit, 4 lemons, and 2 sweet oranges also makes an extremely delicious breakfast treat.

❋ MANDARIN

❋ SWEET ORANGE

❋ SEVILLE ORANGE

❋ LEMON

❋ GRAPEFRUIT

❋ LIME

❋ THE CALAMONDIN
This cross between a mandarin and a kumquat (× Citrofortunella microcarpa, syn. C. mitis) is one of the best to grow in pots or tubs.

FIGS & MULBERRIES
Ficus carica & Morus nigra, rubra, and alba

THESE TREES ARE BOTH GREAT SURVIVORS, hanging on in old gardens long after the lawns and walls on which they were displayed have disappeared. Both give an air of distinction to a garden, for they are fruit with an ancient lineage and make splendid specimen trees, although figs need protection from cold winds and are unlikely to succeed in very cold areas. Figs can be grown successfully in cool greenhouses or splayed out as espaliers on a warm wall. The mulberry, which makes a big, bushy round-headed tree, needs an expanse of lawn to set it off properly. Although both lose their leaves in winter, the trees, starkly stripped, still contribute to the garden scene. They have the attribute of all true aristocrats: good bones.

❦ MULBERRIES

❦ BROWN FIGS

❦ GREEN FIGS

Cultivation

Where space is limited, a fig can be grown in a large pot to stand in a sheltered corner, but a mulberry needs space. It will gradually develop into a tree at least 20ft (6m) high and 15ft (4.5m) wide. You sometimes see veteran trees leaning on their elbows in a relaxed way, which makes them spread even further.

SITE AND SOIL Figs are very forgiving trees. They will tolerate air pollution and even seem to prefer low-nutrient soil. Their architectural foliage is pleasing, but if you want them to fruit you will have to provide them with sun and shelter, which may mean a south-facing wall or cool greenhouse. A mulberry needs deep, well-drained, rich soil that does not dry out in summer. In cold climates, you can try growing hardier red or white mulberries.

PLANTING Both figs and mulberries are best planted in spring (see page 176). Figs do well in large tubs, which you can protect or bring inside in climates with cold winters. In the garden they fruit more freely if the roots are restricted. Dig a hole about 3ft (1m) deep and wide, and line it with bricks or concrete slabs. Plant the fig inside this box, mixing in plenty of bonemeal with the soil.

ROUTINE CARE Mulch trees thickly with compost in late spring. Water mulberries if necessary in summer. Water fig trees in dry weather while the fruit is swelling, but do not overwater while the figs are ripening or they may split.

PRUNING Mulberries bleed badly if cut, so should not be pruned on a regular basis except to cut out dead wood or crossing branches. Remove cold-damaged shoots and overcrowded young growth from fig trees in midspring. If necessary, you can thin out branches again in midsummer. With figs that fruit twice a season in warm climates, be sure to save plenty of new growth for the second crop. For fan-shaped espaliers, take out one of the oldest branches each year to persuade the tree to throw up more productive young growth from the base.

YIELD AND HARVESTING Yields depend on winter weather and the age of the tree. Wait until the fig droops on its stem to harvest, with the skin just beginning to split and a drop of nectar hanging from the eye. The easiest way to gather mulberries is to spread sheets out under the tree and shake the branches.

PESTS AND DISEASES Neither is usually troubled by pests; gray mold/*Botrytis* may attack young fig shoots (see page 193).

RECOMMENDED CULTIVARS

FIGS
'Brown Turkey': *the hardiest, producing chocolate-colored fruit with deep red flesh.*
'Texas Everbearing': *provides two crops per season in southern climates.*
MULBERRIES
'Illinois Early': *delicious red and white hybrid.*
'Wellington': *abundant, extremely fine fruit.*

PRODUCING MORE FIGS
In summer, you can encourage a fig tree to produce more fruit by pinching back new shoots to 5 or 6 leaves. This prevents the tree from putting its energy into making unwanted growth.

MEDLARS & QUINCES
Mespilus germanica & *Cydonia oblonga*

MEDLARS AND QUINCES are as attractive in bloom as any purely ornamental tree, and by planting one or the other you have the added advantage of an autumn crop. Both fruit make excellent jellies. The quince is a favorite in Turkey, though elsewhere it is seldom grown as a commercial crop. It blooms later than an apple tree and is less prone to frost damage. Like figs and mulberries, medlars and quinces bring an air of ancient peace to a garden. The medlar, with its angular branches, makes a tree wider than it is high, casting dense shade. Where soil and weather conditions suit it, the leaves flame into an orange, yellow, and red blaze before falling in autumn. Quince tree leaves turn clear butter yellow.

❀ MEDLARS

❀ QUINCES

Cultivation

Quinces usually make round-headed trees not more than 12ft (3.5m) tall, but where they are happy they can reach 20ft (6m). 'Orange Dwarf' stays under 15ft (4.5m), great for small yards, but be sure to allow them room for expansion. All cultivars are self-fertile and should start to crop by the time they are 6 years old. In Europe, the medlar tree has been cultivated since ancient times and bears fruit that looks like large, swollen, bronze rosehips. Watch out for suckers on medlars, which are often grafted on to hawthorn rootstock.

SITE AND SOIL Quinces like warmth and a deep rich soil that is not too alkaline. They love moisture, so you sometimes see old specimens growing by the side of ponds. A damp corner of the garden will suit them just as well. Medlars are hardier than quinces and will succeed in any ordinary well-drained garden soil.

PLANTING Plant any time after leaf fall, digging a hole large enough to accommodate the roots easily, and stake the trees to provide support for their first year (see page 176). Keep the ground around the trunks clear of grass or weeds.

ROUTINE CARE Mulch thickly around the trees every spring.

PRUNING Thin out crowded branches of quince trees if necessary during winter. Treat medlars in the same way, removing branches that are dead, weak, or crossing over each other.

YIELD AND HARVESTING Expect about 50lb (23kg) of quinces and perhaps 30lb

(14kg) of medlars from a mature semi-dwarf tree. Pick quinces in mid-autumn before the first frost. Store them in trays in a cool dark place where they will keep for up to a month. Keep quinces as far away as possible from other fruit. Quinces have a very strong aroma, which can be used to scent a room, but the scent will be picked up by other fruit nearby. Medlars are still very hard when you gather them from the tree in late autumn. In the 16th and 17th centuries in England, the fruits were stored in damp bran or sawdust until they were "bletted"; that is, until the flesh had become soft, brown, and faintly alcoholic. Then the pulp was sucked straight from the skin, like wine from a winebag.

PESTS AND DISEASES Leaf spot can sometimes be a problem on quinces. Spray with a fungicide as the leaf buds burst, and again after the fruit has set. Medlars are usually trouble-free.

RECOMMENDED CULTIVARS

MEDLARS
'Nottingham': *prolific, often bearing fruit when only 3 years old.*
QUINCES
'Champion': *large, apple-shaped fruit.*
'Orange Dwarf': *handsome bushy tree with yellow fruit.*
'Pineapple': *large, pear-shaped fruit.*
'Smyrna': *strongly aromatic with good quality fruit.*

NUTS

THE MOST USEFUL NUTS FOR THE GARDENER are hazelnuts and filberts. They make a good informal hedge and are extremely decorative in winter, hung with long, soft catkins and, where squirrels allow, produce heavy crops of nuts in the autumn. Left to themselves they make useful thickets, which you can plunder for stakes, bean poles, and twiggy stems to weave into decorative supportive lattices for your peas and beans. Other nuts, such as walnuts and almonds, are better used as specimen trees. Almonds are breathtaking in spring, iced all over with pink blossoms. Walnuts are grander, more restrained – and slow. You may have to wait 20 years for a crop but you will have, meanwhile, the pleasure of anticipation.

Cultivation

Country of origin is the best guide to the conditions these nuts need in order to bear good crops. Hazelnuts (*Corylus avellana*) and filberts (*Corylus maxima*) do well in the Pacific Northwest. The hazelnut is a rounded nut, only partly covered by its husk. A filbert is longer and enclosed completely by the husk. Walnuts (*Juglans regia* and *J. nigra*) also generally do better in cool climates, but almonds (*Prunus dulcis*) are natives of North Africa and fruit most successfully in California.

SITE AND SOIL Hazels will grow in sun or partial shade, doing best in deep, damp alkaline soils. Almonds are not as fussy about soil as they are about having a warm climate. A walnut is long-lived, so you need to think carefully about its planting position. It may live there for 200 years, spreading eventually to make a tree 100ft (30m) high and at least 50ft (15m) wide.

PLANTING Plant in spring in cool climates, or fall in warm climates. Choose only young walnut trees since they resent being moved when they are older.

POLLINATION Hazels are wind-pollinated, with male and female flowers borne on the same bushes, but for the best crops, plant several different cultivars together. Most walnuts and almonds need cross-pollination with a compatible cultivar in order to produce a crop.

ROUTINE CARE Water until trees are well established, and mulch well.

PRUNING When hazels are 4–5 years old, start to cut out some of the oldest stems at ground level to encourage new shoots.

Walnuts bleed horribly when cut and fortunately require no regular pruning. It may sometimes be necessary to remove a crossing branch. Do this in midspring or late summer. Do not let the tree develop a forked trunk. Almonds need an open-center framework.

YIELD AND HARVESTING Yield varies enormously according to age and climatic conditions. Expect about 25lb (11kg) of nuts from a hazel, 20lb (9kg) from an established almond, and 50lb (23kg) from a full-grown walnut. Hazelnuts fall to the ground when they are ripe, but almonds can be harvested from the tree when the shells split. Husks still cling around the shell of walnuts when they are ready to harvest in autumn and must be removed before you store the nuts. Use gloves. The juice stains skin a startling dark brown.

PESTS AND DISEASES Squirrels are the chief pest of all nut trees. No other pest can be compared.

RECOMMENDED CULTIVARS

HAZELNUT
'**Ennis'**: *a new cultivar from Oregon State University with bountiful, extra-large nuts.*
'**Contorta'**: *an ornamental tree with twisted stems and nuts.*
FILBERT
'**Purpurea'**: *decorative purple-leaved tree with well-flavored but small nuts.*
WALNUT
'**Broadview'**: *Persian walnut with thin shells.*
'**Thomas Black'**: *classic black walnut.*
ALMOND
'**All in One'**: *unique self-pollinating tree.*

IN THE KITCHEN

Nuts store beautifully in their shells so were once highly valued as a winter food. We still associate them with Christmas fare: ground almonds make marzipan for the cake, and roast chestnuts are served with the turkey. This compote of dried fruit and nuts is popular in Islamic countries. It is traditionally made with seven fruits, and seven passages from the Koran are read before eating.

AFGHAN COMPOTE
Serves 4–6

about 1 cup (125g) each of small dried apricots and dark seedless raisins
about ½ cup (60g) each of golden raisins, shelled walnuts, pistachios, and almonds (unsalted)
6 cherries (fresh or canned)
heavy cream, to serve

1 Wash the dried fruit, put it in a serving bowl with just enough cold water to cover, and set aside in a cool place for a couple of days.
2 Put the almonds and pistachios in a bowl and cover them with boiling water. Cool, then slip the skins off the nuts.
3 Add the walnuts, almonds, and pistachios to the soaked fruit. Decorate with cherries. Put the bowl in the refrigerator for a day or two before serving with cream.

CULINARY NOTES

❧ A fresh, home-grown walnut is worth the years of waiting. Its soft and creamy texture bears no relation to that of the dry, slightly rancid, store-bought nuts that masquerade under the name around Christmas.

❧ Ground hazelnuts can be used successfully to thicken soups. They are also delicious combined with cauliflower and celery.

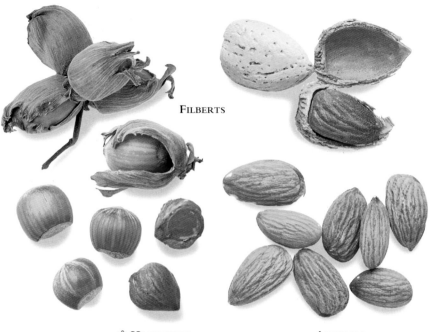

FILBERTS

ALMOND DELIGHT
An almond, its branches covered with fragile blossoms, makes an enchanting sight on a clear spring day. To produce a good harvest of nuts, though, it must have a warm site.

❀ **HAZELNUTS**

ALMONDS

WALNUTS

UNRIPE WALNUTS WITH HUSK

SOFT FRUIT & VINES

THE MOST SPECTACULAR GRAPES are not necessarily those with the best fruit, so you will have to decide which of the two is more important: appearance or taste. All grapes, though, have handsome foliage that can be used to good effect on arbors, trellises, and pergolas. *Vitis vinifera* 'Purpurea' provides a striking contrast for a scrambler such as *Clematis flammula,* or you could combine its purple leaves with pale blue clematis and deep red climbing roses. Soft fruit, such as red currants and gooseberries, are no less decorative when trained. Grow gooseberries as mop-headed standards to mark the corners of an herb garden. Train red currants on wires as U-shaped cordons to make a very unusual, airy screen. Strawberries, particularly the alpine kinds, are pretty enough to grow as groundcover. They will spread successfully in any moist, rich soil.

BLAZING BLUEBERRY
Blueberries will be happy only in acid soil, where they can be used to good effect as groundcover under other lime-haters, such as azaleas and rhododendrons. The late summer crop of berries is followed by a brilliant blaze of orange from the leaves before they fall.

REFRESHING GRAPES
This grape is planted outside the greenhouse, but the rods, or stems, are trained up inside against the ribs of the roof. The handsome foliage makes a dappled pattern against the light and provides useful natural shading for crops growing underneath.

PERFECT MELON

The fruit of a muskmelon is kept clean by an underlying sheet of plastic. Muskmelons are generally smaller than cantaloupes or winter melons, and in warm climates the vines can be trained over an arbor. In cool areas, all melons benefit from some form of protection.

BLISSFUL HARVEST

Autumn-fruiting raspberries, such as this cultivar 'Autumn Bliss', are not attacked by birds in the way that summer-fruiting ones may be. This is an advantage, since it saves the trouble of protecting the crop with nets. Use them to make a hedgelike screen in the garden.

STRAWBERRY COVER

Cloches, like these old-fashioned handlights, are both practical and decorative. They will protect fruit and help it to ripen a little faster. Strawberries such as these that bear large fruit will need fresh ground every few years, but alpine strawberries can be left to wander at will.

RASPBERRIES *Rubus idaeus*

ALTHOUGH NOT PARTICULARLY ORNAMENTAL in themselves, raspberries, trained neatly on wires, make useful summer screens in a garden or can be used to divide a fruit patch into different sections. Plant them corner to corner in a square plot to make four triangular spaces for gooseberry bushes, currants, and strawberries (see the plan for a soft fruit garden on pages 23–24). Potentially, this is a more decorative way of using them than simply planting them in traditional parallel rows. Autumn-fruiting raspberries grow much more densely than summer-fruiting cultivars and make great thickets of canes (stems). Apart from providing a delicious crop at an unexpected time of year, autumn raspberries seem to have the added advantage of being not nearly as tempting to birds. Do not plant other fruit too close to the rows because it is likely to be overwhelmed.

RASPBERRIES

Cultivation

Raspberries need moisture if they are to thrive, and a relatively acid soil. They also need support. You can fence them in between two sets of parallel wires, or grow in a single row tied to wires stretched between 1.8-m (6-ft) posts (see page 180).

SITE AND SOIL Raspberries like a deeply dug, light, moist soil. They are often disappointing in heavy soils. If it bakes in the summer sun, heavy soil has a tendency to crack and this would disturb the fine surface roots that feed the canes. They grow best in slightly acid soils (pH 6.5–6.7) and will succeed in light shade.

PLANTING Plant bare-root plants in early spring in cool climates, or late fall in warm climates, setting the roots no more than 3in (7cm) below the soil surface. They will not grow if they are planted too deeply. Water container-grown plants well. Set plants 15–24in (38–60cm) apart. If you are planting more than one row, allow at least 4–6ft (1.2–1.8m) between the rows. Cut down the canes to about 9in (23cm) after planting to encourage new growth to shoot from the base.

ROUTINE CARE Mulch the rows in early spring with manure or compost, but not mushroom compost, which is alkaline. Keep the ground free of weeds. Do not dig deeply around the raspberries because they resent any disturbance to their shallow roots. Water well, if necessary, during the summer.

PRUNING After summer cultivars have

fruited, cut out the old canes close to the ground and thin out new canes, leaving no more than 5 or 6 strong stems at each original plant. Tie in new canes to their wires, if using this method of support. In late winter, cut off the top of each cane just above the top wire. Autumn-fruiting raspberries need different treatment since they carry fruit on canes formed earlier in the same season. Cut the old, fruited canes to the ground in late winter and thin out the thicket of new growth gradually as it grows during the season.

YIELD AND HARVESTING Summer-fruiting varieties may be early, mid- or late season, bearing crops from mid- to late summer. Autumn-fruiting raspberries can be gathered from early to mid-autumn. Expect about 12lb (5.5kg) of summer raspberries from a 10-ft (3-m) row and half that amount from autumn types.

PESTS AND DISEASES In alkaline soils, raspberries may show signs of chlorosis, or yellowing of the leaves (see page 192). Spread sulfur on the soil or fertilize with an acidic fertilizer. Plant virus-resistant varieties to minimize the risk of disease spread by the common raspberry aphid. Cane diseases (see page 193) appear as small purplish spots on the stems in late spring or early summer. Cut out affected canes, and spray every 2 weeks with a fungicide from when the flower buds begin to open until the end of flowering. Protect fruit from birds and squirrels with netting (see right). Raspberry fruit worm may damage the fruit (see page 191).

RECOMMENDED CULTIVARS

SUMMER-FRUITING
'Algonquin': *thornless red raspberry with disease resistance.* **'Brandywine'**: *tart and delicious hardy purple raspberry.* **'Jewel'**: *black raspberry with good disease resistance.*
AUTUMN-FRUITING
'Autumn Bliss': *high-yielding red fruit with firm texture, resistant to raspberry mosaic virus.*

FRAME THE FRUIT
Summer raspberries often need protecting from birds and squirrels. Make a frame, perhaps in a decorative shape as on page 24, and attach netting to it before the fruit starts to ripen.

IN THE KITCHEN

Summer pudding is one of the great classic dishes of the season and can be made with any mixture of berries you like, although it should always contain a good proportion of raspberries. Make it the day before you want to eat it.

SUMMER PUDDING
Serves 4–6

*1 tbsp (15g) butter
6 slices good white bread,
preferably slightly stale
2lb (1kg) mixed summer fruit
(raspberries, strawberries, blueberries,
black or red currants, et al.)
1 cup (250g) sugar*

1 Butter the inside of a 5-cup (1.25-liter) bowl. Cut all the crusts off the bread and use the slices to line the bottom and sides of the dish.

2 Heat the prepared fruit gently with the sugar in a saucepan until the fruit is just soft. Be careful not to overcook it. Then pour it into the dish without dislodging the bread. The fruit should be close to the top of the dish, but not up to the rim.

3 Use the rest of the bread to make a lid to cover the fruit. Put a saucer on top of the dish, and a weight on top of that to press it down. Leave the weighted pudding in the refrigerator overnight.

4 Unmold the pudding onto a plate and serve with plenty of heavy cream.

CULINARY NOTES

To make a delicious, sharp sauce, press fresh raspberries through a fine-meshed sieve. For a striking, as well as healthy, dessert, serve as an accompaniment to peaches, which are conveniently in season at the same time of year (see page 126 for the full recipe).

LOGANBERRIES & TAYBERRIES

PROMISCUITY GENERALLY GETS BAD PRESS, but in the plant world there is much to be said for it. The wantonness of raspberries and blackberries has produced some fine hybrids. The first was the loganberry, bred over 100 years ago by Judge Logan of California, who crossed a raspberry with a blackberry. A similar cross produced the tayberry, whose parents were a blackberry called 'Aurora' and a tetraploid black raspberry known tersely as No 626/67.

LOGANBERRIES

Cultivation

Both plants are very vigorous, so their long canes need tying to wires or against fences. They grow best in the Pacific Northwest. If frosted, the canes may die back. The plant itself usually recovers.

SITE AND SOIL All the hybrid berries like roughly the same treatment. They hate waterlogged soil and are unlikely to do well where there is only a thin layer of soil over limestone.

PLANTING Plant in fall in warm climates or early spring in cool climates. Set plants quite shallowly in the soil to encourage plenty of suckers. Leave 10–12ft (3–3.5m) between plants.

TRAINING If you are training hybrid berries on wires to make a screen, put in posts that stand at least 6ft (1.8m) high, at convenient intervals. Stretch the first wire between them just under 3ft (1m) from the ground with another 3 parallel wires above, attached at regular intervals. Tie the growths securely along the wires, keeping the new canes bunched in a fountain in the middle and the older fruiting growths trained horizontally away from the center (see page 180). When you have finished picking the fruit, cut out the old canes, unbundle the new ones, and tie them in where the old ones were.

ROUTINE CARE A spring mulch of manure or compost will conserve moisture and help feed the plants. In really cold areas, you may find it best to leave the bundle of new canes lying on the ground

TAYBERRIES

all winter and tie them up in spring. Research has shown that canes treated like this suffer less from die-back.

YIELD AND HARVESTING Expect about 5lb (2.5kg) of fruit per plant after the first year, and 14lb (6kg) when mature. The fruiting season lasts from mid- to late summer.

PESTS AND DISEASES Maggots of the raspberry fruit worm may tunnel into the fruit. If you must, spray plants with a contact insecticide (see page 191).

RECOMMENDED CULTIVARS

LOGANBERRIES (R. URSINUS VAR. LOGANOBACCUS)
'Logan': *big red berries with special flavor and thornless stems.*
TAYBERRIES
Larger and sweeter than the loganberry with bountiful black berries.

BLACKBERRIES *Rubus fruticosus*

IN SOME AREAS, BLACKBERRIES are so prolific in the wild that gardeners may wonder whether they should give them space in the garden. But modern cultivars bear bigger fruit than wild brambles and, carefully trained, will make useful, windproof screens. Thorny cultivars such as 'Darrow' grow upright and make a prickly barrier against marauding animals. Other cultivars, such as 'Black Satin', have no prickles. Thornless types tend to droop and do best if supported. Blackberry leaves that are deeply cut like parsley are very decorative, and, in some areas, turn rich shades of orange and red in autumn. Blackberries crop well in shade, so consider training one on a north wall.

WILD BLACK-BERRIES

CULTIVATED BLACKBERRIES

Cultivation

Even the less vigorous varieties of blackberries need plenty of space, so bear this in mind before planting. Train blackberries against a fence or wall or along parallel wires that have been stretched between posts (see page 180). You can also use blackberries in a hedge (see the plan on page 27), the way they grow naturally in the wild. If you are planting a new hedge, let the trees get established before putting in the blackberries, or else they may be smothered in the blackberries' prickly embrace.

SITE AND SOIL Blackberries grow best in ground that retains moisture and is not too alkaline. You can improve the soil by digging in plenty of manure or compost before planting. Since they do not flower until early summer, blackberries can be grown in frost pockets and do best in sun but tolerate light shade in warm climates.

PLANTING Plant in late autumn or at any time up until early spring. Cut the canes (stems) down to about 9in (23cm) immediately after planting. If you are growing two or more plants, set them at least 12ft (3.5m) apart. If you are using an especially vigorous variety, increase the spacing to 15ft (4.5m). Train the new canes against a wall or fence, or along parallel wires. If planted in a hedge, blackberries need no formal training.

ROUTINE CARE Water, if necessary, in dry spells during summer. Mulch each spring with manure or compost.

PRUNING As with raspberries and loganberries, the fruited canes should be cut out each year after the crop has been gathered. With a late-fruiting variety this may not be until early autumn. Tie in the new canes to replace the old (see page 180). Remove suckers from the roots of upright blackberries; they can spring up anywhere. Thin out thick clusters of canes to let the sun in and air penetrate.

YIELD AND HARVESTING Expect about 10–20lb (5–9kg) of berries from one plant, depending on variety, from late summer to early autumn. Some cultivars will continue to provide fruit into mid-autumn.

PESTS AND DISEASES Gray mold/*Botrytis* may attack the fruit, especially in wet summers (see page 193). Pick off the worst-affected fruit or spray the plants at flowering time with a fungicide. Spraying will need to continue every 2 weeks throughout the summer.

RECOMMENDED CULTIVARS

'Black Satin': *large, sweet berries on suckerfree, thornless, disease-resistant plants.* **'Chester'**: *delicious fruit, a hardy plant without thorns.* **'Darrow'**: *slightly tart, medium-sized berries appear early on hardy plants.* **'Hull'**: *large fruit with exceptionally high yields on thornless stems.*

❀ OREGON THORNLESS

The variety 'Oregon Thornless' has leaves as intricately cut as parsley. Trained as a screen or against a wall, fence, or trellis, it makes a decorative feature in any part of the garden.

IN THE KITCHEN

Wild berries, like blackberries, make excellent jelly. Since the fruit is free, you don't worry that the yield is lower than for jam. If you cannot find enough blackberries, combining them with apples makes an equally good jelly, though with a less intense flavor.

BRAMBLE JELLY
Makes about 1½lb (750g) for every 1lb (500g) sugar used

8lb (4kg) blackberries
juice of 3 large or 4 small lemons
(or 2 tsp citric acid)
3½ cups (900ml) water
sugar (see below)

1 Wash the fruit and put in a stockpot with the lemon juice (or citric acid). Add the water and simmer slowly until tender. The fruit should be gently broken down during this process.

2 Strain the resulting pulp through a scalded jelly bag. For sparkling clear jelly, do not squeeze the bag.

3 Measure the juice into the cleaned pan, bring to the boil, then add the sugar, using 1lb (500g) for each 2½ cups (600ml) of juice.

4 Stir well, then boil rapidly without stirring until the setting point has been reached – do not boil for longer than 10 minutes. Skim any froth from the surface and pour into warm, sterilized jars as quickly as possible. When the jars are filled, seal them using your favorite canning method.

CULINARY NOTES

❦ To make a good jelly you need pectin (the natural setting agent present in fruit), acid, and sugar in the correct proportions. You can try making jelly with apples and plums, apples and blueberries, or red currants and raspberries.

BLUEBERRIES *Vaccinium* spp.

BLUEBERRIES WILL SUCCEED ONLY in the kind of moist, peaty soil in which rhododendrons flourish, and the best way to grow them is in an informal border or woodland setting among other lime-hating shrubs. White flowers, tinged pink, appear in little tassels during late spring and early summer. In autumn, the whole bush turns into a fiery blaze of red, orange, and copper.

Cultivation

The modern cultivated blueberry is a mixture of several wild North American species including *Vaccinium corymbosum*, the swamp or highbush blueberry, which is a shrubby, woody plant common in eastern North America. The blue-black fruits, covered in a grayish, silvery bloom, are ready in summer. It is not worth bothering with blueberries unless you can supply the very specific growing conditions that they need. They will not survive in ordinary soil, and certainly not in alkaline or heavy clay soil. An alternative is to grow them in large pots or tubs filled with peat-enriched soil, but for this to be successful you would need a nonalkaline water supply.

SITE AND SOIL Blueberries should be planted in damp, peaty soil with a pH lower than 5.5. They like well-drained ground and the position should be relatively open, although they will grow in sun or partial shade.

PLANTING Plant in spring in cool climates, or fall in warm climates (see page 176), using 2- or 3-year-old plants and setting them about 5ft (1.5m) apart.

POLLINATION To ensure good pollination, two different cultivars should be planted together.

ROUTINE CARE The plants should be protected from birds as soon as the fruit begins to ripen. Work a little acidic fertilizer into the soil around plants in spring and mulch with an acid compost. Water regularly in dry summers.

PRUNING Start pruning the plants in winter by cutting out dead or damaged

BLUEBERRIES
'Bluecrop'

branches together with a proportion of the old, darker-colored wood. In spring, lightly trim the tops of the bushes to help keep them compact.

YIELD AND HARVESTING Expect about 6lb (3kg) of fruit from a fully established, mature bush. You will need to pick over the bushes several times since the berries ripen over a relatively long period during late summer and early autumn.

PESTS AND DISEASES Blueberries do not generally get attacked by pests or diseases, but they will start to show signs of chlorosis if the soil is not sufficiently acid (see page 192).

RECOMMENDED CULTIVARS

'Berkeley': *large, prolific, pale blue berries on a vigorous spreading bush.* **'Bluecrop'**: *firm, good-quality berries among leaves that color well in autumn.* **'Earliblue'**: *one of the earliest to mature.* **'Herbert'**: *said by connoisseurs to have the best-flavored fruit.*

STRAWBERRIES *Fragaria × ananassa*

NOTHING SPEAKS OF SUMMER so eloquently as a dish of strawberries, eaten warm and richly glowing, straight from the garden. Recent breeding has concentrated on producing fruit that travels well. Gardeners can happily ignore this criterion and choose cultivars purely on the basis of taste. The strawberry is the only fruit that carries its vital working parts on the outside. The seeds dotted in the flesh are the true fruit – the berry is just the carrier. When choosing cultivars, try June-bearing, everbearing, and day-neutral types, and do not forget the alpine strawberry, which makes an excellent edging for potager or path. The berries are small but there are plenty of them, and they do not seem to be attacked by birds.

Cultivation

You can pick ripe strawberries most of the summer and on into fall if you grow June-bearing, day-neutral, and everbearing strawberries. Choose cultivars with exceptional flavor. Let the commercial growers have the ones that ship well. Bear in mind, though, that if you do grow your own, children, birds, and slugs will always find some ripe berries before you do.

SITE AND SOIL To grow good crops you must have ground that is in good condition: deep, porous, and well-fed. Prepare beds in summer, digging in plenty of manure. Old gardening books recommend trenching 3ft (1m) deep. That is pure sadism.

PLANTING You must buy certified virus-free stock. Plant in early spring and rotate the patch every 3 years so you renew the plants in fresh ground (see propagating by runners, opposite). This can be difficult to arrange in a small space: the plan on page 25 shows one way, using a combination of strawberries with other soft fruit. Plant rooted runners in late summer, or in autumn in warm climates, so that the plants can settle in before winter. Strawberry plants should be set 18in (45cm) apart in rows 3ft (1m) apart. Set alpine types at 12in (30cm) intervals.

ROUTINE CARE A dressing of potassium sulfate in late winter will help to develop flavor. Spread straw around plants as the fruits form (see opposite). Plastic mulch is sometimes used but seems to encourage gray mold/ *Botrytis*. Nip off runners as they form, unless you need to raise fresh plants. After cropping, cut off the old leaves (see

opposite) and dress the ground lightly with a general fertilizer. Discard old plants after 3 years, starting a new bed with freshly rooted runners.

YIELD AND HARVESTING Some cultivars yield much more heavily than others, but flavor tends to decrease as productivity rises. Expect about 2 cups (250g) of fruit from each plant. Alpine strawberries crop intermittently from midsummer to autumn. Everbearing strawberries are not in fact perpetual but carry a second, lighter crop in the autumn. The June-bearing type can be early or late, depending on the cultivar. Day-neutral strawberries produce crops on and off through the summer.

PESTS AND DISEASES You may need to net crops against birds. Slugs can also be a problem. Gray mold/ *Botrytis* is the worst disease (see page 193) since it rots the berries, covering them with fungus. It is worst in wet summers. If prevalent, spray with fungicide as the first flowers open and repeat every 2 weeks until the fruit starts to ripen. Water plants in the morning rather than the evening so that flowers and fruit dry off quickly.

RECOMMENDED CULTIVARS

'Baron Solemacher': *has the useful habit of growing in neat clumps without runners (alpine).* **'Catskill'**: *large and dark red.* **'Honeoye'**: *early variety that crops heavily.* **'Surecrop'**: *June-bearing with rich, sweet fruit.* **'Tribute'**: *day-neutral with solid fruit and disease resistance.* **'Tristar'**: *day-neutral with smaller summer fruit but exceptional disease resistance.*

IN THE KITCHEN

The advantage of growing your own strawberries is that you can pick them when they are at the peak of perfect ripeness. A squeeze of lemon juice on the fresh fruit intensifies the flavor.

STRAWBERRY SHORTCAKE
Serves 6

For the shortcake
2 cups (250g) flour
2 tsp baking powder
½ tsp salt
1 tbsp sugar
½ cup (125g) butter, cubed
2–3 tbsp milk
For the filling
500g (1lb) strawberries
1 tbsp sugar, or to taste
1¼ cups (300ml) whipping cream

1 Grease two 9-in (23-cm) cake pans and preheat the oven to 450°F (230°C).

2 Sift flour, baking powder, and salt into a bowl and sprinkle in the sugar. Rub in the butter using your fingers until the texture resembles breadcrumbs. Add just enough milk to bind the mixture, working it in with a knife.

3 On a floured surface, divide the dough in half and, with the palm of your hand, press out each half into a circle about 6in (15cm) across. Put each circle of dough into a cake pan and press it out gently to fill the whole tin. Bake until the shortcake is a golden color, about 15 minutes. Let cool.

4 Halve the strawberries, reserving some to use whole to decorate the top, and sprinkle with sugar.

5 Whip the cream until thick and spread half over one shortcake circle. Put halved fruit on top and sandwich with the second circle. Spread the rest of the cream on top. Decorate with whole strawberries.

❋ ALPINE STRAWBERRIES

EARLY-
FRUITING
STRAWBERRY
'Honeoye'

JUNE-BEARING
STRAWBERRY
'Surecrop'

PROPAGATING BY RUNNERS

1 To keep strawberries fruiting well, you will need to renew them every 3 years. Select some of the runners that develop on the plants, and let them take root in the surrounding soil.

2 Once they are growing well, carefully lift the rooted runners with a handfork, then sever them from the parent plant. Transplant these new plants to a fresh bed that has been dug and manured.

PROTECTING FRUIT
Spread a generous layer of straw under and around the plants once the berries begin to form. This keeps the strawberries free from soil and well aired.

CLEARING FOLIAGE
After the fruit has finished cropping, chop off all of the leaves to within 4in (10cm) of the crown, and remove the old straw to discourage pests and diseases.

BLACK, RED & WHITE CURRANTS
Ribes nigrum & R. rubrum

FOR THE GARDENER, there are three different kinds of currant: black, red, and white. For the botanist, there are only two, for the white currant is nothing more than a variant of the red, *Ribes rubrum*. For translucent, luminous beauty, nothing can match the red currant, which you often see glowing in the still-life paintings of Dutch artists. Though they are most often grown as ordinary bushes, red and white currants can be trained into highly decorative cordons to make screens around a vegetable patch. Black currant bushes are living medicine chests. Half a dozen of these tiny fruit have more Vitamin C in them than the biggest lemon. Choose compact varieties such as 'Ben Sarek' if you are gardening in a small space.

BLACK CURRANTS

RED CURRANTS

WHITE CURRANTS

Cultivation

Currants grown in bush form need no support, but if you decide to grow red or white currants as single- or two-stem cordons (see page 174), they will need to be trained on a wall or fence, or tied in to wires between posts. The eventual height of bushes depends on the cultivar but usually extends to about 4–5ft (1.2–1.5m). Black currants have a tendency to grow into large, spreading bushes; red and white currants produce more upright shapes. As cordons, red and white currants will reach 5–6ft (1.5–1.8m).

SITE AND SOIL All currants do best in open situations but will tolerate some shade. Black currants are greedier feeders than red and white currants. Dig in plenty of manure or compost before planting.

PLANTING Plant in fall if possible (see page 176) because currants break dormancy in early spring. Black currants should be set more deeply than they were growing in their containers. Leave 5–6ft (1.5–1.8m) between bushes. Cut down all stems of black currants to within 3–4in (7–10cm) of the ground immediately after planting to promote fresh growth.

ROUTINE CARE Mulch in spring with a thick layer of manure and topdress red and white currants with potassium sulfate, about 1oz (30g) for each bush. Do not disturb the roots by digging around bushes, but keep the ground well weeded.

PRUNING Black currants are treated differently from red and white currants, since they fruit on 1-year-old wood; the other two fruit on spurs made on old wood. When black currants have fruited, cut out the old wood, as shown below, leaving the pale stems that will produce the next season's fruit. Since red and white currants bear fruit on old wood, pruning is less drastic. After fruiting, or during fall and winter, shorten branches by about a third to keep the bushes compact. On red and white currants grown as cordons, cut the lateral branches back to within 1½in (3cm) or so of the main stem (see page 178).

YIELD AND HARVESTING Currants are ready to pick in mid- and late summer. Expect about 10lb (5kg) of fruit from each bush when they are fully established.

PESTS AND DISEASES Protect fruit from birds. Avoid pine blister rust disease by growing rust-resistant cultivars such as 'Consort'. Because rust kills pines, some areas outlaw currants.

RECOMMENDED CULTIVARS

BLACK CURRANTS
'Ben Lomond': *medium-sized bush bearing heavy crops of large fruit.* **'Ben Sarek'**: *compact bush, with good crops of large fruit.* **'Consort'**: *rust-resistant; sweet-musky fruit.*

RED CURRANTS
'Jonkheer van Tets': *large fruit on early-cropping, upright bush, mildew resistant.* **'Red Lake'**: *popular variety, upright bush bearing very large fruit.*

WHITE CURRANTS
'White Grape': *best for flavor, with large fruit on an upright bush.* **'Wilder'**: *long-bearing with sweet-tart fruit.*

PRUNING BLACK CURRANTS
After fruiting, cut out at least a third of the old, dark wood, leaving the new, pale stems, which will bear fruit the following season. This does not apply to red and white currants (see left).

GOOSEBERRIES *Ribes uva-crispa/R. hirtellum*

"THE FREEDOM OF THE BUSH should be given to all visitors," wrote Edwardian epicure and fruit-grower Edward Bunyard. He was thinking of the European gooseberry in its dessert state – squishy, sweet, highly scented – a state that has almost been forgotten, for gooseberries are usually gathered hard and green for cooking. Plants can be grown as very pretty, yard-high tree forms, but they need strong stakes since the stems are spindly.

Cultivation

Gooseberries are found wild in most northern temperate zones and seem to flourish in cool, moist, high places. They can be grown as bushes, cordons, or standards. The height varies with the cultivar. Bushes generally grow to about 4–5ft (1.2–1.5m) and cordons to 5–6ft (1.5–1.8m).

SITE AND SOIL The soil should be well drained but moisture retentive. On dry ground, the fruit will not swell properly. Gooseberries thrive in sun or partial shade.

PLANTING Plant in fall if possible, since they break dormancy in early spring. Bushes are best grown on a short stem to prevent suckering at ground level. Set bushes about 5ft (1.5m) apart and do not plant too deeply. Cordons can be set just 12in (30cm) apart.

ROUTINE CARE Mulch with manure or compost in early spring. Water newly planted bushes in summer, if necessary. Feed each winter with potassium sulfate, using 1oz (30g) for each bush. Remove any suckers that sprout around the base.

PRUNING Gooseberries do not need regular pruning, but it is easier to pick the fruit if you remove some of the growth every winter to keep the center of the bush open. On cordons, shorten the side growths to 3 buds, and cut the branches of standards back by at least a third.

YIELD AND HARVESTING For cooking, green fruit can be picked in late spring and early summer. Dessert fruit should be left to ripen on the bush. Expect 6–10lb

❀ **GREEN GOOSEBERRY** 'Invicta'

❀ **RED GOOSEBERRY** 'Whinham's Industry'

(3–5kg) of fruit from a bush, 2–3lb (1–1.5kg) from a cordon.

PESTS AND DISEASES American gooseberry mildew, a form of powdery mildew, is the most damaging disease (see page 194). Prune to keep bushes open so that air can flow through. If necessary, spray with a systemic fungicide or plant the resistant cultivar 'Invicta'. Net bushes if birds attack the flower buds.

RECOMMENDED CULTIVARS

'Careless': *mildew-resistant, bearing pale green fruit on a spreading bush.* **'Invicta'**: *vigorous, spreading bush, immune to mildew.* **'Leveller'**: *ripens into an excellent dessert gooseberry, extra large, greenish yellow.* **'Whinham's Industry'**: *upright bush with dark red fruit, good cooked or eaten as dessert.*

IN THE KITCHEN

Gooseberries (and white currants) make a refreshing white wine. To make wine, you need large sterilized containers that can be corked with an air lock. Gases can then escape while the wine is fermenting.

GOOSEBERRY WINE
Makes 1 gallon (4.5 liters)

2lb (1kg) green gooseberries
3 sterilizing tablets
4 quarts (4.5 liters) water
½oz (15g) pectin-destroying enzyme
2¼lb (1.1kg) sugar
1 level tsp yeast nutrient
1 heaped tsp wine yeast

1 Crush the uncooked gooseberries in a clean plastic bucket. Dissolve 2 sterilizing tablets in the water and add to the fruit. Then add the enzyme and stir.

2 Seal the bucket with plastic wrap or a lid and let the mixture steep for 48 hours in a warm place. Strain through several layers of cheesecloth into a fresh plastic bucket. Squeeze out all the liquid.

4 Dissolve the sugar in 2½ cups (600ml) boiling water. Let this syrup cool, then add it, with the yeast nutrient, to the liquid. Make up the volume to 4 quarts (4.5 liters) with more water if needed.

5 Pour the liquid into its fermenting container and add the wine yeast. Keep under air lock at about 60°F (15°C) until it stops fermenting (bubbling). This may take 12 weeks.

6 Siphon off the wine into a container of the same volume (taking care not to siphon off any sediment from the bottom of the original container). Add another sterilizing tablet and fit a new air lock. Let stand until clear. This will take a few weeks rather than days. Bottle in sterilized bottles. Store the wine in a cool place.

GRAPES *Vitis labrusca, V. rotundifolia & V. vinifera*

GRAPES MAKE UP THE BIGGEST single fruit crop in the world. Given the amount of liquid that finds its way down the throats of wine buffs each year, this is not surprising, although gardeners will probably not be growing grapes for their alcoholic potential. The vines are blessed with an elegant, venerable habit of growth and excellent shading foliage. Trained over a seat or an arbor, they give just the right air of productive ease in a garden. Combined with clematis, grapes are ideal plants for a pergola. In hot climates, they will make a shaded roof over a terrace, where you can sit in dappled light (see the plan on page 45). In a conservatory, a grape vine will provide useful summer shading for the plants inside. Some varieties are more tolerant of cold than others. One of the most widely grown in North America is 'Concord', a cultivated form of the native species *Vitis labrusca*. Vines grown in Europe are generally derived from a different species, *Vitis vinifera*.

Cultivation

Correct pruning and training are essential, whether you are growing grapes outside or under cover. Most make far too much growth, which must be restricted if the plants are to be persuaded to fruit.

SITE AND SOIL Although they are fairly hardy, grapes will ripen their crop most successfully where summers are long and warm. 'Concord' is among the hardiest and may survive in areas where the somewhat more tender *Vitis vinifera* types such as 'Chardonnay' and 'Merlot' will shiver and sulk. French-American hybrids combine the hardiness of American species with the dignified flavor and growth of European vinifera grapes. Southern growers enjoy vigorous muscadine grapes, which thrive in heat.

PLANTING Grapes grow best in fertile, well-drained soil and full sun. Before planting, it is wise to build a trellis to support your grapes. Plant in spring in cool climates or fall in warm climates. Plant American and French-American hybrids about 8ft (2.5m) apart; vinifera cultivars about 5ft (1.5m) apart; muscadine grapes at 20ft (6m) apart. Conservatory beds should be filled with a rich mixture of good garden soil and manure.

ROUTINE CARE In cold climates, protect questionably hardy and grafted vines during winter, then mulch all vines in early spring with compost or well-rotted manure. Vigorous growers may also need a small dose of nitrogen fertilizer. Water as needed to provide an inch of moisture a week. After fruit sets, thin the bunches, leaving one for every 12in (30cm) of stem. As the grapes begin to swell, cut out the smallest and most overcrowded fruit in the center of the bunch. In a conservatory, keep the atmosphere humid and ventilate well as soon as the vines begin to flower. Pollinate the flowers by hand with a soft brush (see page 177). Thin the bunches of grapes, leaving one for every 12in (30cm) of stem. As the grapes begin to swell, thin as per grapes grown on a trellis. Give a liquid feed every 10 days until the grapes have fully ripened, and make sure the air is less damp and ventilating well. Rest the vines in winter by reducing the temperature, untying the branches from the wires, and laying them on the ground. Tie them back up in spring.

PRUNING AND TRAINING When grown on a trellis, limit your grape vine to a single stem or trunk. In spring, cut back the vine you planted the previous year, then allow a single shoot to grow up a stake toward the trellis, strung with two horizontal wires, set at 3ft (1m) and 5½ft (1.7m) high. When the main trunk reaches each wire, allow only a single horizontal shoot to stretch along the wire in each direction. Cut out all other shoots that arise off the trunk in spring. In summer, thin out any other excess growth to allow sun to penetrate to both top and bottom layer and also to the interior of the vine. An alternative for vigorously growing vines is to train them to a T-shaped trellis. When grown under glass in a conservatory, grape vines should be trained on wires set about 12in (30cm) apart and at least 6in (15cm) away from the glass. The leading shoot should be trained vertically and the lateral shoot horizontally, along the wires. When the vines have flowered, prune the laterals back, leaving just 2 leaves beyond the clusters of fruit. Any subsequent shoots breaking from the laterals should be pinched out, leaving 1 or 2 leaves at most. In autumn, after fruiting, cut the leading stem back to firm, well-ripened wood and cut the laterals back to 2 buds.

YIELD A mature vinifera vine will yield about 15lb (7kg) of fruit, often more for American and muscadine grapes.

PESTS AND DISEASES Powdery mildew is the most serious disease (see page 194) and is most likely to strike where plants are underwatered. Spray with a fungicide to control powdery mildew and also gray mold/*Botrytis* (see page 193), which is usually worst on outdoor vines in wet years. *Phylloxera* is a serious insect problem on vinifera grapes. Plant only cultivars grafted on to *Phylloxera*-resistant rootstock.

RECOMMENDED CULTIVARS

VINIFERA
'Müller-Thurgau': *prolific and fragrant white wine grape.* **'Siegerrebe'**: *white wine grape that also can be eaten fresh.*
FRENCH–AMERICAN
'Johannes Seyve': *prolific pink grapes for wine or fresh eating.* **'Rayon d'Or'**: *pink grapes perfect for wine.*
AMERICAN
'Concord': *classic blue grape for juice or fresh eating; vigorous, hardy vines.* **'Niagara'**: *popular white grape for juice and fresh eating; also hardy.* **'Valiant'**: *extra-hardy with moderately sized, early, blue grapes.*
MUSCADINE
'Summit': *sweet pink grapes on disease-resistant plant.* **'Supreme'**: *large, late, and lovely black grapes.*

IN THE KITCHEN

Grapes add texture to the creamy, smooth mix of a dessert like *Crème brûlée*. Large grapes should be halved and their seeds taken out. Smaller seedless grapes can simply be washed and used whole.

CREME BRULEE
Serves 4

1lb (500g) grapes
4 egg yolks
½ cup (90g) brown sugar
2½ cups (600ml) light cream

1 Deseed the grapes if necessary and arrange them in a thick layer on the bottom of a flameproof dish.

2 Beat the egg yolks in the top of a double boiler. Heat the cream gently and pour it over the yolks. Mix well.

3 Heat some water in the lower part of the double boiler, set the mixture over it in the top part of the pan, and keep stirring until it begins to thicken. It is important that the mixture does not boil. When it has thickened, pour it over the grapes and leave overnight in the refrigerator.

4 The next day, cover the cream with an even layer of brown sugar, then put the dish under the broiler until the sugar has caramelized. Let it cool and chill before serving.

CULINARY NOTES

❧ Homegrown black grapes have a beautiful bloom on the skin that is very easily rubbed off and spoiled. Handle bunches with care, and bring them to the table displayed on a few of their own handsome leaves.

❧ Grapes also look beautiful divided into small bunches and piled in a glass bowl, together with sparkling ice cubes and a scattering of small flowers such as blue borage.

❀ BLACK GRAPES

❀ WHITE MUSCAT GRAPES

TYING IN SHOOTS

In spring, tie the rods (branches) back on to the wires using strong twine. They should spend the winter lying on the ground so that as the sap rises, buds break evenly all the way along the stems.

MELONS *Cucumis melo*

ANYWHERE WITH A WARM growing season over 80 days long can grow melons, trailing perhaps between tall sheaves of sweet corn, or sitting proudly like kings on little heaped thrones of manure and compost. In growth, they look like squash, but you need to thin the fruit so that no more than four melons are allowed to develop on a plant. In cool climates, look for early cultivars including cantaloupes – small, round fruit with heavily netted skin – such as 'Earligold', or miniature watermelons – with green rinds and succulent, juicy flesh – such as 'Sugar Baby'. The most successful type in cool areas is the muskmelon 'Ogen'. It has a yellow ring with green ribs and orange-tipped green flesh.

❀ MUSKMELON 'Ogen'

❀ HONEYDEW MELON

Cultivation

To produce the best fruit, melons need a long, warm growing season. In cool areas, fruit will ripen more quickly if you train vines over hard surfaces, such as concrete or paving stones, that store and reflect heat.

SITE AND SOIL Provide full sun and rich, moist, well-drained soil that has a pH close to neutral. Melons also grow well in large containers if kept well watered and fed, but you may have to support the fruit in a net sling as it gets heavier.

SOWING Sow seeds 4 weeks before the last spring frost, setting each on edge ½ in (1cm) deep in a 3-in (7-cm) pot of peat-based mix. Water and cover with clear plastic. Keep at about 70°F (21°C) until germination. Plant out after the last spring frost. Do not disturb the roots.

TRANSPLANTING Set plants in their final quarters from late spring. Melons grow best on a slight mound with a wall of compost built up around the edge to retain water. Set the plants 1m (3ft) apart.

ROUTINE CARE The main stem will produce laterals (side stems), which you should stop when they have made 5 leaves. From these laterals will come sublaterals, which you should pinch out at 3 leaves. The flowers that will eventually become fruit form on these sublaterals, so pinch out growing tips to force the plant to concentrate on producing fruit rather than foliage. Keep the soil moist and the air as well ventilated as possible. In rainy weather, pollinate the flowers by stripping the petals from a male flower and pushing it into a female flower. Female flowers have slight swellings just underneath the flowerheads. One male flower will pollinate at least 4 females. Pollination is best done at mid-day. Thin the fruit, if necessary, leaving no more than one melon per sublateral. Place tiles underneath to keep the fruit off the soil.

YIELD AND HARVESTING Expect 4 fruit from each plant. Do not pick melons until absolutely ripe. The all-embracing scent will tell you when to pounce.

PESTS AND DISEASES Because melons, like cucumbers, are cucurbits, they may suffer from cucumber mosaic virus. The leaves crumple and become flecked with yellow spots. There is no cure. Cover seedlings with floating row covers to avoid wilt-carrying cucumber beetles.

RECOMMENDED CULTIVARS

CANTALOUPE TYPE
'Earligold': *one of the best for growing in cool conditions.* **'Minnesota Midget'**: *small, sweet, fast-ripening fruit.* **'Ogen'**: *small, round, yellow fruit with green ribs.*

HONEYDEW TYPE
'Earlidew': *matures early even in cooler areas.*
WATERMELONS
'Moon and Stars': *heirloom with star-speckled leaves and rind.* **'Sugar Baby'**: *mini-watermelon for cooler climates.*

KIWI FRUIT & PASSION FRUIT
Actinidia spp *& Passiflora* spp.

BOTH FRUIT GROW ON EXTENSIVE twining vines, neither of which is very hardy. The tropical kiwi, or Chinese gooseberry, has big, round leaves covered with a gingery fuzz when young. The fruit has a brown, furry coat and, where it gets sufficient heat and a long enough growing season, will ripen outside to be harvested in autumn. The passion fruit, a cousin of the common passion flower, *Passiflora caerulea*, has showy white flowers with purple centers in midsummer, set off against handsome, three-lobed leaves. Outdoors in cool climates, the plant is likely to be cut down each year by frost so that growth has to start from the base again in spring. This makes the flowers late, so the fruit then has insufficient time to ripen.

☙ KIWI
FRUIT

☙ PASSION
FRUIT

Cultivation

In mild but not tropical climates, give these plants the hottest spots you can find in the garden, training them on a sunny wall. In cool climates, grow hardy kiwis (*Actinidia arguta*). If the conditions suit them, these vines can be rampageous. In order for tropical kiwi fruit to ripen, the vine needs an 8-month growing season; hardy kiwis only need half of that. To get any kiwi fruit at all, you will need two vines: a male and a female. Passion fruit is even more tender and is likely to succeed outside only where winter temperatures rarely fall below 45–50°F (8–10°C). Even though crops might be capricious, both plants have handsome foliage and can be planted to grow over an arbor or shed to provide a leafy backdrop for a scattering of clematis or some other flowery climber.

SITE AND SOIL Both these vines do best in rich, well-drained ground.

PLANTING Set out plants in late spring when all danger of frost has passed. They both need to be trained and tied in to supports. These need to be strong for a kiwi vine, which can be up to 27ft (9m) long and heavy with it. Plant male and female plants next to each other but leave 14ft (4m) between each pair.

POLLINATION Female kiwi plants will set fruit only when there is a male vine nearby. Most passion fruits are self-fertile.

ROUTINE CARE Both plants are greedy for food and water. Mulch liberally in spring with manure or compost, and water regularly throughout the growing season.

PRUNING Growth is rampant in the right conditons and may need curbing to persuade the plants to concentrate on the job at hand. For the gardener, this means the production of fruit rather than foliage. Kiwi vines fruit on the shoots that break from the first 3–6 buds of the current year's growth. Treat them like grapes (see page 181), summer pruning new growth to a point just beyond the setting fruit. Winter pruning can be more drastic. If necessary, remove whole stems. Prune passion fruit in early spring, thinning out overgrown plants and pinching back the lateral (side) shoots to about 6in (15cm).

YIELD AND HARVESTING Expect about 20lb (9kg) of fruit from both tropical kiwi and passion fruit vines, more from hardy kiwis, but only once the plants have become well established. This may take 7 years. Pick the fruit when, like a peach, it gives slightly under thumb pressure.

PESTS AND DISEASES These crops are generally trouble free.

RECOMMENDED CULTIVARS

KIWI FRUIT
'Haywood': *the most reliable female kiwi fruit available.* **'Tomuri'**: *a good male.*

PASSION FRUIT
Little selection of passion fruit has taken place, and there are few cultivars to recommend.
'Purple Granadilla': *bears purple fruits that are 3in (7cm) long with orange flesh, and white flowers with purple centers.*

3

PLANNING & CULTIVATION TECHNIQUES

IN THIS FINAL SECTION are some ground rules that you may find useful. Humus and hardening off, intercropping and insects, pricking out and pollination: they are all here, explained in a way that makes them simple to follow. Garden rules, however, exist only to be broken. Your own ability to tune in to the ebb and flow of the seasons and your plants' reactions to those changes will, in the end, be much more useful than any other source of knowledge. Learn, too, to be sanguine. Even if you follow all the rules you may still have disasters. Do not worry. There is always another spring.

SIZING UP THE OPTIONS

THE OPTIONS AVAILABLE to kitchen gardeners will depend entirely on the space available. You can grow vegetables on a balcony, but you would not expect to make an asparagus bed there. If all you have is a windowsill, you may become the world's expert on growing basil or arugula, but you are unlikely to be able to pull a decent carrot. Finding the right place for the right plant is the secret of success in gardening, and it is as true for fruit and vegetables as it is for flowers. Some vegetables will grow in partial shade. Some demand sun. Some want to gorge on food and drink. Others will spin a crop out of little more than thin air. When planning what you want to grow, you must consider the plant's needs as well as your own.

THE ALTERNATIVES

Once you grasp the notion that fruit and vegetables do not necessarily have to be grown in seclusion, away from the rest of the plants in the garden, all kinds of possibilities arise. Instead of planting a rose on a west wall of your house, you may put a pear there and train its branches into a flattened fan so that it can blossom and fruit in the shelter of the wall. Instead of raising a dividing screen of wooden fencing, you may think of planting a loganberry or tayberry and training it on parallel wires to make a highly productive partition. You may think of bringing an artichoke into the flower border to give

height and architectural substance to flowers that are lacking in both. Or you may edge a path with crinkled parsley, perhaps planting it alternately with groups of chubby violas. And you may decide for once to do without the petunias in the hanging basket and fill it with tumbling bush tomatoes. All these things are possible and look beautiful as well as providing food. There is no pleasure to equal that of picking your own supper on a summer evening. The pleasure is more muted when trying to hack a parsnip out of frozen ground, but even that may have a masochistic charm. And you can dream of the parsnip purée (see page 105) that will be the reward for your labors.

LETTUCE ALL THE WAY
Nowadays, you can grow lettuce with frills and flounces in red, bronze, or 40 different shades of green. Use them as foliage plants among pot marigolds and hot-looking zinnias.

TUNNEL VISION
In midsummer, roses are at their height, here creating a perfumed tunnel through a traditional kitchen garden. They have been imaginatively interplanted with kiwi fruit and grapes that will reach their peak later in the season.

SCREEN PLAY
This cottage garden is just beginning to burst into growth with its neat rows of vegetable seedlings. The wigwam and woven willow screen, which acts as a partition – and will later support a fast-growing hop – make good focal points when there is less greenery about.

PLUMMY TONES
No garden is so small that vegetables cannot be used to stunning effect. Here, a ring of young cabbage plants make a bold swath of leaves around a potted shrub. The midnight-colored flowers of the iris, once they open, will underline the cabbages' dusky tones.

ACCENT ON COLOR AND SHAPE
Though all have their role in the kitchen, the herbs and vegetables here have been chosen just as much for their colors and shapes. The round flower heads of leeks add a sculptural touch to a colorful arrangement of flowering chicory, nasturtiums, chard, and fennel.

FRUITFUL FEATURES

When sizing up the options, think hardest about the features that will be the most permanent. These are likely to be fruit trees. Could you fit an apple tree onto the lawn? The answer is probably yes, but your life will be made easier if you choose a tree trained as a half-standard with at least 3ft (1m) of clear stem before the branches start to arch out. This will develop into a fine tree, will be easy to mow under and to sling a hammock from, and be infinitely more beautiful to look at than a squat bush reined in by a dwarfing rootstock. Could you make better use of the paths by turning one of them into a tunnel dripping with grapes (if you are a romantic) or scarlet runner beans (if you take a more pragmatic view)? Again the answer is probably yes. Tunnels can

be permanent structures – hoops of iron joined by crosspieces – for the grapes, or temporary. For the scarlet runner beans you could make a tunnel from poles bent and lashed together over the path and joined at the sides with horizontal poles. This would suit a cottage garden where you might have zucchini and alliums bobbing around busily under the beans.

Deciding what to grow has to come after sizing up the options. You might not have enough space to do all that you want, nor enough sunny sites to grow your chosen crops. However many decorative designs you dream up for the leek bed, it will be a waste of ground if your family is resolutely antileek. With some vegetables, such as tomatoes, there is no such thing as too much. Not only are tomatoes decorative, they can be trained to grow in vertical space, rather than

horizontal, which is always at a greater premium. Tomatoes also make attractive centerpieces for the formal beds of a potager. They crop well on balconies, too, where you could make a miniature potager with a grow bag planted with tomatoes on stakes, surrounded by well-watered pots of salad vegetables, such as cut-and-come-again lettuce, and arugula.

If the way things look is as important as the process of producing food, you will find yourself choosing vegetables for appearance as well as for taste. You will plant the parsley-leaved blackberry, 'Oregon Thornless', and not mind that it crops more lightly than the standard kind. You will want yellow zucchini and tiger-striped tomatoes, red-stemmed Swiss chard, and purple-podded snap beans. If you choose carefully, you can have the best of both worlds: bounty and beauty.

SORTING OUT THE SPACE

THE SIZE OF A GARDEN need not limit your ambition. Indeed, the smaller it is, the greater the need for the gardener to feel that every square inch is earning its keep. There are several ways you can bring this about. One is to consider the way the garden is laid out. You need bold, simple lines, with paths wider than you ever thought necessary and beds bigger than you ever thought possible. Introducing key plants, or highlighting existing ones, is another way to pull together a design that somehow always seems to have something missing. There is no strict formula for sorting out the space: each individual gardener finds his or her own solution. We may start working from the same set of principles, but we should finish with completely different results that reflect what we want from our own particular patches.

INTERNAL DIVISIONS

Imagine the average backyard. The usual arrangement is for the house to give on to a small paved area, with a central lawn beyond and narrow flowerbeds running along either side. At the end there may be a shed or a set of swings. How would it be if, for a start, you did away with the lawn and divided up the space in a more engaging way? If you have children, this may not be an option, but for the moment, concentrate on the space – the former lawn space – and its potential. If you are sitting on the paved area right outside the house, or looking out of the windows, you will want something there to catch the eye. The garden itself should appear as luxuriant as possible. We are not talking about fearful gardening here.

Faced with a plot of ground that needs dividing up, many gardeners turn first to the edges and work their way around the boundaries, digging borders that are usually too narrow. Perhaps this is a remnant of some atavistic urge to mark territory. If, instead, you think out from the center of the space toward the edge, quite different patterns will emerge.

DIAGONAL PLAN If the squarish space in front of you were divided with a giant X to mark the lines of two new diagonal paths, as in Plan 1, several advantages become clear. Space is apportioned in a clean, simple way, creating the maximum area for growing flowers, fruit, and vegetables in the four triangles formed by the X. It becomes possible to create an eyecatching display alongside the paved

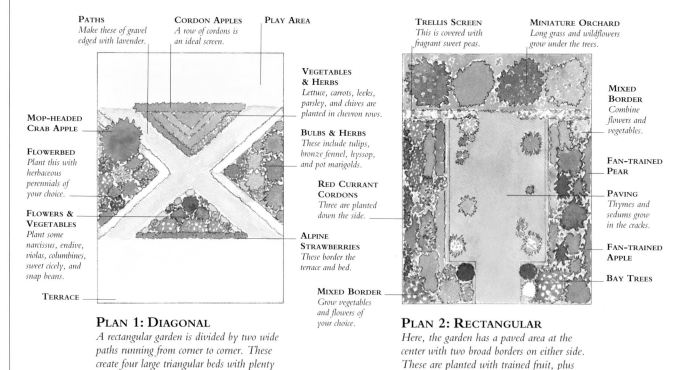

PATHS
Make these of gravel edged with lavender.

CORDON APPLES
A row of cordons is an ideal screen.

PLAY AREA

MOP-HEADED CRAB APPLE

FLOWERBED
Plant this with herbaceous perennials of your choice.

FLOWERS & VEGETABLES
Plant some narcissus, endive, violas, columbines, sweet cicely, and snap beans.

TERRACE

VEGETABLES & HERBS
Lettuce, carrots, leeks, parsley, and chives are planted in chevron rows.

BULBS & HERBS
These include tulips, bronze fennel, hyssop, and pot marigolds.

RED CURRANT CORDONS
Three are planted down the side.

ALPINE STRAWBERRIES
These border the terrace and bed.

MIXED BORDER
Grow vegetables and flowers of your choice.

TRELLIS SCREEN
This is covered with fragrant sweet peas.

MINIATURE ORCHARD
Long grass and wildflowers grow under the trees.

MIXED BORDER
Combine flowers and vegetables.

FAN-TRAINED PEAR

PAVING
Thymes and sedums grow in the cracks.

FAN-TRAINED APPLE

BAY TREES

PLAN 1: DIAGONAL
A rectangular garden is divided by two wide paths running from corner to corner. These create four large triangular beds with plenty of space for an eyecatching display of plants.

PLAN 2: RECTANGULAR
Here, the garden has a paved area at the center with two broad borders on either side. These are planted with trained fruit, plus flowers and vegetables to suit personal tastes.

area outside the house, where you most need something to admire. And the crossing of the paths in the middle creates a pivot for the design. The two diagonal paths need to be wide. This is possible since there is untrammelled planting space in between. So be generous.

The style of planting in the four triangles can be formal or not, depending on taste. Each of the four pieces of ground should have one big, outstanding specimen: a giant fennel, perhaps, or a neat, mop-headed crabapple tree. Depending on the size of the garden, the far side of the X-shape may mark the back boundary, or you may be able to keep the set of swings or shed area. Hide this from view with a bold semiscreen. You do not want anything solid, or your eye will bounce off it like a rubber ball. Nor do you want anything fussy. This is where fruit trees, planted in rows of slanting single-stem cordons or splayed out as fans or espaliers, make an ideal screen.

RECTANGULAR PLAN You might like the idea of a rectangular paved area in the middle of the plot, as in Plan 2, with wide borders of mixed vegetables and flowers on either side, and a miniature orchard at

the end. A trelliswork screen covered with sweet peas divides the orchard from the rest of the garden, and cracks between the paving stones are planted with mats of thyme and fleshy-leaved sedums.

WINDING PATH PLAN This divides the garden with a path that winds up through the center. The thick planting of lobelia makes the flagstones look like stepping stones in a river of blue. Stepover apples (like a long, low, one-tier espalier, see page 175) have been planted along its edge. Other fruit trees and bushes include plums, a quince, and a mixture of currants. Vegetables share the beds with flowers, while squash have room to roam under the fruit trees.

SYMMETRICAL PLAN A fourth option, shown in Plan 4, has rectangles of grass either side of a central path, with plants contained in raised beds built at the sides. The path could be made of bricks or stone. Tomatoes tumble over the edges of one raised bed with sunflowers and sweet corn behind. The other raised bed combines vegetables, herbs, and flowers. Three wigwams at the end add height, and are used to support scarlet runner beans, clematis, and *Cobaea scandens*.

GETTING STARTED

New gardeners are usually told that they must draw out a plan on paper before they start flailing around with spades and wheelbarrows. Because this is the way professional designers work, it is assumed that this is also best for amateurs. The problem with paper designs is that they tend to get over-complicated. The obvious is avoided at all costs. Another difficulty with paper is that it cannot contain all the information you need to make the right decisions. You will get this only as you prowl around your patch, taking in slight rises and falls in the ground and the consequences these will have on your design. Then you become aware of things beyond your boundary that you would rather not see, things that a well-placed plum tree may be able to conceal. You see where the sun falls and which patches are permanently in shade, and the problems the wind might cause for a too hastily erected wigwam of peas. Above all, working on the ground you develop a proper sense of proportion. Think simple is the best advice. And think big, however small your plot.

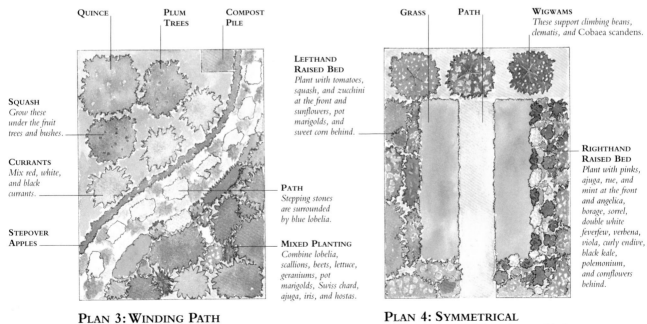

QUINCE PLUM TREES COMPOST PILE

GRASS PATH WIGWAMS
These support climbing beans, clematis, and Cobaea scandens.

LEFTHAND RAISED BED
Plant with tomatoes, squash, and zucchini at the front and sunflowers, pot marigolds, and sweet corn behind.

SQUASH
Grow these under the fruit trees and bushes.

CURRANTS
Mix red, white, and black currants.

STEPOVER APPLES

PATH
Stepping stones are surrounded by blue lobelia.

MIXED PLANTING
Combine lobelia, scallions, beets, lettuce, geraniums, pot marigolds, Swiss chard, ajuga, iris, and hostas.

RIGHTHAND RAISED BED
Plant with pinks, ajuga, rue, and mint at the front and angelica, borage, sorrel, double white feverfew, verbena, viola, curly endive, black kale, polemonium, and cornflowers behind.

PLAN 3: WINDING PATH
A path of flagstones surrounded by blue lobelia meanders through the garden, dividing it into two large planting areas filled with fruit, vegetables, and flowers.

PLAN 4: SYMMETRICAL
This very symmetrical design has raised beds around its sides, two patches of grass, and three wigwams of climbing plants that act as a focal point as well as a screen.

CHOOSING PATHS

PATHS DEFINE THE MAIN LINES OF THE DESIGN in a garden. They do not all need to be of equal importance. The main thoroughfares may be wide and hard-surfaced, but there may be an interconnecting web of narrow paths between beds that are no more than beaten soil. You need to get these lines of communication sorted out before you proceed with the rest of the plan for your plot. You need also to think of the kind of surface you want to use on your paths. The most sympathetic coverings in terms of looks and texture will probably also be the ones that need most care and maintenance. If you do not like weeds, but have an equal antipathy to weedkiller, then you had better start learning to love concrete.

SIMPLE SURFACES

The way you treat the paths in your garden will be dictated by cost as well as taste. The simplest, least expensive method is to leave them as beaten soil, but your design will have lost contrasts of color and texture between paths and vegetable beds. They will also be muddy after rain. The advantage of trodden soil paths is that they cost nothing and are easily rerouted if you feel like a change in layout.

Straw has a rustic look and is, in rural areas at least, easy to get hold of. It quickly sops up moisture in the soil and treads down to make friendly paths in vegetable gardens, especially those made in the cottage style.

Another inexpensive treatment is to cover them with ground or chipped bark, although like straw it will need regular replenishing. It is not a good idea if you already use a good deal of the stuff as a mulch on your borders. Used on both, your garden will begin to look like a demonstration plot for the timber industry's waste products. Lay the bark over black plastic if you want to cut down on weeding, but not if you like the idea of the bark itself slowly transmuting to soil. Ground, composted bark disappears faster but gives a smooth, sleek finish. Chipped bark is coarse and rustic in effect. Both are dark and molasses-colored.

GRAVELS

Gravel, if you have not used it elsewhere, makes a good path, although it sticks to the bottom of your shoes and then magically unsticks as soon as you walk into the house. The noise that it makes when you walk on it is very satisfying, so crunchy and distinctive that police forces now recommend it as a useful deterrent to burglars. Plants will seed themselves into it; bulbs (and weeds) will grow through it. This may be the effect that you want. If you like the idea of gravel but want to retain it as a formal, clean, unplanted area, put landscape fabric down first.

Different gravels give different colors and textures. Stick to one kind and make sure that it complements the color and texture of the brick or stone of the buildings around you. For a serene, calming finish, rake the gravel in parallel lines with a wide-tined rake. Gravel can be used in combination with other materials – perhaps a few paving stones set at regular intervals all the way down the path.

Rolled gravel is a mixture of sand, gravel, and pebbles often used in traditional kitchen gardens to provide a firm surface for heavily used work routes. It must be properly rolled, so that the constituents bind together to make a hard, durable crust. The best rolled gravel paths are made with a "batter," a slight hump in the middle, so that water is shed from the center to run along gutters on either side.

EDGINGS

If you use bark or gravel, both of which dislodge easily, you will probably need an edging to the beds, to prevent the one straying into the other. Lengths of board, about 3in (7cm) deep, are simple to set

STRAW PATH
Straw makes a good surface over a path of beaten soil, especially in a cottage garden. It feels pleasant underfoot and soaks up moisture.

GRAVEL PATH
Gravel is easy to lay and has an attractive, crunchy texture, but it does have a tendency to stray, especially if the path is on a slope.

STRAW
A good choice in rural areas, but it needs regular replenishing.

BARK CHIPS
This makes a natural-looking path and is comfortable to walk on.

GRAVEL
Choose a color and type that will blend in well with the surrounding area.

with a few wooden pegs bashed into the ground to keep path and bed where you want them. Avoid the rolls of corrugated plastic edging. It draws attention to itself without having the looks to warrant it. If you use more permanent forms of paving for the paths, you can dispense with fixed edgings, relying on borders of parsley, alpine strawberries, and the like, to keep the soil vaguely in place. There will always be some sweeping up to do. Birds do not understand the pleasures of clean paths, and some have beaks that excavate as efficiently as a bulldozer. In an ornamental kitchen garden, the paths will always tend to be on a lower level than the beds. The mulching that should be an annual routine gradually builds up the level of the soil, which is then more likely to topple onto the paths. In this respect, plants make better nets for catching the soil than narrow wooden boards.

PERMANENT PATHS

Old bricks make good paths. Professional bricklayers will roll their eyes knowingly if you use indoor bricks outside. Yes, they do flake in winter, but they do not disintegrate entirely, and the texture and color of ordinary bricks is infinitely more pleasant than the unvarying liverish look of what is called engineering brick. Stableyard bricks are equally good, shallower and cross-hatched on the top with a regular diamond pattern.

To do the job properly, you need to excavate the soil to a level of at least 7in (18cm) plus the thickness of the brick. Lay down crushed stone 6in (15cm) deep along the path and top it off with a layer

HERRINGBONE BRICK PATH
A pattern like this can be used to add a further decorative dimension to a potager and give it a pleasantly unhurried air. Plainer patterns tend to give a path a more purposeful look.

of cement, about 1in (2cm) thick. Lay the bricks on the cement, leaving narrow gaps between them. Fill the gaps with more cement, mixed very dry. Press the mixture down between the bricks with a trowel or stick, running the top of a stick along the joints to take away any surplus. Wipe the bricks clean before any spare cement hardens and becomes impossible to remove.

Some of the best paths, such as those at Sissinghurst, the famous garden in Kent, England, are made from a random selection of bricks, cobbles, and rubble. Some patterning of the materials – using bricks in threes, incorporating roundels made from bits of blue and white china, making parallel lines of cobbles down the

COBBLESTONE PATH
Although they can be a little hard on the feet, cobbles are extremely pleasing to the eye and make another attractive option, particularly when mixed with single rows of brick.

sides – gives a better effect than total anarchy. The advantage of this sort of path is that it gives a home to all kinds of bits and pieces that you do not want to throw away. Gertrude Jekyll used to sink families of clay flowerpots, one inside the other, to fill the open centers of the millstones that were such a feature in Edwardian gardens designed in the Arts and Crafts style.

Asphalt is perhaps the most unpleasant surface in the garden, but concrete runs a close second. On an uneven surface, it cracks and becomes as lethal as it is ugly. If you have such a path, forget about repairing it. Invite around some aggrieved friends and get them to work out their frustrations by smashing up the whole thing. You can then cart it off to the dump.

PAVING PATTERNS
Bricks, being relatively small paving units and very regular in shape, can be laid in a variety of patterns. Stretcher bond may mirror the pattern of a house wall. Herringbone is much more decorative but leaves you with the interesting problem of what to do with the triangular spaces that it produces at the edges. Basketweave is equally comfortable and less problematical to lay. When working with large, irregular slabs of stone, patterning is not as easy. Artificial stone does not have quite the same appeal, but it is inexpensive and comes in even shapes.

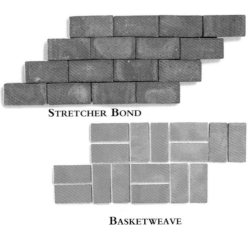

STRETCHER BOND

BASKETWEAVE

ARTIFICIAL STONE

SCREENS & STRUCTURES

THE NEED FOR A FOCAL POINT in a planting dawns on you gradually. If you want your garden to be comfortable and unselfconscious, you tend not to use words like focal point. But in certain places, the eye needs something to rest on, to bring the area into focus. A good focal point should seem inevitable, avoiding any uneasy sense of manipulation. It should show that it is important, without divorcing itself from the rest of the garden. A bench or seat might do the trick, particularly if you signal its significance by giving it pots for companions, or by surrounding it with a bower or an arbor swathed in grapes and honeysuckle. You can use tailor-made wigwams to bring height and consequence to a low planting of vegetables and herbs. The structure itself is appealing but it is practical, too, and can support useful crops of climbing beans and peas.

RURAL RETREAT
A seat at the end of a path, inviting you to sit down, is bound to attract attention. Choose a style in keeping with the garden. The woven willow seat above is perfect in a country setting.

USING SCREENS

Hazel and willow are the materials traditionally used to make structures such as wigwams and hurdles for the garden. Both are pliable, easy to get hold of in rural areas, and both grow quickly from clumps that are regularly "stooled" (cut down in rotation) to provide a nonstop supply of stems.

Boundaries made from willow or hazel hurdles will not be long lasting and are best used for internal divisions. They blend sympathetically with plants around them and can be used, like wigwams, to support climbers or trained fruit. You might think of stretching willow hurdles end to end to divide a fruit plot from a flower plot. Use them to support a loganberry, whose stems can stretch out along the structure. The loose, woven pattern of these supports means that you will easily find spots to tie the stems in place. Plant golden hops to twine over a hazel hurdle such as the one on the right. Hops die down completely in winter and allow you to get in and repair the hurdles where necessary.

The crisscross, open lattice, made from pieces of softwood, also makes a decorative structure in the garden and

would be suitable for a light boundary fence. A screen such as this would be strong enough to support the weight of a colonizing pumpkin or an assortment of squash. Alternatively, you could use it to provide the background for a row of slanting cordon apples.

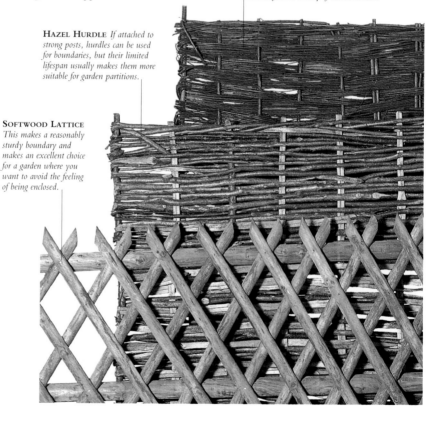

WILLOW HURDLE *The fine stems of willow make a dense yet elegant screen. Choose from a variety of natural colors.*

HAZEL HURDLE *If attached to strong posts, hurdles can be used for boundaries, but their limited lifespan usually makes them more suitable for garden partitions.*

SOFTWOOD LATTICE *This makes a reasonably sturdy boundary and makes an excellent choice for a garden where you want to avoid the feeling of being enclosed.*

SCREEN ASSORTMENT
Hazel and willow hurdles and lattice fencing can all be used in decorative ways in the garden, adding a soft, rustic air. Grow a loganberry against a hurdle, and festoon the lattice with eccentrically shaped squash.

WIGWAMS TO SCARECROWS

You can buy already-made wigwams of metal or wood but, with a little practice, you can also make your own. Professional basketmakers usually work sitting down. They would start a wigwam, such as the one shown below, with the bunch of hazel sticks clasped between their knees. As they progress, working farther and farther down the spiral of the wigwam, the whole structure is pushed under and between their knees. You might find it easier to start off by sticking the uprights in the ground, using a garbage can lid or the wheel of a bicycle to mark out the size and shape of the base. Hazel or willow can be used for the uprights, and willow,

bittersweet, grape vines, or prunings of clematis stems for the woven spiral that holds the whole thing in place. Freshly cut stems do not need to be soaked, but you would need to soften up material that has been cut and stored by soaking it in water for a few hours. You can make the thin wands of willow that you use for the weaving even more supple by swinging them around against your finger and thumb, like a cowboy in a Western about to lasso a steer.

In the wigwam shown below there are 18 uprights, which makes a very stable structure. You could use less, but there should not be too much space between the uprights, if the wigwam is to make a bold feature in your planting. Structures

such as this do not last forever. Eventually the bottoms of the uprights will begin to rot and, as the wood ages, it will become more brittle and more likely to snap under the weight of the growth it is supporting. If you have the necessary space, bring wooden structures such as this under cover in the winter after you have gathered in all your crops.

Once you have realized the potential of materials such as willow and hazel, all kinds of possibilities open up. You may even feel you could tackle something similar to the basketwork seat opposite. You may start dreaming about a futuristic scarecrow, with a body made from bowed lengths of hazel and willow crosspieces for its arms. Dream on. Then get weaving.

WIGWAM STYLES
Wigwams can be as simple or as elaborate as you choose to make them. This one has only two woven bands. More, as at right, make a stronger structure.

HOW TO MAKE YOUR OWN WIGWAM

1 Take 9 uprights, 7–10ft (2–3m) high, and bind them at the top with fine willow wands. This number will make a stable structure. You may find it easiest to work with the uprights stuck in the ground. Soak the wands first only if they have been stored.

2 Tie 2 long, thin, flexible wands into the top. Start to weave them into bands around the wigwam, taking one under and the other over each upright. Keep the weaving under tension as you go.

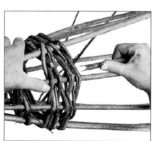

3 When you have woven 2 bands, take another 9 stakes, with one end sharpened on each, and push the sharpened end into the second band between each upright, to give 18 uprights altogether.

4 Continue weaving the wands in a spiral down the wigwam. Keep the uprights evenly spaced. Slot in new wands as needed, tying them in at the bottom.

FINISHED WIGWAM

UNDERSTANDING THE SOIL

VEGETABLE HEAVEN IS A SOIL that is well-drained, fertile, open, and neither too acid nor too alkaline. If you have an old garden, someone else might have already converted the underlying sand or clay into a workable tilth. If not, grit your teeth and prepare to mulch, mulch, mulch. Soil is a mixture of bits of rock, water, air, and organic matter such as rotted leaves. Sandy soils (ideal for carrots, which swell easily in this friable medium) are made from relatively large bits of rock; clay soils (good for brassicas, which prefer a solid soil) from small particles. One is called light, the other heavy. Adding bulky manures is arguably the best way to improve soil structure. The extra humus closes up the big spaces in sandy soils and makes it capable of holding more water. In clay soils, humus adds extra air spaces between the too closely packed particles and so improves drainage.

LIMING
Acid soils can be limed to make them a little more alkaline. Spread ordinary lime (calcium carbonate) thinly and evenly, then rake it in. Wait three months before sowing or planting.

HOW SOIL WORKS

No amount of chemical fertilizer will improve the structure of your soil. Before plants can take up food, they need roots that can find it. Plant roots need passages along which they can run and from which they can then absorb the nutrients necessary for healthy growth. Humus – decayed vegetable matter – helps to create these vital passages. In city gardens it may be difficult to acquire bulky manures, but make a resolution to haul in a sack of

TYPES OF SOIL
What you grow and how you grow it is to some extent determined by the type of soil. The five main kinds each display certain characteristics that make them reasonably easy to recognize.

some nourishing mulch once a week until the whole plot has been covered. It will pay enormous dividends in improved growth. If you have space, you can make your own compost (see page 163) and add that to the soil. Homemade compost should have the texture of rich fruitcake.

The minerals that plants need for healthy growth are generally lumped together under the heading trace elements and include boron, copper, iron, manganese, and zinc. In fertile soils they are present naturally; lack of them shows up in plant deficiency diseases. Organic animal manures are rich in trace elements, so if you use these regularly, you are unlikely to have problems. Magnesium deficiency (which makes leaves turn brown and wither) is more prevalent on

acid soils than on alkaline ones. Chlorosis is more likely on limy soils: leaves that should be bright, pulsating green turn a pallid, sickly yellow. It is caused by the fact that the plant cannot absorb the minerals it needs from the soil because they are locked up by too much lime. Correct the imbalance by watering with a solution of chelated iron, or sequestrene.

ACID OR ALKALINE?

Acid and alkaline are terms that apply to the pH (the potential of hydrogen) in the soil. The scale runs from 1 to 14 with neutral at 7. Most vegetables and fruit do best in this middle range. Asparagus is not

SILT
Silt is fertile and retains moisture well but is easily compacted. It has a rather silky feel if you squeeze it.

ALKALINE/ CHALKY
Usually pale, shallow, and stony. It drains freely and is moderately fertile.

CLAY
Clay is heavy, slow to drain, and often quite sticky. It can be hard to work but is full of nutrients.

SANDY SOIL
Light, gritty-textured, and free-draining, sandy soil is easy to work, but it needs lots of humus to make it fertile.

PEAT
Rich in organic matter, peat looks very dark and crumbly. It retains moisture well and makes an acid soil.

happy on very acid soils, while blueberries demand it. Generally, though, good fertility and drainage have a greater effect on growth than the precise nature of the pH level. There are simple kits available with which you can gauge the pH level of your soil, but always take readings from more than one location.

You can tinker with acid soils by adding extra lime if you want to make them more amenable to the growing of vegetables, especially brassicas. Do not add it at the same time as manure, or the chemical reaction with the nitrogen in the manure that is produced may harm plants. The nitrogen will also be wasted. It is far more difficult to convert an alkaline soil to a comfortable home for lime-hating plants. Raspberries, for instance, always look happier in slightly acid soils than they do in heavy, alkaline clay ground.

CULTIVATION METHODS

Prepare ground for planting only when the soil is dry enough not to stick to the bottom of your boots (autumn and midspring are often the best times). Only masochists make digging loom large in the gardening calendar.

On heavy ground, you dig to expose clods of soil so that they can be broken up by frost. You dig to get air into compacted soil, to bury weeds or other organic material, and to give robins a decent breakfast. Digging no longer has the heroic status it once had, along with

bastard trenching and double digging, which was twice as backbreaking. On light soils, forking over will often be enough. Mushroom compost or any other weed-free compost that you can spread thickly on top of the ground will eventually be pulled down into the soil by worms. That is a lot less trouble than doing it yourself.

If you are making a new bed, it may not be necessary to dig the soil at all. If you garden on light, sandy soil, weedkill it thoroughly, mulch heavily, and plant directly into the ground. Heavy ground, or areas that have been well-trodden or compacted, need more attention.

Digging improves drainage and introduces air into soil that has been packed hard by feet. Heavy clay soils should be dug in late autumn, light soils as late as possible in spring. Light soils do not need to be broken down by frost. The main problem here is hanging onto water and nutrients. By leaving the soil firm over winter, you will be helping it to hold as much water as possible.

THE NO-DIG METHOD

If you have a light, well-drained, fertile soil, the sort of soil that everyone dreams of, then you may well be able to run a fruit and vegetable garden without ever having to dig at all. Some light forking and hoeing to get rid of weeds will be all that is necessary. To maintain fertility you will have to mulch heavily. The no-dig

method works well in areas of the garden where you have permanent crops such as fruit bushes or asparagus. You can use it successfully in ground that you use for transplanted crops such as tomatoes, zucchini, and leeks, and also for growing potatoes (see page 102).

It is more difficult, however, to produce the fine tilth needed for seedbeds without doing any digging. A mulch in these circumstances is a hindrance rather than a help.

FORKING
Light soils will probably need forking over only to loosen and aerate the surface layer. Work when the ground is moist but not waterlogged. Light soil is best prepared in spring and then mulched to conserve moisture and nutrients.

DIGGING THE KITCHEN GARDEN

1 If the soil is heavy, or if you are making beds in new ground, you will probably have to dig. To make it less difficult, keep the spade upright as it goes into the soil.

2 Do not try to load too much on to the blade, especially if the ground is heavy, and bend your knees as you lift the spade. The whole task will be much less backbreaking.

3 Turn the soil over to introduce air. You can also bury annual weeds or incorporate organic matter. On heavy ground, dig before winter so that frost breaks up heavy clods.

MULCHING, FEEDING & WATERING

IF YOU TAKE CARE OF THE MULCHING, the feeding and watering will mostly take care of themselves. A mulch works like a biodegradeable blanket – by putting a layer of rotted leaves, barnyard manure, grass clippings, or compost on top of the soil you can control weeds, retain moisture, improve soil structure, add nutrients (slowly), and keep plants and crops clean. Thick and regular mulches will make watering and feeding far less imperative. Mulches made of materials that have been plants themselves once add a complex cocktail of nutrients to the soil. They also improve its condition, since earthworms gradually pull the mulch underground and aerate the soil. Without these air pockets, roots cannot easily penetrate the soil. By mulching, you feed the soil, not the plants. Soil that is in good condition is the key to successful gardening.

MULCHING

Spread mulches thickly over the soil to stop weeds from growing, although no mulch will stop determined perennials such as bindweed. If they are intended to conserve moisture, do not apply mulches when the ground is dry.

LEAF MOLD The easiest place to make leaf mold is inside a cage made of chicken wire where the leaves will gradually rot down. You will need a space about 4ft (1.2m) square. If you do not have room for this, pack leaves into plastic garbage bags instead. The best leaves to use are beech and oak. Leaves with thick midribs, such as ash and horse chestnut, take much longer to disintegrate. Making leaf mold is a useful way of exploiting nature's own mulch. It improves soil structure and also, over time, releases valuable nutrients.

MANURE A valuable source of organic matter, although manure is best used when well-rotted. Stables and chicken coops are good sources. Old, well-rotted manure is dry and easy to handle.

GRASS CLIPPINGS These are usually available without too much trouble and are excellent around soft fruit bushes.

COMPOST If you have room to make a compost pile (see opposite), you need never be short of mulch. Any organic material (except meat and fat) – such as vegetable peelings, weeds, leaves, hair – can be added. Covering the pile with an old carpet also hurries things along, as does watering and turning the pile a few times. The hotter you can make your compost, the better: heat destroys weed seeds.

MUSHROOM COMPOST Where it is available, this makes one of the best mulches, but it is alkaline so do not use it around crops that need an acid soil, such as blueberries.

HOW TO MULCH
Mulches need to be spread at least 2–4in (5–10cm) deep in order to keep down annual weeds and conserve moisture in the soil.

FEEDING

Fertilizers are compounds that you use to replace nutrients taken from the soil. They can be organic or inorganic, and a fierce debate rages as to the benefits of one against the other. Organic fertilizers supply nutrients of plant or animal origin; extract of seaweed, blood meal, and bonemeal are

TYPES OF MULCH
Use whatever organic materials you can get hold of. The five suggested below are easy to make or to buy, but you could also use straw, shredded bark, or alfalfa, if available. All are excellent but react in slightly different ways.

LEAF MOLD
A fine, crumbly substance made by stacking fallen leaves in a heap and leaving them gradually to rot down.

MANURE
Few mulches benefit the soil as much as manure, but it needs to be well-rotted.

GRASS CLIPPINGS
These are satisfactory as long as herbicides are not used on the lawn.

COMPOST
Most plant material can go on the compost pile. It will rot down finally to resemble soil.

MUSHROOM COMPOST
Easy to use and sterile, but it is alkaline, so should not be used around plants that need an acid soil.

typical. These are broken down by bacteria in the soil and then drawn in by the plants' roots. Inorganic fertilizers are either manufactured or are of mineral origin, such as ammonium sulfate or green-sand. Organic fertilizers may be cheaper but tend to work more slowly than inorganic ones.

Using high-octane inorganic fertilizers is like using hard drugs. Instant benefit is cancelled out by long-term problems. Only plants growing in unnatural circumstances (usually confined in pots or hanging baskets) are likely to need manufactured fertilizers. They work fast. That is one of the reasons they are popular. But they feed the plant rather than the soil. This upsets the delicate balance of the soil's own life that includes important, invisible microorganisms.

Nitrates promote rapid growth, but plants fed in this way grow artificially fast, which may have a detrimental effect on taste. They often have too high a water content and, being sappy, are more open to attack by pest and disease. Which leads you to reach for a different bottle . . . Neither inorganic nor organic fertilizers are enough on their own. You need to add organic matter to the soil to enhance fertility and structure. Back to the mulch.

WATERING

Watering gardens is a luxury, not a prerogative. Plants growing in restricted spaces, such as pots, need frequent drinks. The rest of the garden should not, if you use organic manures to enhance the water-retaining capacity of soil. The crops that respond best to watering are leafy ones such as lettuce, cabbage, and spinach. Crops that bear seeds and fruits, such as beans, peas, and tomatoes, are best watered while the plants are in flower and the fruits are swelling. Transplants of brassicas, celery, and leeks need frequent watering until established. Overwatering of root crops such as carrots after a long, dry spell tends to make the roots split. Again, mulching is the long-term solution.

COMPOST CORNER
Think twice about what you throw away; it may well be put to better use on the compost pile. You can soon build up enough crumbly compost to mulch large areas of the garden.

MAKING A COMPOST PILE
For the best results, build up the pile in layers of about 6in (15cm). Scatter manure, or another material rich in nitrogen, between the layers to help speed the rotting.

Mix grass cuttings with other garden waste. They impede air circulation if added in too thick a layer.

Add most any kind of organic garden or kitchen waste, but do not include diseased plants, meat, or fat.

Sticks and twigs make a good base layer. They allow air to circulate in the pile.

CROP ROTATION

THE FIRST THING that beginner vegetable gardeners need to know about crop rotation is that vegetables will not necessarily curl up and die if they are not moved to new homes each year. For many years crop rotation, along with double digging and bastard trenching, was one of the great shibboleths of vegetable growing. But the best gardeners are not those who rely on rules but those who use their eyes, take the trouble to learn the vagaries of their own plot, work with the weather, and have respect for their soil. Good gardening depends on finding the balance between what you want the plants to do and what they want you to do. Plants are successful because each has managed to adapt, over the years, to a particular set of conditions. Learn to recognize each plant's needs. Crop rotation should reflect those needs, not become an end in itself.

THE REASON WHY

The most persuasive argument for the practice of some form of crop rotation has to do with the soil. Each different type of vegetable crop – brassicas, onions, legumes (podded vegetables), or root crops, such as potatoes – needs a slightly different cocktail of nutrients and trace elements from the soil. If you always grow your cauliflowers in the same place, it is likely that the soil there will eventually become drained of the ingredients that cauliflowers want the most. By moving them on to a different part of the garden, you give the soil in the first plot a chance to recover and replenish itself using the liberal supplies of compost and manure that you will, of course, be giving it.

The case for avoiding disease by rotating crops is less convincing. If your brassicas are struck by clubroot, they will do better if you plant them in fresh ground the following season. But the spores of clubroot, which causes distorted roots in members of the brassica family, can live for more than 20 years in the soil. Even if you practice a 5-year rotation, those spores will still be lurking when the brassicas eventually return to their original plot. The spores of the fungus that causes white rot in onions are equally long-lived. Also, in a small garden, it is unlikely that any of your plots will be distant enough from each other to prevent pests and diseases drifting over the unmarked boundary lines. Your best defense against disease, in plants as with people, is to take every possible step to prevent it from breaking out in the first place. Be sanguine in those seasons when aphids outnumber predators and the noise of flea beetles jumping off cabbage leaves is louder than the crunch of your foot on the snails that are eating the lettuce.

THE MAIN GROUPS

Traditional crop rotations revolve around three main groups of vegetables. First are the legumes or podded vegetables, the peas and beans. Their group also includes vegetables such as sweet corn, zucchini, and tomatoes that do not fit tidily into any other compartment. Legumes are followed by the brassicas, which include rutabagas, turnips, kohlrabis, and radishes, as well as

LEGUMES (PODDED VEGETABLES)
The roots of legumes – all the peas and beans – form nodules that are packed with nitrogen and will help to enrich the soil. At the end of the season, cut the plants at the base of the stems, leaving the roots to break down in the ground.

BRASSICAS
Leafy brassicas, such as cabbages, cauliflowers, broccoli, and kale, are all hungry for nitrogen. If possible, plant them in a patch of ground that was used the previous season for growing legumes and that has also been well-manured.

ROOT VEGETABLES
Beets, carrots, and the like do not demand much nitrogen, and so usually follow brassicas in a rotation. Potatoes and Jerusalem artichokes, which produce a mass of tubers and roots, are ideal for breaking up newly cultivated ground.

more obviously cabbagelike vegetables, such as cauliflowers, Brussels sprouts, and broccoli. Finally, there are the roots and tubers: beets, carrots, Jerusalem artichokes, parsnips, and potatoes. In a 3-bed rotation, onions will be included with the legumes. In a 4-bed rotation, the onion tribe has a section of its own.

An inflexible attitude is not likely to help your vegetables as much as a commonsense appraisal of their needs. If you have a sunny, south-facing plot, it would be a wasted opportunity to use it for peas or cabbages, which do not need that kind of situation. Tomatoes and sweet corn, however, will be unlikely to crop successfully without it. If one area of your garden soil is noticeably lighter and drains more freely than another, then carrots will do better there than in the stiff ground that seems to suit cabbages.

In drawing up a plan, you also need to be realistic about what you like to eat and have the skill to grow. If you are not fond of cabbages and are unsuccessful in raising cauliflowers, it will be a waste of space to include them in a rotation.

How a 3-Bed Plan Works

Most gardeners will need only to use a simple 3-year, 3-bed rotation. The easiest way is to list the vegetables you want to grow and split them into the 3 main groups (in rotation terms, beds really means groups, not actual growing beds). Draw a rough plan of the garden, then mark which crops can go where using a different color for each group. The following year, move the crops accordingly. Fit in fast-growing crops wherever there is a convenient gap.

Year 1

Year 2

Year 3

3-Bed Rotation

Peas	Brussels sprouts	Beets
Beans	Cabbages	Carrots
Celery	Cauliflowers	Chicory
Onions	Broccoli	Jerusalem artichokes
Leeks	Kohlrabi	Parsnips
Lettuce	Rutabagas	Potatoes
Spinach	Turnips	
Sweet corn	Radishes	
Tomatoes		
Zucchini		

4-Bed Plan

In a 4-bed rotation, onions can be hived off into a separate group along with leeks, garlic, and shallots. Lettuce and other fast-growing salad crops, such as arugula, can be fitted in wherever there is a spare patch of ground.

Year 1

Year 2

Year 3

Year 4

4-Bed Rotation

Scarlet runner beans	Brussels sprouts	Onions	Peppers
Snap beans	Cabbages	Shallots	Tomatoes
Peas	Cauliflowers	Leeks	Celery
Broad beans	Broccoli	Garlic	Celeriac
Sweet corn	Oriental vegetables	Zucchini	Beets
	Rutabagas	Lettuce	Carrots
	Turnips		Parsnips
	Radishes		Potatoes

5-Bed Plan

A 5-bed rotation is for gardeners with lots of space, who like to lie awake at night dreaming up ever more complex ways of utilizing it. Here, the onion family has a section of its own, as do the potatoes and other root vegetables.

Year 1

Year 2

Year 3

Year 4

Year 5

5-Bed Rotation

Broad beans	Cauliflowers	Zucchini	Onions	Potatoes
Scarlet runner beans	Broccoli	Sweet corn	Garlic	Parsnips
Peas	Cabbages	Tomatoes	Leeks	Carrots
Snap beans	Turnips	Celery	Lettuce	Beets
	Radishes	Celeriac	Shallots	Rutabagas
	Brussels sprouts			Jerusalem artichokes
	Oriental brassicas			

GROWING METHODS

THE WAY THAT YOU GROW IS INFLUENCED by the kind of soil that you have. If you garden on heavy ground, the idea of creating deep beds that will need little attention once made may be more compelling than if you have light, free-draining soil. On this type of easy-to-work ground, some gentle hoeing, weeding, and mulching may be all that is needed. If you live in a frost pocket, where winter comes early and spring late, you have more reason to try out floating row covers to extend the growing season. Some cultivation methods relate to particular crops. You will need to hill soil up around potatoes to prevent tubers from developing poisonous green patches, and force Belgian endive if you are to produce fat, white buds.

DEEP BEDS

The deep bed system is not as luxuriously sybaritic as it sounds. It is a way of growing plants in a series of beds, no more than 5ft (1.5m) wide, that are divided by narrow paths about 12in (30cm) wide. This sort of layout means that you can do all the planting, weeding, and general cultivation from the paths without ever treading on the soil. This stops it from becoming compacted, and helps drainage and soil structure. To make the beds it is essential to dig the ground thoroughly and clear it of all perennial weeds. After that, heavy mulches of bulky organic matter must be applied regularly, making the beds higher than the paths. That is why they are called deep beds. What you lose on the paths you gain by more intensive cropping in the beds. Plant in short, fairly close rows running across the beds. Because you are planting closely, you must feed the soil well. The best way is with a bulky organic mulch of well-rotted manure or compost. The initial labor of making the beds is perhaps daunting but, once made, they are easy to maintain.

FLOATING ROW COVERS

Plastic covers have been used for many years by professional growers to protect crops and accelerate growth. Various types of materials – including perforated or fleecy ones – are now available to the amateur grower. They do not guard against frost, but you can use them to warm the soil or to give extra protection to early crops. Brassicas, lettuce, early potatoes, radishes, and onions may all benefit from being covered for the first 4–5 weeks of the growing period. The film must be well anchored at the edges, either by being buried in the soil or weighted down with stones or boards. If the edges are well sealed, it will also give protection against pests such as cabbage maggot, carrot rust fly, flea beetle, and cabbage white butterfly. Soft, fleecy films may be left in place over crops such as lettuce for the entire growing period. Sometimes called "floating mulches," films and fleece do not do what mulches do (keep down weeds, retain moisture, feed soil) but help to raise the temperature of the soil and guard against weather and pests.

FLOATING ROWS COVERS

An early crop of lettuce will grow faster under a fleecy film that keeps in warmth. The film will also give some protection against insect pests as well as predatory birds or rabbits.

DEEP BEDS

This system is ideal for heavy ground since it cuts down on digging and relies on replenishing the soil's fertility by heavy mulching. The layout of narrow beds and paths also makes organizing the rotation of crops a simpler proposition.

FORCING RHUBARB

Put tall, chimney-shaped terracotta pots over rhubarb plants for an early, succulent crop. Stretching for the light at the top, the stems grow much longer than they would otherwise do.

INTERCROPPING

On fertile soil you can increase yields by intercropping, a way of squeezing more produce from less ground. It works only if plants are fed and watered well. You need to combine complementary crops – two that grow in different directions or one that grows faster than the other. Radishes are a classic example, sown between rows of slow-maturing parsnips. You will have harvested the radishes before the parsnips need the space. Sweet corn mostly needs vertical space. Intercrop by planting bush tomatoes or trailing squash beneath. Small cos lettuce can be grown between garlic, or try quick-growing mesclun between recently planted-out brassicas.

HILLING UP SOIL

This gives heavy plants such as Brussels sprouts extra stability, especially in exposed areas. Draw up the soil around the stem with a spade or hoe. Hilling up soil around potatoes prevents the tubers from developing poisonous green patches, caused by exposure to light. Start when plants are about 12in (30cm) high, drawing up the soil around the stems. You can bury the lower leaves, but leave the tops uncovered. Soil is hilled up around celery to blanch the stems.

FORCING AND BLANCHING

These processes keep light from stems or leaves. Forcing hurries vegetables into growth; blanching makes them more tender or less bitter. Crops such as rhubarb can be forced with special terracotta pots or a bucket. Celery is usually blanched with a paper collar as well as being hilled up. The hearts of curly endive can be blanched with a saucer upturned over the center of the plant. Belgian endive needs both forcing and blanching. Outside, if the soil is not too heavy or cold, cut any leaves to 1in (2cm) above the neck of the plant and cover the stumps with at least 6in (15cm) of soil. Then put cloches over the top. The process is faster inside.

FORCING AND BLANCHING BELGIAN ENDIVE

After blanching

1 Take the plants that have been lifted, trimmed, and stored in boxes of sand (see pages 66–67), and shorten the roots to 6in (15cm). Fit 3–6 plants upright in a 9-in (23-cm) pot of moist soil, leaving the tops exposed.

2 Invert a similar-sized pot over the top to keep out light and store at 50–65°F (10–18°C) while the blanched chicons develop. This will take about 3 weeks in a warm environment, longer in a cooler cellar.

SOWING INSIDE

TO THE UNINITIATED, SEED SOWING is the impenetrable rite of passage that separates the novice from the seasoned gardener. It is not usually half as difficult, however, as experts try to make it, and you do not need an arsenal of equipment. When you are sowing indoors, heat will make seeds germinate more quickly and plants grow faster than they would otherwise do, but at some stage they must learn to live without it and take on the weather as it really is. The tougher plants have been raised, the better they will cope. The more sparsely you sow, the stronger the plants will be for later transplanting. Greenhouses provide ideal sowing conditions, but there is much you can raise on a light, warm windowsill.

SOWING LARGE SEED

Large seeds, such as those of zucchini, are best sown one or two seeds to a pot. If you sow two seeds, remove the weaker of the seedlings.

SOWING IN A CONTAINER

Make your initial sowing in a clean plastic pot about 5in (12cm) across. It is better to save your seed trays for transplanting out later. Fill the pot with potting soil. Firm it down gently. Scatter the seed as thinly and evenly as possible on top of the soil. Every gardener devises their own favorite way of doing this. Some like to pour it into the palm of one hand, then take pinches of seed between the thumb and forefinger of the other and sprinkle it over the soil. Others are confident enough to scatter seed directly from the packet with a series of gentle taps. Cover the seed with a thin layer of potting soil or vermiculite. Many gardeners find vermiculite much better and easier to use as a seed covering. It is a lightweight mineral rather like mica that

retains moisture but also drains quickly. Perlite, made from expanded granules of volcanic minerals, has the same qualities. You do not have to worry about the exact depth of a covering of vermiculite the way you do if you are using soil mix. Water thoroughly before sealing the pot in a cocoon of plastic wrap, which will stop the potting mixture from drying out.

Once the seed has germinated, take the cover off of the pot and keep the soil damp but not saturated. Turn the pot around regularly since seedlings always lean toward the light. Damping off may be a problem with seedlings raised inside. They suddenly collapse at the point where stem meets soil, and entire pots of seeds may be affected. Overwatering is the most common cause, but it may also arise from using old potting mixture in dirty pots.

Large seeds, such as those of cucumbers and melons, can be sown in single 3-in (7-cm) pots, setting one or two seeds on edge in each pot. If you sow two, you will need to remove the weaker of the two seedlings after they both have germinated. Seeds sown in this way can stay in their pots until planted outside.

PRICKING OUT

Seedlings grown *en masse* in a 5-in (12-cm) pot need to be moved on to fresh quarters sooner rather than later. Growing close together, they quickly get leggy and then keel over at the slightest disturbance. One evening when you feel in need of some calming, therapeutic activity, fill some full-sized seed trays with potting soil, gently firm down the surface, and, with

SOWING

1 *Fill the seed tray or pot with potting soil. Firm it down gently. In trays, use a piece of wood to do this. In a pot, soil can be firmed using the base of a second, empty pot.*

2 *Scatter the seed as evenly and thinly as you can over the soil mix. The thinner you sow, the better the chance of producing healthy seedlings with good, sturdy stems.*

3 *Cover the seed with a thin layer of potting soil or vermiculite, then water carefully with a fine-nozzled can. Cover with plastic wrap or a sheet of glass to stop the soil from drying out.*

SIMPLE PROPAGATOR

A unit like this fits neatly on to a windowsill and can be used for germinating seeds or to protect seedlings that have just been transplanted.

your finger, poke a grid of holes in the soil mix, 6 along the long side and 4 along the short. With a stick, or some similar implement, gently ease up a few seedlings at a time from the pot. Pick each one up by one of its lowest leaves and drop it into one of the holes you have made in the soil. Set the seedlings deep, so that the first pair of leaves sits near the surface of the soil mix. Firm the mix around them gently with your fingers. When the whole tray is planted, water thoroughly with a fine-nozzled can.

Seedlings of tomatoes that have germinated and grown for the first part of their lives in a 5-in (12-cm) pot should be transplanted out into 3-in (7-cm) pots, one plant in each pot. Fill the small pots with potting soil, make a hole down through the center of the soil with your finger and drop in the seedling, setting it deeper than it was originally growing. Firm the soil around the stem. Plants that resent having their roots disturbed, such as Chinese cabbages, can be tranplanted out

into cell packs. These are specially modified planting trays divided into separate small compartments that can be anything from ½–2in (1–5cm) across. You can improvise by using egg cartons. Sow in the lid and transplant seedlings into each of the compartments. The advantage of cell packs is that the roots do not have to compete with one another for nutrients and are less easily disturbed when being transplanted. You can also sow 2 or 3 seeds directly into modules and thin them after they have germinated.

HARDENING OFF

The potting mix in the cell packs or the tray into which you have transplanted the plants should contain enough food for the seedlings to survive on until they can be planted outside. Watering is important, as is hardening off the plants, which means getting them acclimatized to the real world. Do this gently, putting the trays out on warm days and bringing them in at

nights until the plants seem sturdy enough to be planted outside.

You can help to harden off plants inside by nightly brushing their tops with the edge of a piece of thin cardboard. Do this for about a minute each day, brushing in different directions. This flexing of the stems strengthens them, simulating the effect of wind. But even if you brush your plants, you will still have to acclimatize them gradually to lower temperatures outside. If you intend to grow plants such as melons, cucumbers, tomatoes, and eggplants in a greenhouse, rather than outside in the garden, then you will not need to harden them off. They will be living their entire lives in luxurious warmth and shelter.

TRANSPLANTING

Planting out vegetables such as zucchini, cucumbers, or tomatoes that you have been growing under cover in pots is not usually as detrimental to a plant as transplanting it from a drill or seedbed outside (see overleaf). You can ease the rootball out of the pot without disturbing the roots and, if you water them in well, these plants will not usually be too badly hampered. In general, the earlier seedlings can be transplanted to their permanent quarters, the better. Move lettuce when they have about 4 leaves, and cabbages and other brassicas when they are about 4in (10cm) high.

PRICKING OUT

1 *Seedlings are vulnerable when being rehoused, so handle them as gently as possible. Pick them up by their leaves rather than their stems, which are easily damaged.*

2 *Transplant the seedlings into a tray or cell packs. First make a grid of holes in the soil, then ease in the seedlings one by one with the help of a narrow stick or fine dibber.*

TRANSPLANTING

When planting outside, make the hole large enough for the seedling to be set a little deeper than it was when it was growing in its pot.

SOWING OUTSIDE

VEGETABLES ARE MORE OFTEN grown from seed sown directly in the ground than by any other means. Seed of frost-tender vegetables such as zucchini is sown inside in order to get as long a growing season as possible, but many vegetables such as carrots and beets do not need this treatment. Some vegetables are sown in short rows in seedbeds and transplanted to their final growing positions later. Brassicas and leeks are often treated in this way, although in very windy situations both could be raised under cover and grown in pots and trays and then planted outside in the garden later. Other vegetables such as parsnips and peas are sown in the positions they will occupy for the whole of their growing lives. Remember this when preparing the site for sowing. Do not expect seeds to hoist great clods of soil on their backs in their struggle to reach the light.

SOWING

PREPARING THE GROUND If you are sowing outside, good preparation of the seedbed is the single most important factor in getting seed to germinate. Some soils are easier to work than others. On sandy soil you may only have to clear the soil of weeds and rake it in order to create the fine, crumbly tilth that a seed likes to lie in. On clay, you will hope that frost will have helped to break down obdurate clods of soil during winter. Banging with the back of a rake also helps. The smaller the seed you are sowing, the finer the tilth should be.

SOWING IN A TRENCH This is the usual way to grow vegetables from seed. Stretch out a line (usually strong twine attached to a short stake or peg at either end) to make a straight row and dig out a trench. The depth of the trench should depend on the size of the seed, shallow for small seed, deeper for large seed. Scatter small seed as thinly as possible along the trench to try to avoid, as far as possible, the need for thinning. Seed such as beet or parsnip can be sown "at stations"; that is, in little groups of 2 or 3 seeds spaced at intervals. Leave only the strongest seedling to grow at each station. Cover carefully with soil. If the ground is very dry, water the trench before sowing; otherwise, water afterward with a fine-nozzled can.

SOWING IN A WIDE TRENCH Use wide, flat-bottomed trenches for vegetables that grow in broad rows such as peas and cut-and-come-again crops like oriental mesclun. The trench should be roughly 9in (23cm) wide. You can make it with either a hoe or a spade. Space peas evenly along the trench, but broadcast seed of cut-and-come-again crops as thinly as you

SOWING IN A TRENCH

1 *Using pegs and twine, mark a straight line and dig a trench as close to it as possible with the back edge of a rake or the corner of a hoe. Scatter seed along it as thinly as you can.*

2 *Carefully pull back the soil over the seed with a rake, then firm down the soil with the flat back of the rake or by treading lightly along the trench. Water well if the soil is at all dry.*

SOWING IN A WIDE TRENCH

1 *Make a wide, flat-bottomed trench either by pushing the soil out with a spade or pulling it along with a hoe. Space large seed evenly along the row, but broadcast small seed thinly.*

2 *Cover the trench with the soil you have removed, then smooth it over carefully. Peas will need protecting from birds and mice with lengths of chicken wire laid over the ground.*

BROADCASTING SEED

1 Rake the soil to produce a fine tilth before sowing, and scatter the seed as thinly as possible. Sprinkle a thin line of sand to mark the edge of the patch, if necessary.

2 Carefully rake the soil in the opposite direction to cover the seed and firm it down very lightly with the back of the rake. Water the area well using a fine-nozzled can.

can. Cover the trench with the soil you have removed and smooth it over carefully.
BROADCASTING SEED To broadcast seed is to scatter it over a relatively wide area, rather than confining it to a single row. It is a technique that is most useful where the garden is divided into a series of deep beds (see page 166), with each bed bearing a different crop. Broadcasting can also be used when you are filling part of a formally patterned potager and the plan calls for blocks of crops rather than rows.

THINNING

Seed that is sown directly, such as carrot and beet, may need to be thinned to allow each plant the chance to develop its full potential. If you practice the art of sowing thinly, you can escape this wasteful task. Pests and diseases will do their own grim thinning, so carry out yours in stages, nipping off tiny seedlings rather than uprooting them and disturbing the roots of neighbors. It is particularly important to

avoid thinning carrots, because the smell of bruised seedlings will act like a magnet for the carrot rust fly, and the tiny holes give it ready-made points of entry.

TRANSPLANTING

Vegetables such as leeks, Brussels sprouts, and other brassicas are often grown in nursery seedbeds. These are small patches of ground where you can rake the soil to a mouthwatering tilth and use it to sow seeds in short rows. At some stage the plants will need to be moved to their final growing positions. Try to do this when the soil is damp and the weather overcast, so that the uprooted plants will not have to struggle too much to find their feet.

Dig up the plants with as much soil as possible around the roots, then replant them in a hole which accommodates the rootball comfortably. Replant brassicas deeper than they were growing in the seedbed, so that their lowest leaves are level with the soil. Plant leeks in holes made with a stick or dibber. Thinnings of crops such as lettuce may be transplanted with success if the soil is moist and the temperature moderate, but you cannot transplant tap-rooted vegetables such as parsnips or carrots successfully.

THINNING SEEDLINGS
All plants need sufficient space to develop to their full size. If you sow sparsely enough, there may be no need to thin seedlings. However, if thinning is necessary, nip off the unwanted plants at ground level and remove them to avoid unnecessarily attracting pests or diseases.

TRANSPLANTING LEEKS
Make a hole at least 6in (15cm) deep with a dibber or stick. Drop in the seedling so that it develops a good length of white stem as it grows. Water well to wash soil over the roots.

PLANTING BRASSICAS
When transplanting, set plants a little deeper than they were before. Brassicas need to be planted with their lowest leaves at soil level.

PROPAGATION

PROPAGATION CAN EASILY BECOME an obsession. There is no more wildly parental feeling than seeing your first cutting turn into a grown-up bush. In the kitchen garden, cuttings will mostly be of soft fruit, such as black currants, gooseberries, or blueberries. When you become more ambitious, you may turn your hand to figs. Fruit such as blackberries and loganberries require no effort at all, for wherever the growing tip of a stem touches the ground, it will produce a fresh plant. Several of the shrubby herbs will obligingly start growing extra roots if soil is piled around the stems, a technique known as mound layering. Vegetables are grown mostly from seed, but rhubarb and globe artichokes are perennials and produce offsets around the edge of the clump. A sharp spade is what you need here to separate the siblings from their parent.

DIVIDING

RHUBARB Dividing is one of the easiest ways of increasing your stock of plants, and, in the kitchen garden, rhubarb is a prime candidate for this type of propagation. Wait until the leaves die down in autumn before taking the spade to it (see right).

GLOBE ARTICHOKES You need to replace these on a regular basis, since old plants become woody and unproductive. As artichokes start into growth in spring, they produce a circlet of offsets around the woody crown, each offset made up of a plume of leaves sprouting from the same point. Drive a sharp spade down alongside the clump to detach the offset, which may or may not have roots (if not, it will quickly grow some). Plant the offset in fresh ground, burying it only just sufficiently to keep it standing upright, and water it frequently. The outer leaves will die back, but the plant will renew itself very quickly. Leave at least 4ft (1.2m) between newly planted offsets.

TAKING CUTTINGS

SOFT FRUIT BUSHES In order to propagate currants or gooseberries, you need a spare patch of ground where you can line out cuttings for a year. Propagate gooseberries, red currants, and white currants by taking hardwood cuttings in mid-autumn from vigorous, clean, well-ripened stems (see right). Remove the lower buds that would normally produce shoots, since these bushes are grown with a short main stem. Black currants are dealt with slightly differently. A black currant bush should constantly renew itself by

DIVIDING RHUBARB

1 When the foliage dies down in autumn, lift the plant or scrape away the soil to expose the buds. Drive a spade down between them, making sure that each section has a good bud.

2 Replant the sections in their new quarters, spacing them about 3ft (1m) apart. Set them so that the bud just shows above heavy soil, or 1in (2.5cm) below the surface in sandy soil.

HARDWOOD CUTTINGS

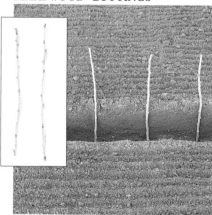

1 Take 12–15 in (30–38 cm) long hardwood cuttings in the fall. For gooseberries and red and white currants, remove all but the top 4–5 buds and insert the cuttings 6in (15cm) deep in a narrow slit in prepared ground. Firm the soil.

2 By the following autumn the cuttings will have produced roots. Carefully lift the new plants and transplant them to a freshly prepared plot. On windy days, roots dry out quickly. Protect them, if necessary, with a plastic bag.

sending up stems from below ground level. Take hardwood cuttings 8–10in (20–25cm) long, in autumn, and leave all the buds intact. Bury the cutting so that only 2 buds show above ground. With luck, each buried bud will produce a shoot, so that when you dig it up the following autumn it will have 3–4 good stems.

FIGS These take longer to find their feet. For cuttings, choose 12in (30cm) sections of well-ripened wood (not from a growing tip). Bury them up to half their length in well-drained soil in a sheltered, sunny spot. After 2 years, transplant the new tree to its final growing position.

BLUEBERRIES These are propagated from softwood cuttings taken in early summer. Choose growth 4–8in (10–20cm) long and strip off all but the top 3 leaves. Set each cutting in a 3-in (7-cm) pot of sandy, acid soil mix. Water, and cover pots with clear plastic, or put them in a propagator at a temperature of 65°F (18°C). Rooting will take 3–6 weeks. As cuttings begin to grow, harden them off and pot on into larger pots of soil mix. Plant out in autumn.

LAYERING

CANE FRUIT Blackberries, loganberries, and other hybrid berries like tayberries are easily propagated by tip layering (see below).
HERBS Many shrubby types such as sage,

rosemary, and thyme can be propagated by mound layering (see right). In spring, pile free-draining soil over the base of the plant. If your soil is sticky, mix it with some sand or potting soil. Replenish the mound with fresh soil through summer, if necessary. This treatment stimulates new roots to grow on the branches covered with soil. Hyssop, lavender, lavender cotton (*Santolina*), and winter savory can also be propagated by mound layering.

STRAWBERRIES These increase by means of runners (see page 143). All summer, mature plants send out long stems that, when they find a piece of bare ground, will produce a small plantlet that quickly grows into a new plant. If you have just planted a strawberry bed, you must spend the first 3 years nipping off most of the runners since the plants need to concentrate their efforts on producing fruit. But strawberries generally lose vigor after 3 years, so you should leave enough runners in place to produce a supply of new plants. The lazy (but effective) way is to let the runners root themselves where they will. Alternatively, you can sink 3-in (7-cm) pots of soil mix into the ground and peg down a runner into each. Whichever method you choose, you need, in early autumn, to cut the young plants from their runners and plant them out in a new bed of fresh, well-fed ground. Old plants should be destroyed.

MOUND LAYERING THYME

1 *In spring, pile free-draining soil over the base of the plant, leaving only the tips exposed. Replenish, if necessary, in summer.*

2 *By late summer or autumn, new roots will have formed on the stems. Carefully scrape away the soil and cut off the sections of rooted branch to plant out in well-prepared ground.*

TIP LAYERING A BLACKBERRY

1 *To propagate blackberries, loganberries, and other hybrid berries, poke the growing tip of a stem into the soil with the tip pointing down. Bury it about 4–5in (10–12cm) deep. This is best done in summer.*

2 *In a few weeks a new growing tip will emerge, roots will form, and, in autumn or early spring, you can sever the new plant from its parent to set out in its new position. If necessary, pot it up for planting out later.*

Choosing Fruit Trees

MUCH PLEASURE IN A DECORATIVE KITCHEN GARDEN can come from trained fruit trees, perhaps curving to make a tunnel of blossoms over a path, or splayed out on walls to make geometric espaliers and fans. Use parallel sets of cordons to screen off one part of the garden from another, or set low hedges of stepover apples around your salad plot. These low apple hurdles look equally good stretched out in front of a flower border. Fans of peaches and apricots are practical as well as beautiful. Spreadeagled on a sunny wall, the blossoms are protected from frost, and the fruit has the best possible chance of ripening. The simplest route to success is to buy fruit trees that are already trained into the shape you want.

TREE STYLES

CORDONS These are the answer where quality rather than quantity of fruit is the goal. A cordon is a single-stemmed tree that is usually planted at an angle of 45 degrees to reduce vigor and produce as much fruiting wood as possible within easy reach. Cordons need to be tied on to parallel wires stretched between posts. They are normally grown on dwarfing rootstocks. Several different cultivars of apples and pears can be grown together to make a fruitful screen. Double cordons are grown upright, the two arms making a goblet shape.

BUSH TREES Bushes start fruiting when they are very young, are easy to pick and spray, but difficult to mow the lawn under.

HALF-STANDARDS AND STANDARDS These are the apple trees of picture books.

Half-standards have a clear stem of at least 4ft (1.2m) while full standards go up to 6ft (1.8m) before the branches break from the trunk. Their height makes spraying and picking slightly more difficult to manage, but they are infinitely more pleasing to look at than a dwarfed bush. When you plant a half-standard, you dream of picnicking in its shade, of slinging a hammock from its branches. There is no such romance with a bush.

FANS These are more often used for cherries, plums, peaches, and pears than they are for apples. The name explains the shape, which looks particularly good against a stone or brick wall. The branches are best trained on rigid poles of bamboo and, as with all trained fruit trees, summer pruning is essential.

ESPALIERS An espalier is trained to make several flat tiers of branches, like a

FINE FIGS
Whether fanned out over a clean, whitewashed wall or basking outdoors in a warm, sunny site, figs have an architectural quality that remains unmatched by any other fruit.

wedding cake. It may have two, three, or four sets of parallel branches, depending on the space available. Naturally, they take up more space than cordons, but they can be used in the same way to make a screen. The branches need to be tied up regularly as they grow, and careful pruning

GUIDE TO TREE STYLES
From slanting cordon to tall-stemmed standard, the different styles of fruit tree all have a role to play in the decorative kitchen garden. While cordons will squeeze into the smallest plot, standards look romantic in flower-strewn grass. Pruning espaliers and fans can become a strangely satisfying and rewarding task.

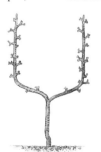

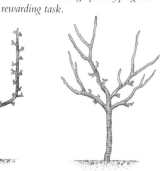

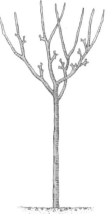

CORDON   DOUBLE CORDON   BUSH   HALF-STANDARD   STANDARD

is imperative if the espalier is to keep its formal, two-dimensional shape. If the main trunk is trained on a curved hoop over a path, espaliers can be used to make beautiful fruit tunnels.

STEPOVER A stepover tree is a miniature espalier, with one set of arms, growing out about 12in (30cm) above the ground.

The style of tree you choose must consider site, cultivar, and rootstock. Some of the most fussy dessert pears such as 'Marie-Louise', 'Winter Nelis', and 'Glou Morceau' are best grown as fans or espaliers against a wall, but a vigorous apple such as 'Bramley's Seedling' would not be a good choice for a trained tree. If you have poor soil, then you are unlikely to succeed with dwarfing rootstocks. They are demanding and need weed-free soil as well as careful feeding and watering.

ROOTSTOCKS

Fruit trees are usually grafted on to rootstocks that control the rate at which they grow, and the size they reach. As a rule, dwarfing rootstocks bring a tree into production earlier but demand ideal growing conditions. Good grafts are imperceptible. Bad ones are like a crooked elbow. Sometimes the rootstock makes a bid to take over the graft, called suckering. If it happens, the suckers should be cut or pulled out as soon as you see them.

A good nursery will offer fruit grafted on to more than one type of rootstock, so you can choose the right one for your particular needs. You might want to grow the dessert apple 'Discovery'. This is of

medium vigor, so you would not generally want it on the extremely dwarfing M27 stock. As a cordon in a restricted situation on good soil, you might choose M9 as the rootstock. On poor soil, you would be better off with MM106. This would also be the best choice for growing 'Discovery' as an espalier or fan, but if you wanted to grow it as a half-standard you need to look for a tree grafted on MM111 stock.

BACK TO THE WALL
Any stretch of wall, whether on the house or part of a boundary, can be used to train a fruit tree. The blossoms of this old pear have enhanced the mellow brick for many a season.

ROOTSTOCKS

APPLES

M27 Extremely dwarfing. Trees unlikely to exceed 6ft (1.8m) height or spread. Crops at 2–3 years. Can, with care, be grown in pots. Succeeds only in very fertile soil and needs permanent staking.
M9 Very dwarfing. Produces trees from 7–8ft (2–2.5m) high and wide. Crops at 3–4 years. Slightly more tolerant than M27, but needs good soil and permanent staking.
MM106 Ideal for the average garden. Produces trees from 12–16ft (3.5–4.8m) high and wide. Crops at 4–5 years. Does not need permanent staking. Vigorous even on poor, sandy soils.
MM111 Vigorous. Produces trees from 15–18 ft (4.5–5.5m) high and wide. Used for standards and half-standards. Trees do not start fruiting for 6–7 years.
M25 Ideal for orchard and specimen trees, forgiving of poor conditions. Produces trees from 16–18ft (4.8–5.5m) at maturity.

PEARS

QUINCE C Produces trees about 10ft (3m) high and wide that start fruiting earlier than those on Quince A. Suitable only for very fertile soils or for cordons.
QUINCE A Semivigorous. Good all-around performer. Produces trees from 12–15ft (3.5–4.5m) high and wide. Said to be more cold-resistant than Quince C.
PEAR ROOTSTOCK Pears on pear roots, not necessarily their own, grow slowly to produce beautiful trees. Suitable only for standards or half-standards.

PLUMS

PIXY Dwarfing. Produces trees 10–15ft (3–4.5m) high and wide. Suits only very fertile soil. Trees need permanent staking.
ST JULIEN A Semivigorous. Produces trees up to 20ft (6m) high and wide. Compatible with all cultivars.
BROMPTON Good for standards in orchards. Produces trees 25ft (7.5m) high and wide.

PEACHES AND NECTARINES

ST JULIEN A Semivigorous. Produces a fan 12–15ft (3.5–4.5m) wide.
BROMPTON More vigorous. Produces fans 15–20ft (4.5–6m) wide.

APRICOTS

ST JULIEN A Produces a fan about 15ft (4.5m) wide or similar-sized bush.

CHERRIES

INMIL Most dwarfing rootstock available. Produces trees little more than 6–7ft (1.8–2m) high and wide. Needs a great deal of attention.
COLT Old and reliable. Produces trees from 15–20ft (4.5–6m) high and wide.

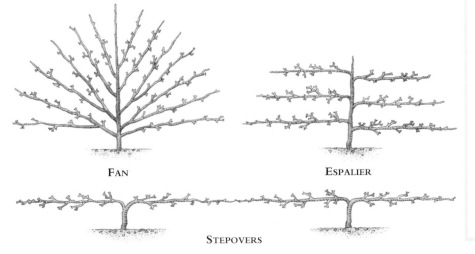

FAN

ESPALIER

STEPOVERS

PLANTING & POLLINATION

TAKE TIME TO PLANT A FRUIT TREE. The task deserves your full attention, for a fruit tree has the potential to be one of the longest-serving features in your new kitchen garden. That ultimate potential is unlikely to be realized if you cram a tree into a measly little hole with its roots coiled around as dizzily as vipers in a basket. Excavate generously, remain oblivious to the ringing of the telephone, the temptation of the coffee pot, or any other distraction, and do not leave the tree's roots drying in the wind while you dig. Consider your tree's sex life as well. Some fruit trees are self-fertile, which relieves you of any further worry on this score. Others need pollinating partners not more than a bee's hop away.

PLANNING A FRUIT BUSH

1 *Dig a hole larger than the bush's rootspan. Spread out the roots evenly in the hole and lay a stake across to indicate soil level. Make sure that the bush is not too high or too low.*

2 *Fill in the hole, first with soil mixed with a little bonemeal, working it around the roots, then backfill. Firm it down so that there are no air pockets, and water well.*

PLANTING

If your fruit tree comes in a container, do not plant the pot as well as the contents. There is a certain logic in doing so (plant easier to move if you have made a mistake, roots not disturbed, job quicker and simpler) but it does nothing for the plant's long-term future. Roots must run. Autumn is generally the best time to plant since fruit trees are dormant then and can settle themselves in, getting their roots firmly plugged into supplies before having to fuss about flowering.

Make a hole bigger than the one you first thought of, and have a bucket of soil mixed with bonemeal standing by. Ease the tree out of its container, then settle it so that the stem sits at the same level in relation to the ground as it was in the pot. Put in a short stake, to stand about 20in (50cm) above the ground, for half-standard and standard trees. Always plant with the join of the graft above soil level; otherwise, the plant that has been grafted may try to make its own roots and the benefit of the rootstock will be lost. Spread the roots out comfortably, so that the main ones go off in different directions, and work a bit of the soil and bonemeal in around the roots. Backfill and water the plant thoroughly – a drench, not a sprinkle. If it is very dry, mulch around the base of the tree after watering.

POLLINATION

Many fruit trees need to be cross-pollinated if they are to produce fruit. The job is usually done by insects, who transfer pollen from the anther of a flower on one tree to the stigma of a flower on another. Some fruit trees, such as sour cherries, are self-fertile, in which case you can expect fruit even if you have only one tree in the garden. Some trees, such as the 'Conference' pear, are technically self-fertile, although this will set fruit more readily if it is also cross-pollinated by another type of pear. Where trees need to be cross-pollinated, the pollinator obviously needs to be in bloom at the same time as the tree it is pollinating.

Most specialist nurseries number the fruit trees in their catalogs to indicate the different flowering seasons (see opposite). The apple 'Discovery', for instance, might be paired with 'Egremont Russet', the

PLANTING A FRUIT TREE

1 *Dig a hole large enough for the roots to spread out comfortably inside it. If planting half-standard or standard trees, drive in a short stake. Lay a stake across the hole to check the planting depth. The graft (inset) must be above it.*

2 *Work some soil mixed with a little bonemeal in around the roots, then fill in the hole with soil and firm it down, especially around the trunk. Use a tree tie to attach the stake to the tree, and water in thoroughly.*

HAND-POLLINATION

Peaches and nectarines flower before most insects are around, so help pollination by using a camelhair paintbrush to shift pollen from one flower to the next. Repeat as new flowers open.

'Beurré Hardy' pear with 'Doyenné du Comice'. While most fruit trees are diploids, with two basic sets of chromosomes, a few are triploids with three and this makes them sterile. These need to be pollinated by two different cultivars. 'Ribston Pippin', 'Bramley's Seedling', and 'Jupiter' are triploid apples, 'Jargonelle' is a triploid pear.

The other vital factor in pollination is a good supply of insects. Commercial growers arrange for hives of bees to move into their fruit orchards. Others release specially bred bumblebees to work in their greenhouses. Bees have suffered appallingly from the thoughtless use of insecticides. Think before you spray.

Both peaches and nectarines are self-fertile, so you do not have to plant different cultivars to ensure pollination. But to ensure a good set of fruit, you can help the process of pollination by transferring pollen with a paintbrush, as above. Unless doors are left open, trees grown in greenhouses will always have to be hand-pollinated. Traditionally, this job was done at noon and the greenhouse floor damped down immediately afterward to help the fruit to set.

POLLINATION GROUPS & RECOMMENDED CULTIVARS

APPLES

Early flowering: 'Akane', 'Anna', 'Carroll', 'Discovery', 'Duchess', 'Egremont Russet', 'George Cave', 'Grenadier', 'Lodi', 'Parkland', 'Transparent', 'Vista Bella'

Mid-season flowering: 'Bismarck', 'Cortland', 'Cox's Orange Pippin', 'Delicious', 'Empire', 'Freedom', 'Golden Delicious', 'Gravenstein', 'James Grieve', 'Jonathan', 'Liberty', 'Macoun', 'McIntosh', 'Mutsu', 'Norland', 'Red Baron', 'Ribston Pippin', 'Spartan', 'Spigold', 'State Fair', 'Sunset', 'Wagener', 'Wealthy', 'Wolf River', 'Worcester Pearmain'

Late flowering: 'Ashmead's Kernel', 'Bramley's Seedling', 'Ellison's Orange', 'Gala', 'Golden Russet', 'Granny Smith', 'Idared', 'Jonagold', 'Jupiter', 'Kidd's Orange Red', 'Laxton's Superb', 'Monarch', 'Northern Spy', 'Novaspy', 'Orleans', 'Rhode Island Greening', 'Rome Beauty', 'Suntan', 'Tydeman's Late Orange', 'Winesap'

Triploids: apples needing two pollinators include 'Bramley's Seedling', 'Gravenstein', 'Jonagold', 'Jupiter', 'McIntosh', 'Reinette du Canada', 'Ribston Pippin', 'Spigold', 'Suntan'

PEARS

Early flowering: 'Ayres', 'Clapp's Favorite', 'Earlibrite', 'Harrow Delight', 'Marguerite Marillat', 'Moonglow', 'Rosée de Juliette', 'Summercrisp'

Mid-season flowering: 'Aurora', 'Bartlett', 'Beurré Hardy', 'Bosc', 'Conference', 'Devoe', 'Douglas', 'Beurré Hardy', 'Doyenné du Comice', 'Jargonelle', 'John', 'Lincoln', 'Max-Red Bartlett', 'Merton Pride', 'Nova', 'Rescue', 'Santa Claus', 'Spartlett', 'Twentieth Century'

Late flowering: 'Anjou', 'Comice', 'Duchess', 'Dumont', 'Highland', 'Joséphine de Malines', 'Kieffer', 'Luscious', 'Seckel', 'Winter Nelis'

PLUMS, GAGES, AND DAMSONS

Plums exhibit a range of self-fertility and self-sterility. Consult catalogs and experts for specific details. Some of the plum family, such as 'Bluefre', 'Green Gage', 'Iroquois', 'Mirabelle', 'Opal', 'Prune', 'Stanley', and 'Sugar', are self-fertile, but crops are much improved if you provide a suitable pollinator.

European: 'Bluebell', 'Bluefre', 'California Blue', 'Coe's Golden Drop', 'Earliblue', 'Iroquois', 'Italian Prune'/'Fellenberg', 'Lombard', 'Mirabelle', 'Mohawk', 'Opal', 'President', 'Prune d'Agen', 'Seneca', 'Stanley', 'Sugar', 'Veeblue', 'Verity', 'Victoria', 'Yellow Egg'

Gages: 'Golden Transparent Gage', 'Green Gage'/'Reine Claude', 'Laxton's Gage'

Japanese: 'Brookgold', 'Burbank', 'Early Golden', 'Methley', 'Redheart', 'Santa Rosa', 'Shiro', 'Starking Delicious', 'Weeping Santa Rosa'

Japanese-American hybrids: 'AU Producer', 'AU Roadside', 'Early Golden', 'Elite', 'Kahinta', 'La Crescent', 'Perfection', 'South Dakota', 'Superior', 'Tecumseh', 'Toka', 'Waneta'

Damsons: 'Blue Damson', 'Farleigh', 'Prune'/'Shropshire'

PEACHES AND NECTARINES

Peaches and nectarines are self-fertile but may need hand-pollinating if there are no insects on the wing to do the job.

APRICOTS AND CHERRIES

Apricots are self-fertile but may need hand-pollinating. All varieties of sour cherry are self-fertile and will pollinate sweet cherries such as 'Napoleon Bigarreau' that flower at the same time. With the exception of 'Stella', sweet cherries are not self-fertile.

MELONS, KIWI, AND PASSION FRUIT

Pollinate by stripping the petals from a male flower and pushing it into a female flower. The females are the ones with slight swellings just underneath the flower heads. One male flower will pollinate at least four females. Pollination is best done at midday. Female kiwi plants will set fruit only when there is a male plant growing close by. The passion fruit is self-fertile.

PRUNING & TRAINING TREE FRUIT

PLANTS DO NOT DIE if they are not pruned. There is no phantom pruner in the wild, flitting about with pruning shears to get wild blackberries into shape or to trim up the crabapples. Gardeners prune fruit trees to enhance fruiting, to maintain the style or shape of a tree that is growing in a particular way (as with a cordon or an espalier), or simply because they are neat-minded. Accept that the diagram in your manual will never look like the tree that confronts you in the garden. Once you understand the principles, the practice becomes easier to carry out.

PRINCIPLES OF PRUNING

You cannot rely on pruning alone to contain the size of a tree. If an apple has been grafted on to M25 rootstock, it will always have the will to do what destiny dictates: grow into a big, beautiful, prize-fighter of a tree. Heavy pruning will lead only to renewed efforts on the tree's part to fulfil the imperative of its genes. If you want a small tree, choose a cultivar that is only moderately vigorous and check the rootstock on which it has been grafted. If you buy a tree trained as a cordon, espalier, or fan, the appropriate rootstock is likely to have already been chosen for you.

Most apples and pears produce their fruit buds on new shoots that develop from short, woody clusters known as spurs. These are called spur-bearing trees.

A few cultivars, such as the apples 'Bramley's Seedling' and 'George Cave' and the pears 'Jargonelle' and 'Joséphine de Malines', are tip bearers, producing their flower buds on the ends of two-year-old shoots. If you are constantly cutting these back, there is little chance of getting any fruit. Tip-bearing cultivars are not a wise choice for cordons or espaliers.

Before you plunge in, brandishing a pruning saw, remind yourself why you want to prune. It may be to maintain the tree in a particular form, to increase vigor, to encourage more fruit buds to form, to improve the quality or quantity of the fruit, to thin out overcrowded branches (which will in turn help prevent diseases), or to cut out diseased or dead wood. Just as you need to balance suitable rootstocks with particular styles of tree, so you should regulate your pruning to the vigor of the cultivar. Winter pruning stimulates a tree to produce more growth, so the more vigorous a tree is, the more lightly it should be pruned. But, if a tree has weak, droopy branches, it can be pruned hard.

APPLES AND PEARS Trees growing as bushes, half-standards, and standards will need only winter pruning, if you prune them at all. They will grow and fruit quite happily, although not at maximum potential, if you leave them alone. If you prune, do it on the replacement principle. Encourage new growth by cutting back some of the old growth at the ends of the branches, making the cut where there is a new shoot waiting to take over.

On trees growing as single or double cordons, espaliers, and fans, summer pruning is more important than winter pruning since it is by this means that you control the amount of growth that the tree produces. To summer prune, cut back the new leafy shoots that have been produced during spring and early summer. If the shoot is growing directly from one of the main arms of the tree, cut it back to the third leaf above the basal cluster of leaves. Leave the cluster itself intact. If the shoot is springing from a knobby spur formed by previous pruning, cut it back to just one leaf above the cluster. Do this in

PRUNING AND TRAINING A SINGLE CORDON

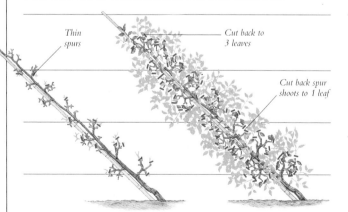

Thin spurs

Cut back to 3 leaves

Cut back spur shoots to 1 leaf

1 In winter, thin out buds on spurs that have become congested, especially on old trees. Check, too, for loose ties or wires.

2 In summer, cut back shoots from spurs to 1 leaf above the spur. Cut back other shoots to 3 leaves above the basal cluster.

PRUNING AND TRAINING A DOUBLE CORDON

Cut stem

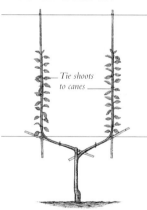

Tie shoots to canes

1 In winter, cut a very young, single-stemmed tree to 10in (25cm) from the ground, just above 2 good buds, one at either side.

2 As the shoots grow, train them to bamboo stakes attached to wires, first at an angle and then vertically. Prune as single cordons.

mid- to late summer, when the greenish stems of the shoots have started to turn brown. In winter, you may have to shorten any other long shoots that have grown since summer pruning.

A fan is slightly less rigid in its underlying structure than a cordon or espalier. You can continue to tie in sideshoots springing from the main branches, until all the space between them is filled. After that, you must summer prune sideshoots, cutting them back to one leaf above the basal cluster. If one of the main stems starts to outgrow its space, cut it back to a strong replacement shoot, which you can tie in in its place.

PLUMS AND PRUNES Freestanding trees require little pruning. Simply take out dead wood and any thin, overcrowded growth. Any cutting should be done in late spring or summer. This reduces the risk of spores of silverleaf getting into the system.

Fans require more attention. Shoots sprouting from the main framework should be nipped out in two stages. In midsummer, pinch back all sideshoots to leave about 6 leaves. These will be the shoots that bear fruit in the subsequent summer. When they have fruited, cut back these sideshoots by half, to about 3 leaves. Any shoots that are pointing directly forward or backward into the wall should be completely removed.

PEACHES AND NECTARINES These can most conveniently be grown as fans. Make life easy for yourself by buying a ready-trained tree. The fruit is borne on the shoots produced in the previous season. Take out any shoots that you do not want (including those pointing either forward or back) in spring, leaving 3 growth buds on each lateral branch. In early summer, prune back each of these 3 shoots to 6 leaves. When you have picked the fruit, cut out the shoot that bore it and tie in a replacement shoot. On freestanding trees, trim out crowded or crossing branches in summer. In midspring, prune back any shoots killed by winter frost.

APRICOTS Fan apricots are treated in a similar way to peaches. Aim to build up a series of fruiting spurs about 6in (15cm) apart all the way along the branches of the fan. Do this by pinching back the lateral growths in early summer, leaving about 3in (7cm) of each growth in place. Any growths springing from these laterals

should be pinched back, leaving just one leaf. Keep tying in the new growth on the ends of the main branches of the tree to maintain the fan shape. No regular pruning is needed for established bushes.

CHERRIES Sweet cherries growing as standards or half-standards do not need pruning. Simply cut out any dead wood and remove crossing branches. Sour cherries fruit only on new wood, so you must prune to force the tree to produce

plenty of the necessary growth. When a wall-trained tree has fruited, cut out the long growths at its extremities so that it will make new shoots in the center, or else the tree will bear fruit only at the tips of its branches. Tie in as many new shoots as you can fit in among the main branches.

CITRUS FRUIT Citrus trees do not need regular pruning. Trim new growth in early spring, if necessary, to keep the plants balanced and shapely.

PRUNING AND TRAINING AN ESPALIER

APPLES AND PEARS
Train new branches to form horizontal tiers. In summer, cut back shoots from the main stems as inset below, and cut back those arising from spurs to 1 leaf above the spur.

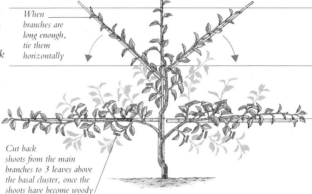

When branches are long enough, tie them horizontally

Cut back shoots from the main branches to 3 leaves above the basal cluster, once the shoots have become woody

PRUNING AND TRAINING A FAN

PLUMS
In midsummer, cut back all sideshoots from the main framework to 6 leaves. After fruiting, cut them back further to 3 leaves. These shoots will bear the following season's fruit. Cut out entirely shoots growing forward or backward.

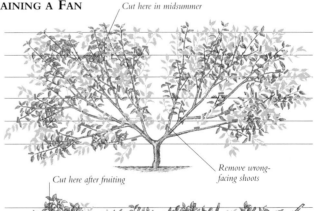

Cut here in midsummer

Remove wrong-facing shoots

SOUR CHERRIES
In late summer, cut off growths at the extremities of the branches to encourage the tree to produce new shoots in the center. The following season's fruit will be borne only on new wood. Cut out entirely shoots growing forward or backward.

Cut here after fruiting

Remove wrong-facing shoots

PRUNING & TRAINING SOFT FRUIT & GRAPES

WITH SOFT FRUIT, as with tree fruit, you can choose to grow canes or bushes in a decorative manner. Train loganberries or blackberries to make screens or garden dividers, or grow a standard, mop-headed gooseberry on a 4-ft (1.2-m) stem to rise up among your annual flowers. Red currants respond to being trained, too. You can turn them into double cordons, which grow in the shape of a wine goblet, the two stems trained out and up from a single, clear trunk. Of this group, grapes need the most careful pruning. In good soil, they tend to develop too much leaf, so you must prune to remind them to flower and fruit. Where you are growing grapes to cover an arbor you need not be too particular about the pruning.

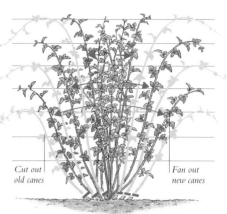

TRAINING BLACKBERRIES
Keep the new canes bunched in a fountain in the center. After cutting out the fruited canes in autumn, fan out the new growth and tie it in.

CANE FRUIT

RASPBERRIES These need pruning every year, but this is a simple process. After summer cultivars have fruited, cut out the old canes close to the ground and thin out the new canes, leaving no more than 5 or 6 strong stems growing from each original clump. Tie the new canes to supporting wires, if you are using this method. In late winter, cut off the top of each cane just above the top wire. Autumn-fruiting raspberries need slightly different treatment since they carry fruit on canes formed earlier in the same season. Cut the old, fruited canes to the ground in late winter and thin out the new growth gradually as it grows during the season.

HYBRID BERRIES If you are training hybrid berries such as loganberries or tayberries on wires to make a screen, put

the first wire about 3ft (1m) from the ground, with several parallel wires above. Tie the growths securely to the wires, keeping the new canes bunched up in the middle and the older, fruiting growths trained along the wires away from the center (see training blackberries above). After picking the fruit, cut out the old canes, unbundle the new ones, and tie them in where the old ones were.

BLACKBERRIES These are treated in the same way as hybrid berries. Cut out the fruited canes each year after the crop has been gathered. With a late-fruiting cultivar such as 'Himalaya Giant', this may not be until mid-autumn. Fan out and tie in the new canes to replace the old. With 'Himalaya Giant', which does not produce canes quite as freely as other blackberry varieties, a proportion of the old wood may be left in place each season.

SOFT FRUIT BUSHES

BLUEBERRIES Bushes can be trimmed, rather than severely pruned. Start in winter by cutting out dead or damaged branches together with a proportion of old wood. In spring, shear lightly the tops of the bushes to keep them compact.

CURRANTS Red currants and white currants are pruned in the same way, but black currants are treated differently. Red and white currants fruit on spurs made on old wood, while black currants fruit on young, one-year-old wood. When they have finished fruiting, cut out at least one third of the old, dead wood, leaving as much of the new, light brown growth as possible, to bear the following season's fruit. Since red and white currants fruit on old wood, pruning can be less drastic. After fruiting, or during the autumn and winter, shorten branches by about one third to keep the bushes shapely and compact. On red and white currants grown as cordons, cut the lateral branches back to within 1in (2cm) of the main stem.

Red currants are very good trained as goblet-shaped double cordons. Allow a rooted cutting to grow up as a single stem, without any side branches. Plant it against parallel wires that will support it. When it is well established, cut the stem back to about 10in (25cm) from the ground, leaving a strong bud on either side below the cut. These two buds will break into sideshoots, which you should train on canes set at an angle of 45 degrees. When the tips of these shoots are at least 18in

TRAINING RASPBERRIES

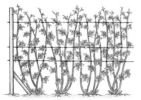

POST AND WIRES
This method of support takes up the least space. The posts need to stand 6ft (1.8m) high, with three parallel wires stretched between, the first 30in (75cm) from the ground.

PARALLEL WIRES
Canes need no tying with this system. Put up two rows of posts 30in (75cm) apart with two wires along each row. Crisscross twine between them to support the canes.

TYING IN
Tie in securely the strongest of the new canes as soon as the old ones have been cut down. The lacing method shown here, where twine is twisted around and along the wire, holds them neatly in place.

Cut out old stems

PRUNING BLACK CURRANTS

After fruiting, cut at least one third of the old, dead stems to ground level. Prune off any excess side growth to keep a fairly upright shape.

PRUNING GOOSEBERRIES

1 *Cut out a proportion of old stems each year in late autumn or winter to prevent the center of the bush from getting congested, and shorten any stems that are unnecessarily long.*

2 *Prune to give the bush an open center. This will allow air to circulate between the branches and so deter gooseberry mildew. It will also make picking the fruit a less prickly task.*

PRUNING A CORDON GRAPEVINE

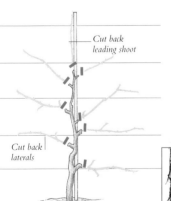

Cut back leading shoot

Cut back laterals

1 *In the autumn or early spring, cut the leading shoot back to well-ripened wood. You should also cut all laterals back to 2 buds so that spurs develop at these points.*

Pinch out weak flower trusses

Cut here after flowering

Take out the second lateral shoot springing from each spur when the first one is growing well.

2 *In spring, thin spurs to 2 laterals (inset). In summer, prune laterals to 2 leaves beyond the end cluster of fruit. Pinch out any weak flower trusses.*

(45cm) apart, lower the training canes to an angle of 30 degrees and attach more canes vertically to the wires. Continue to train the two sideshoots in the new vertical position. Prune them as you would a single cordon.

GOOSEBERRIES These will bear fruit even if they are not regularly pruned, but it is easier to pick the fruit if you remove some stems each year to keep the center of the bush open and shorten long branches that may be weighed down by berrries. Shorten the side growths on cordons to 3 buds, and cut the branches of standards back by at least a third to keep a well-shaped head.

GRAPES

CORDONS When grown under glass, grapes should be trained on wires set about 12in (30cm) apart and at least 6in (15cm) away from the glass itself. The leading shoot should be trained vertically, and the laterals horizontally along the wires. When the grapes have flowered, prune the laterals back, leaving 2 leaves beyond each cluster of fruit. Any subsequent shoots breaking from the laterals should be pinched out, leaving 2 leaves at most. After fruiting, cut the leading shoots back to well-ripened wood and cut the laterals back to 2 buds.

WALL-TRAINED GRAPES Train grapes on walls by allowing, at most, 3 or 4 main stems to develop from a single rootstock. After the first season's growth, cut back the branches by two thirds, and repeat this in early autumn each year until all the available space is filled. On young plants, tie in the laterals and let them grow to about 24in (60cm) before pinching them out. On mature plants, the laterals should be stopped just beyond the clusters of flowers, leaving no more than 2 leaves. Sublaterals (shoots springing from the sideshoots) should be stopped at one leaf.

THE GUYOT SYSTEM Grapes growing outside can also be trained according to the Guyot system, named after its inventor. For this you need parallel sets of wires spaced 12in (30cm) apart, stretched between posts or fastened to a wall. After planting the grapes in the dormant season in late autumn, cut the previous season's growth back hard, leaving no more than 2 buds. During the first summer, train a single shoot vertically up the wires, tying it in at regular intervals. Prune away any other shoots that develop. In autumn or early winter, cut back this shoot, leaving about 30in (75cm) of growth. Undo the ties and retie this stem horizontally along the bottom wire.

The next season, shoots will break from this stem. Train them vertically up the wires. When the fruit has been gathered, cut out all except 2 shoots nearest the original rootstock. Shorten these to 30in (75cm), then tie them along the bottom wire. Train the new summer shoots to the wires vertically, then repeat the process of cutting out most of the growth and selecting new shoots to tie in on the lowest wire every autumn or early winter.

GROWING IN GREENHOUSES

THE CHIEF BENEFITS OF A GREENHOUSE are the extra warmth and shelter it will give to plants, although it can also be decorative in its own right. Under glass you can extend the growing season and grow fruit and vegetables that may not survive outside in the garden. Unfortunately, greenhouses also provide ideal living conditions for pests as well as plants. Be prepared for armies of whitefly and spider mite. The options available will depend on the type of structure you have. Old-fashioned kitchen gardens may have lean-to greenhouses built against a sunny wall, where apricots, peaches, and nectarines can be trained in fans. Protected from frost, trees blossom fearlessly and fruit ripens easily. Grapes, too, benefit from the shelter of a greenhouse, but the rootstock is best planted outside, with the trunk leading in through an opening in the side.

HEADY DAYS OF SPRING
Peaches and nectarines put on a sumptuous display in this traditional greenhouse long before the rest of the garden has sprung into action.

CHOOSING A GREENHOUSE

Freestanding aluminum greenhouses with floor-to-ceiling glass walls are one of the most popular options for amateur gardeners. Although maintenance is minimal and the design allows maximum light to reach the plants, this type can be cold, and condensation may be greater than in a similar house made of wood. But wood, even cedar, needs looking after. The cheapest option is a floating row cover, made from plastic stretched over big metal hoops. Unfortunately, these add nothing to the decorative value of the garden. Even plastic that has been treated against ultraviolet light rarely lasts for more than three years, and it is easily punctured or torn in high winds.

Whatever type of greenhouse you choose, make sure that it can be well ventilated. You need to have roof ventilators equal in area to at least 20 percent of the floor space. If you are away from home for a good deal of time, it may be wise to invest in automatic ventilators. These are often designed around a cylinder of sensitive material that expands or contracts according to the temperature. The cylinder moves a piston rod attached to the ventilator. All automatic ventilators should be marked with the weight they can lift. Check that yours are strong enough for the job.

The heating in your greenhouse will depend on your wallet, but in any case, arrange the space so that you can partition off part of it to keep frost-free in winter. Heating is normally an expensive option,

IN SIMPLE STYLE
A greenhouse can be attractive as well as practical. Wooden structures are more harmonious but need regular maintenance.

although installation is not too costly. Remember that maintaining a winter temperature of 50°F (10°C) costs twice as much as maintaining one of 45°F (8°C). Kerosene heaters are inexpensive, but not as accurate as electric ones. Insulation is the best way to save money. Use heavy-duty bubble plastic clipped to the inside of the greenhouse frame. In areas with cool, short summers, leave this in place on the north side to provide extra protection.

GREENHOUSE CROPS

Even in an unheated greenhouse you can extend the growing season of basic crops such as carrots and lettuce. Tender vegetables, such as eggplants, cucumbers, peppers, and tomatoes, will grow outside, but cannot be set out until all danger of frost is past. In a greenhouse, they can be planted earlier and so will start cropping sooner. Frost-tender herbs such as basil also benefit from the extra warmth (and also grow well under floating row covers). Chard and some oriental vegetables may be hardy, but they will be more succulent if they are grown under cover in winter.

Your greenhouse or floating row cover can also function as a nursery in which to bring on seedlings of tomatoes, zucchini, or peppers that you intend to plant out later on. You can raise seedlings on a windowsill indoors, but light levels are unlikely to be as good as those in a greenhouse, and the temperature may be too warm. Both conditions could induce the seedlings to become leggy and weak.

Grow tomatoes in a greenhouse on stakes rather than as bushes, setting a short, strong stake, about 24in (60cm) high, by the side of each plant, and train them as shown at right. Pinch out the leading shoots by midsummer, or when six clusters have set, if that is sooner.

Damping down helps keep pests at bay. Some of the most troublesome, such as spider mite, thrive in hot, dry conditions. Hose down the floor every day during hot weather to keep the air inside moistly humid. If the weather itself is moistly humid, you need to keep air moving through the greenhouse to stop plants from rotting off.

PLANNING THE SPACE

You can use the space inside a greenhouse more economically if you grow crops in soil borders on either side of a central path. Where greenhouses are set on a solid base in a backyard, all crops will need to be grown in pots or containers. Borders are easier to manage mainly in terms of watering and feeding, but they have an important disadvantage. If you grow the same crop year after year in the same soil, a buildup of salts can occur, causing "soil sickness." This means that crops will not continue to thrive in that position unless the soil is sterilized or replaced. If you have three greenhouse borders, one at either side of a central path and one at the end, you can practice a simple crop rotation. See the plan below for one way of organizing the growing area and taking full advantage of the space available in winter as well as summer.

TRAINING TOMATOES
Set a stake by the side of each tomato plant and tie a double string between the stake and the greenhouse roof. As the plants grow, twist the string around the stems to support them.

GREENHOUSE PLAN: *for a house 10 × 6ft (3 × 2m)*

SUMMER
This plan shows how to use a greenhouse to its full potential all year. In cooler areas, all of these crops benefit from being grown under glass.

CUCUMBERS MELONS

CORIANDER

TOMATOES

BASIL

WINTER
Put the free space to good use by growing a range of fresh salad crops. Choose lettuce varieties that are recommended for winter harvesting.

PEPPERS

EGGPLANTS

GRAPE

CURLY ENDIVE ORIENTAL MESCLUN WINTER MESCLUN

MIZUNA GREENS

ARUGULA

GRAPE

LETTUCE

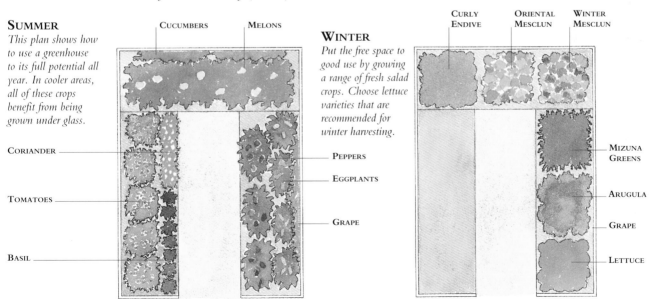

COLD FRAMES, CLOCHES & LIGHTS

IF YOUR YARD IS TOO SMALL for a greenhouse, you can still arrange useful protection for vegetables and fruit by investing in a cold frame, a set of cloches, or individual lights. A cold frame is a kind of doll's greenhouse, unheated as the name suggests, and built with a low, sloping glass roof that you slide on and off depending on the weather. Old-fashioned cloches were always made of glass, which allows the maximum amount of light through onto the crops beneath. Modern cloches are made from various types of plastic and can be either transparent or translucent, ridged or smooth. Victorian lantern lights, or modern replicas, are attractive and easy to move around the garden, but they are expensive. Much cheaper, and a great recycling opportunity, are jars or chopped-off plastic bottles, which can be used to cover seeds or emerging plants.

COLD FRAMES

The warmest type of cold frame has walls of brick or wood rather than glass. Use it to harden off plants raised from seed, before planting them out. Set the young plants as close as possible to the top of the frame by raising the seed trays or pots on piles of bricks or some similar support. Do not leave the frame closed on hot, sunny days because the temperature will rise dramatically and plants will suffer. In the tricky days of late spring, when sudden frosts can wreak havoc, give the frame extra protection by covering the top with sacks, newspapers, an old carpet, or any other material that will provide insulation.

If you do not have a greenhouse, you can use a cold frame to grow crops such as peppers, eggplants, and melons. Position the frame so that it catches maximum sun and is protected from any cold winds.

CUSTOM-MADE COLD FRAMES
Cold frames can be bought in kit form, straight off the garden-center shelf, but if you want to add a certain idiosyncratic charm to the garden, try building one yourself. Recycled materials are ideal: use old windowframes, if you can find them, and reclaimed lumber or bricks.

A FLOATING ROW COVER
Floating row covers, made to whatever length you need, are a cheap method of producing early crops. Stretch them over sturdy, galvanized wire hoops, pushed into the ground at 3-ft (1-m) intervals.

MAKING THE TUNNEL

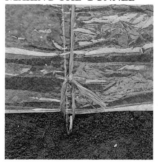

1 *To hold the cover in place, tie a piece of sturdy twine tightly over the top of the tunnel by every hoop. Attach the twine securely to the loops at the base of either side of each hoop.*

2 *Bunch up the cover at the ends and tie it to a stake driven into the ground at an angle. When ventilation is needed, push up the sides of the tunnel between the hoops and the twine.*

OPEN-ENDED CLOCHE
A cloche like this will give temporary protection to a patch of seedlings or a short row of plants. Leave the ends open for daytime ventilation, but close them with a propped-up sheet of glass on cold, frosty nights.

LANTERN LIGHT
Old-fashioned lanterns like this look very pretty, will give cover to reasonably large plants, and are easily moved around the garden.

RECYCLE A BOTTLE
A plastic bottle, chopped in half and placed over seeds or seedlings, will provide warmth, light, and protection from slugs and snails.

You can also use a frame to grow early crops of vegetables such as carrots, lettuce, or radishes. Fork over the soil inside to a depth of at least 6in (15cm) before direct sowing. "Soil sickness" can build up as easily in a cold frame as it can in a greenhouse. Vary the crops that you grow, and keep the soil in good condition by mulching areas that are free of crops in the late autumn and winter.

FLOATING ROW COVERS

The cheapest way of protecting vegetables is to grow them under a floating row cover, made by stretching plastic sheeting over wire hoops (see opposite). These are usually available as kits and provide a protected growing area of whatever length you want, but usually no more than 12–18in (30–45cm) high. Tunnels of this kind are ideal for protecting strawberries and carrots. The strawberries ripen more quickly, and the tunnel keeps them safe from birds. Carrots do not need extra heat to grow well, but a covering of some kind prevents them from being attacked by carrot rust fly (see page 190).

CLOCHES

Cloches can be made of plastic or glass and used singly or put together to form a row. The simplest style is tent-shaped, which you can easily make yourself, either from two sheets of glass held together with a specially designed clip, or from plastic stretched over batons, held together with a clip. For bulkier crops, barn cloches are a better shape. These have tent-shaped roofs supported on two slightly slanting side-pieces. Place them end to end to protect a row, but leave a little space between each one for ventilation.

Plastic does not hold on to heat as well as glass, and temperatures under a glass cloche will usually be 2–3 degrees higher. Glass cloches do not deteriorate with age as plastic does, but they are more fragile – and heavier to move. Sometimes, though, this is an advantage. Wind can get under a light plastic cloche and whirl it away in a fashion that obliterates not only the cloche, but also the crop underneath. You do not have to move cloches to water the crops underneath. Water over the tops of them so that the water drips down and soaks in either side. The roots of the plants underneath will reach out to find it.

Use cloches to warm up and dry out soil before planting and to protect emerging seedlings. With such protection, crops should be ready to harvest 2–3 weeks early. Warming the soil is as valuable as any other benefit of a cloche, for seeds sulk and may rot in cold, wet ground. They are particularly valuable during the last month of winter and the first one of spring, when temperatures fluctuate in a way that is not favorable to young seedlings. Beets, carrots, lettuce, and peas will all benefit from protection.

Later on in the season, use cloches to help along tender vegetables such as snap beans, sweet corn, squash, cucumbers, and tomatoes. In cold areas, use them to warm the soil before transplanting brassicas such as cauliflowers. Leave the cloche in place as long as possible, until the cauliflower outgrows the space. You can also use them to good effect with peas. You may find that the only way to bring a late-sown crop to fruition in cold areas is to cover it with cloches. This would only be possible with a dwarf cultivar. In early autumn, you can extend the growing season by giving protection to carrots and lettuce sown in late summer. You can also use cloches to hasten the ripening of tomatoes or to protect onions drying off for storage.

LANTERNS, BOTTLES, AND JARS

Old lantern lights make attractive covers for plants or patches of seedlings and are easy to remove during the day and replace at night. But for the cheapest covers of all, use upturned jam jars or cut the bottoms off clear plastic bottles. Put these over seeds of plants such as cucumbers, pumpkins, and zucchini while they are germinating. Keep them in place over the seedlings until the nights have warmed up.

HARVESTING & STORING

VEGETABLES AND FRUIT GATHERED FRESH from the garden nearly always taste better than produce that has been stored, however carefully. The exceptions are apples and pears, some varieties of which need to be stored to finish ripening (as with pears) or to develop full flavor (as with late-season apples). By trial and error, you will sort out the crops that you are most likely to use and those that store most successfully. Handle all produce carefully, since cuts and bruises quickly lead to disease. The freezer has revolutionized the whole business of preserving vegetables and fruit. Few people now preserve peas by drying them, but once these were a winter staple. And if there was a glut of tomatoes, you canned them. You can still do this, but it is easier to freeze them. Frozen whole with their skins on, they maintain an excellent flavor.

VEGETABLES

Leafy vegetables such as lettuce and spinach deteriorate fast, but root vegetables can be stored successfully for months given the right conditions. Where you have a range of different-sized vegetables, try to store them so that you can use the smallest first.

LEAF & SALAD VEGETABLES Harvest soft, leafy vegetables and salad crops, oriental brassicas, and spinach early or late in the day, when they are at their coolest. On sunny days lettuce may have heated up considerably by midday. Store in a cool place (for most people, the crisper in the refrigerator) in a loosely folded plastic bag. Red and white cabbages that are not frost-hardy need to be stored on wooden slats or trimmed and hung in nets in a cool, frost-free place. Other winter cabbages and chard can be harvested as needed.

FRUITING & FLOWERING VEGETABLES Late crops of frost-tender vegetables such as zucchini, cucumbers, eggplants, and sweet and hot peppers can be stored in a cool place in loosely folded plastic bags, but they will not keep long. Sweet corn can also be stored in this way but the flavour soon deteriorates. Tomatoes keep successfully in a cool place. Pumpkins and winter squash should be "cured" by leaving them to dry and harden in the sun. They will keep for several months stored in a cool, frost-free place. Hot peppers dry extremely well. Pull up the plants and hang them upside down before picking the hot peppers and putting them in jars or threading them on a string.

PODDED VEGETABLES Pick snap and scarlet runner beans as needed and store in a cool place in loosely folded plastic bags. They will keep only for a short time. Many beans (including limas), peas, and southern peas can be dried. Pull up the plants whole when the pods are mature, then hang them in a cool, airy place. When they are completely dry, shell and store in jars.

BULB & STEM VEGETABLES Leeks can be wrapped in newspaper and kept in a cool place if the ground is likely to freeze hard. Onions, shallots, garlic, and celeriac can all be stored successfully. Proper harvesting is the key to keeping onions, shallots, and garlic. Make sure that the bulbs have been properly dried off before storing them in shallow trays stacked in a well-ventilated but frost-free place. They need drier storage conditions than other vegetables. Moisture starts them into growth again. Onions with thick necks will not keep for long. You can also hang them in cotton or plastic nets or tie or braid them in strings.

ROOT VEGETABLES Harvest potatoes when the ground is dry, so that they are not covered in mud, and store in thick paper sacks, not plastic, which makes them rot. Tie the neck of the sack to exclude light, since it stimulates the poisonous

STORING RED CABBAGES
Pull up red (and white) cabbages whole and store on slatted shelves, with a little straw if you want, the roots dangling through the slats.

HARVESTING SQUASH
Both winter squash and pumpkins should be picked with a piece of stalk still attached. Summer squash will keep for about a week.

STRING OF GARLIC

The most decorative way of storing garlic, as well as onions and shallots, is to make a braid or string and hang it in a cool, dry place.

alkaloids that make green patches on the tubers. Leave carrots, beets, turnips, rutabagas, parsnips, winter radishes, salsify, and scorzonera in the ground for as long as possible. Covering with straw will help to protect them from frost and make lifting easier. They can also be stored in layers in boxes of damp sand, in a cool place. Twist the foliage off first. If you have enough space, make a clamp, the traditional method of storing root vegetables. Kept like this, they should last through most of the winter. Put down an 8–12in (20–30cm) layer of straw on the floor of a cellar or cool storeroom and pile the vegetables in a neat heap on top. Cover with another layer of straw at least as thick as the first and finish with a layer of soil 6in (15cm) deep. Vegetables in a clamp are, of course, much easier to get at than ones stuck firmly in frozen ground, but they may attract vermin.

FRUIT

Soft-fleshed fruit such as peaches and plums deteriorate quickly once they have been harvested, so the most important fruit to store are firmer-fleshed sorts such as apples and pears.

APPLES The ideal place is one that is free of frost and mice, with a temperature of 37–40°F (3–5°C). In practice, it is difficult for ordinary gardeners to attain this. Aim for a steady 45°F (8°C). Pick apples when the stalk parts easily from the branch. Early-maturing cultivars should be eaten straight from the tree. Other apples can be stored in wooden boxes, laid out on slatted shelves, or packed into plastic bags that can hold 4–6lb (2–3kg) of fruit. Tie the bags loosely and punch holes in them so that air can circulate freely. Keep fruit as far as possible from anything strong-smelling such as creosote, onions, and paint, which may taint the flavor.

PEARS The same general principles apply as for apples. The lower the temperature, ideally 32–34°F (0–1°C), the longer they keep. Do not wrap them, since they need picking over frequently. Pears are at their best for a very short period. Bring them a few at a time into a warm room to finish the ripening process. Do not store them in plastic bags because it encourages rot.

QUINCES & MEDLARS Store quinces on trays in a cool, dark place where they will keep for up to a month. Keep them as far as possible from other fruit, which may pick up their strong aroma. Medlars must be stored until soft (see page 133).

CITRUS FRUIT Citrus fruit last a long time provided they are cool and dry. Store fruit in boxes or on slatted shelves.

STORING APPLES

Apples can be stored in wooden boxes or laid out on slatted shelves in a cool place where they are never in danger of freezing. They keep better if individually wrapped, but the advantages must be weighed against the extra work involved.

FREEZING

The quality of frozen produce is greatly affected by the rate at which it is frozen. If vegetables and fruit are frozen slowly, large ice crystals form, spoiling the texture.

Freeze produce quickly (the instruction booklet that comes with the freezer will give details) and do not try to do too much at the same time. If you know that you are going to freeze crops, choose cultivars that have been specially selected for the process.

VEGETABLES

- Lima beans: best frozen while the beans are small and not starchy.
- Sprouting and heading broccoli: cut the florets into suitable lengths.
- Brussels sprouts: choose small, firm sprouts; trim off outer leaves.
- Cauliflower: break into florets about 2in (5cm) across.
- Snap beans: pick the beans while they are still small and freeze them whole.
- Peas: freeze only young peas. Shell them first.
- Spinach: wash thoroughly, drain, and trim the stems.
- Sweet corn: remove the husks and tassels before freezing.
- Tomatoes: freeze whole. To use, slip off skins under running water.

HERBS

- Mint and basil: freeze leaves in small plastic bags.

FRUIT

- Apples: freeze after cooking to a pulp or purée.
- Apricots, nectarines, peaches, and plums: cut in half and remove the pit. Freeze halves in light syrup.
- Blackberries, loganberries, mulberries, and raspberries: spread the fruit on trays to fast-freeze before packing it in containers.
- Sour cherries: pit them first.
- Currants: strip fruit from the bunches before freezing.
- Gooseberries: top and tail first.

PESTS & DISEASES

SOME PEOPLE SEEM TO SEE their gardens only in terms of its pests and diseases, a battlefield where a long war of attrition has to be waged by the gardener against fly, maggot, beetle, blight, and rust. These are probably the same people who write pedantic and complaining letters to their local newspapers and as a matter of principle challenge their check in a restaurant. Gardening does not have to be confrontational in this way. In mixed plantings of herbs and flowers, vegetables and fruit, there is little likelihood that crops will be completely wiped out by bugs. That is a problem that comes with monoculture, when large areas are put down to only potatoes or peas. Diseases can best be prevented by attending to the conditions in which plants grow. If they are growing strongly and enjoying life, they are much less likely to succumb to disease.

BEAT THE BIRDS
Birds are difficult to keep from plundering the strawberries. This pleasing frame has been made from netting attached to young, pliant hazel stems that have been bent over the row.

NATURE'S BALANCE

Bugs exist to feed other creatures. If you annihilate them with insecticides, their hungry predators will have to go elsewhere. Then, when the pests come back, they will not have any enemies. The reason for the existence of diseases such as gray mold/*Botrytis* is not as clear to the gardener but, with plants as with humans, the best strategy is prevention rather than cure. Disease is much less likely to strike plants that are thriving. In Part Two of this book, we have included a list under

each type of fruit or vegetable of the most common pests and diseases to which that plant is prone. There, too, you will find the names of some fungicides and insecticides that may help with specific problems. They are given in recognition of the fact that some gardeners like to know what potion they can turn to if the aphids get out of hand, or what preventative sprays they can use in a season when blight is most likely to strike the potatoes and tomatoes. But serenity in the garden is more easily achieved if you learn to be tolerant of pests and diseases.

Up to a point . . . There is no need to fling the netting off the raspberries and invite the birds in for a feast. But it is not the end of the world if the cabbages have a few outer leaves nibbled by caterpillars, or if a slug has taken an *hors d'oeuvre* from the lettuce.

Now that we buy, rather than grow, so much of our food, we have come to expect an almost unreal perfection in the appearance of fruit and vegetables. Grocery-store lettuce may have been sprayed as many as 11 times before it leaves the farm for the supermarket shelf. No insects lurk in the folds of its leaves. No downy mildew disfigures its appearance. We would complain bitterly to the manager if it did. But there is a lurking suspicion that what we are putting in our mouths is not what is doing our bodies most good. When you grow your own fruit and vegetables, you eat them confident in the knowledge that you have been the arbiter of what they should or should not receive by way of medicine. If the price to pay for that is the odd bit of

STAY SANGUINE
Some damage may be inevitable, but a few slug or caterpillar holes in the outer leaves of a cabbage hardly spell disaster. The leaves will, in any case, probably be discarded in the kitchen.

PREVENT AND PROTECT
Young cabbages, left, are being protected from two different pests. The netting deters birds from pecking the leaves, while the square collars at the base of the plants will stop the cabbage maggot from laying its eggs around the stems. When the maggots hatch, they eat the roots.

FRUITFUL HARMONY
If the soft fruit patch needs a fruit cage, try building one that is as attractive to the human eye as it is offputting to the birds. Here, the supports are arranged like the spokes of a wheel. The netting is attached to the top and sides.

WIRED UP
Plants are at their most vulnerable to attack by birds while they are small. Lengths of chicken wire arched over rows or patches of seedlings will give all the protection that is necessary.

root fly damage to carve off a carrot when you are preparing it, or a few strawberries lost to gray mold, then that is a price worth paying.

It may sometimes seem to the gardener that there are more bad guys than good guys in the garden. There are not, but the good guys are slower on the uptake and the gardener's patience is limited. Aphids are the most common horrors and it *is* offputting when you go to gather Brussels sprouts to find the plant seething with gray hordes. You could spray them with insecticide, but you can also direct a strong stream of water onto them, taking pleasure in knowing they probably won't have the strength to crawl back up the plant. It is in artificial environments such as greenhouses, often without natural predators, that you may feel most need to reach for a bottle. But you could equally well reach for an *Encarsia* wasp (see page 195), which can despatch prodigious numbers of whitefly.

In the natural cycle, a buildup of pests is followed by a buildup of predators. The gap between is nerve-racking, but you learn to trust in nature, which has a longer overview than fidgety humans. The cycle is not helped by the introduction into the food chain of unnatural numbers of predators such as cats. In suburbs and cities, where there are more cats than could star in a million musicals, there are relatively few species of birds. This, in turn, has an effect on the numbers of insect pests.

BOTTLED REMEDIES

Insecticides work in several ways. The simplest are those that kill by contact. You spray the bug. It drops dead. Other insecticides leave a deposit on the leaf that is then eaten by the creature. Caterpillar killers work in this way. Systemic insecticides are more devious. These are absorbed by the tissues of the plant and then get into the sap. The insects are killed by feeding on the plant that you have sprayed. Sap suckers such as aphids and leafhoppers are usually tackled in this way. The least dangerous times to spray are early in the morning (say before 10am) or in the evening (after 6pm) when there are fewer beneficial insects on the wing and bees are less likely to be working flowers. Millions of bees, which do only good in the garden and are essential for pollination, are killed each year by reckless spraying. Spray when foliage is dry and when there is no wind. But remember your allies. If you must spray, avoid using kill-all insecticides that get rid of friends as well as foes. Choose chemicals that are as specific as possible to the problem at hand.

Fungicides can be used to fight against a wide range of common diseases. They can combat powdery mildew, which is particularly prevalent in hot, dry summers, and are also effective against gray mold/ *Botrytis*, which attacks strawberries and many other plants. Leaf spots, such as chocolate leaf spot on broad beans, may also be controlled by a systemic fungicide.

Like insecticides, fungicides work in different ways. The systemic types are absorbed through the leaves into the plant's sap, there killing any fungus spores. Contact fungicides work by making a barrier between the leaf surface and any external spores. They will be effective only if applied regularly, usually at 10–14 day intervals. All fungicides are better at prevention than cure. Unfortunately, most gardeners are better at reacting than predicting. Your best defense is to grow your plants in well-nurtured soil and in the kinds of situation that nature intended for them. They will then be less prone to any kind of disease.

PESTS, DISEASES & MINERAL DEFICIENCIES

PESTS AND DISEASES SORT THEMSELVES quite clearly into the general, like aphids and gray mold/*Botrytis*, that are attracted to a range of plants, and the specific, like asparagus beetle or cane blight, that are particular about their targets. Generally the latter are less of a problem than the former, although when they attack, they may inflict more damage. A gardener also needs to distinguish between problems that can be controlled and those that cannot. Usually pests are more easily dealt with than diseases. There is no sure treatment, for instance, for viruses and southern blight.

PESTS

APHIDS

Aphids – tiny, pear-shaped, stem-clustering insects – share with slugs the dubious honor of being the most commonly complained-about pests in the garden. About 550 types of aphid thrive in North America. They breed prodigiously because, for the whole summer, all aphids are female. Their young grow up in a week and then start to reproduce asexually. Do not even *think* about it. It is too frightening. Aphids are sapsuckers and therefore spreaders of virus diseases that can be more of a problem to the gardener than the pests themselves. Their enemies are ladybugs, lacewings, and hoverflies. Aphids often are a problem in spring, when fast-growing plants are high in nitrogen, which helps aphids reproduce even faster. Avoiding high-nitrogen fertilizers will help eliminate your spring crop of aphids. Ants will place aphids on crops such as nasturtiums and Brussels sprouts. Eliminate the ants and you'll discourage the aphids as well. Watch for aphids on fruit trees and bushes, cabbages, cucumbers, globe artichokes, and more. Some aphids overwinter on different host plants to those that they attack in summer. The black bean aphid often overwinters on euonymus. As well as the problem of their introducing virus

SHOOT DAMAGE
BY APHIDS

diseases, aphids can also reduce a plant's vigor and distort its growing tips. They excrete a sticky liquid known as honeydew that, in its turn, attracts sooty mold. Encouraging their natural predators helps to control aphids. You can also treat them by using an insecticide.

APHIDS ON BROAD BEAN

ONION MAGGOT

If your onions suddenly turn yellow and keel over then you may well have this fly on your patch. The adults look like small houseflies and in late spring lay their eggs in the soil around onion or leek crops. The creamy maggots eat the roots of onions and leeks, then burrow into the bulbs themselves, and continue to fatten themselves up at the gardener's expense. The most dangerous time is in early and midsummer, when young plants may be killed by the onion fly's maggots. The flies themselves overwinter in the ground as pupae. Cover onion plantings with floating row covers to prevent egg laying. Remove and destroy any plants that are affected by this pest. Another strategy for outwitting it is to shift your onion and leek beds each year; in other words, to practice an organized rotation of crops.

WHITEFLY

Whitefly are a particular problem in greenhouses and warm climates where they multiply safe from killing cold. They lay eggs, usually on the backs of leaves, which hatch into tiny, scalelike, sapsucking creatures. The scale pupates, hatching into a fly, and the whole grisly cycle starts again. Yellow sticky traps are effective, as is the parasitic wasp *Encarsia* (see page 195). You can also clear whitefly on the wing with a battery-operated vacuum cleaner.

WHITEFLY NYMPHS   ADULT WHITEFLY

CARROT RUST FLY

The adult fly is inconspicuous. It is its progeny that does the damage. Small underground maggots nibble at carrot roots, causing the tops to wilt or discolor. The first generation of flies hatches in late spring, so damage is most obvious in early summer. Since the adults are incompetent fliers, you can protect crops with barriers of plastic about 30in (75cm) high, or set floating row covers over seedlings (see page 166). You can also time sowings to avoid the peak hatching period: sow in early summer rather than late spring.

CARROT RUST FLY DAMAGE

CELERY FLY

Tiny white maggots, similar to carrot rust fly maggots, tunnel into the celery leaves, causing pale blotches, which later turn dry and brown. Attacks in spring, when celery plants are still young, are the most dangerous. Pick off and destroy affected leaves or spray with a systemic insecticide.

CABBAGE MAGGOT

The small white larvae of the cabbage maggot feed on the roots of brassicas – from cabbages and cauliflowers to kohlrabi – causing the plants to wilt. Young plants may be killed altogether. Several generations of the fly hatch in a single season, usually appearing in midspring, mid-, and late summer. Predatory nematodes and collars around plant stems (see page 57) provide an effective deterrent.

ASPARAGUS BEETLE

These yellow and black beetles are easy to identify. Both beetles and their larvae feed on asparagus foliage and may completely defoliate plants. They are active from late spring to late summer, and overwinter as pupae in the soil. Spray with a contact insecticide and clear away all debris from asparagus beds.

BEETLE LARVAE

ADULT ASPARAGUS BEETLE

SCALE INSECTS

These shield-covered creatures may colonize the stems of apples, cherries, figs, peaches, grapes, citrus trees, and bay trees. They are rarely troublesome, but a dormant oil spray will kill insects and eggs.

SCALE INSECTS

RASPBERRY FRUITWORM

The maggots of the raspberry fruitworm may also attack loganberries and blackberries. The adult beetles hatch from pupae in the soil from midspring onward and lay eggs in the flowers of cane fruit. The grubs eat the center of the fruit as it develops. When it is ripe, they return to the soil to pupate. You can prevent damage by spraying with a contact insecticide when raspberry flower buds swell and open. Loganberries should be sprayed as the petals start to fall, but spray blackberries before the flowers open.

RASPBERRY FRUITWORM DAMAGE

MITES

Mites strike in the garden or greenhouse. Barely visible to the naked eye, they produce threads like a spider's web. Affected leaves are yellow-flecked and turn brown before dying. Crops of citrus fruit, cucumbers, apples, peppers, and strawberries are worst affected, particularly in hot, dry weather. Spray with dormant oil or insecticidal soap. Damp down greenhouses to maintain humidity in winter. The predatory mite *Phytoseiulus persimilis* is an effective biological control under glass (see page 195).

MITE DAMAGE

COWPEA CURCULIO

A curculio is a weevil with a long snout, and this type is particularly prevalent on southern peas (cowpeas). Shake the adult weevils onto newspaper spread under the crop and destroy them. The young spend their entire lives inside the seeds and are a major nuisance while crops are in storage.

FLEA BEETLE

Brassicas of all kinds, including turnips, and radishes, arugula, bok choi, and mizuna greens, as well as eggplants, may be attacked by these tiny beetles. Flea beetles pepper the leaves with holes and leap into the air when disturbed. Seedlings and new transplants are most at risk. The beetles overwinter in plant debris, so clear this away at the end of the growing season. Neem and rotenone are effective controls.

FLEA BEETLE DAMAGE

CUCUMBER AND SQUASH PESTS

These are avid pests of cucumbers and squash but can also attack many other crops. Both the striped and spotted types of cucumber beetles feed on leaves, shoots, and flowers, spreading bacterial wilt that can kill many curcurbits. Protect new plantings with floating row covers and spray flowering vines with rotenone. The squash vine borer is a white caterpillar that tunnels into vines, killing them. Dust vine bases with rotenone and wrap them with nylon hose to protect them.

BIRDS

In the summer, soft fruit such as currants grapes, cherries, strawberries, and raspberries, also larger fruit such as plums and peaches will need some kind of protection. Small plants and bushes can be protected with small-meshed nets. For trees, scaring flash tapes or balloon predators are very effective. Birds may eat newly planted seed, especially sunflower seed. Put floating row covers over plantings.

COLORADO POTATO BEETLE

These beetles, striped with yellow and black, swarm over potatoes and related crops such as tomatoes and eggplants. They and their larvae eat foliage, and can devastate plants in large numbers. Try mulching potatoes with straw and use floating row covers. Spray with Bt formulated for Colorado potato beetles.

APPLE AND PLUM PESTS

Several pests lay eggs in apples, enabling larvae to tunnel through the fruit. Apple maggots attack in early to midsummer. Trap them on sticky red balls, then spray a contact insecticide repeatedly. Plum curculio leave crescent-shaped egg-laying scars. At flower opening and when seen in summer, spray repeatedly with insecticide.

CUTWORMS

Lettuce seedlings seem most often to be attacked by cutworms, which are actually moth caterpillars rather than worms, unpleasantly plump, dark-colored, and about 1½in (3cm) long. They nibble through the base of young plants which, even if not severed completely, quickly wilt and die. Cutworms emerge from the soil to feed at night. You can collect them by flashlight and destroy them if you are not squeamish. Or surround the seedling stem with a collar, a section of cardboard tube sunk a couple of inches deep and protruding a couple of inches high.

CUTWORM

ROOT-KNOT NEMATODES

The root-knot nematode is a baddy with no redeeming features. It is a soil-borne pest that can build up to damaging numbers if provided with susceptible crops. Young nematodes swim to roots of potatoes, corn, tomatoes, peppers, lettuce, and fruit trees, causing the roots to grow into knots with devastating above-ground results. Rotation is the best defense. Do not grow vulnerable crops in the same place more than once every 5 years. Treat affected soil with neem to reduce population numbers.

ROOT KNOT NEMATODE CYSTS

CABBAGE CATERPILLARS

You could forgive cabbage caterpillars if they were content with feasting on the outside leaves of cabbages, cauliflowers, and Brussels sprouts. But they get where we want to be – right in the heart of the plant. Caterpillars may be of 2 different kinds: those of the small cabbage white butterfly are pale green and velvety, while those of the cabbage moth are yellowish green and fairly smooth. Try picking off caterpillars by hand (chickens are very partial to them), or dust the plants with derris, pyrethrum, or Bt, a nontoxic caterpillar disease. Protect susceptible plants with a floating row cover.

CABBAGE CATERPILLARS

SLUGS AND SNAILS

The most bothersome pests in a fruit and vegetable garden are slugs and snails. Although they may not look as impressive as the big, overground monsters, small, black, keeled slugs are the worst offenders, attacking a wide range of crops, including potatoes, tomatoes, and strawberries. But many other crops are at risk, particularly when young and succulent. Try predatory nematodes, a biological control, or use an aluminum sulfate-based slug killer. Catch slugs in small tubs of beer by setting the rim of the tub even with the soil surface.

SLUG AND
SNAIL DAMAGE

DISEASES & MINERAL DEFICIENCIES

BACTERIAL CANKER

Apples, cherries, and plums are the fruit trees most affected by bacterial canker. It invades the stems through leaf scars or wounds, forming abnormal sunken patches. Drops of amber-colored gum may ooze from the affected areas. The stem, then foliage and flowers begin to wither. Control by cutting out and destroying affected branches. Spray with a copper-based fungicide when the petals fall. You will need to follow that up by spraying 3 more times at weekly intervals from late summer onward. Help prevent canker by supporting heavily laden branches of fruit.

BLOSSOM END ROT

Tomatoes, and occasionally green peppers, are most commonly affected by blossom end rot, which is caused by a deficiency of calcium. Underwatering is often the cause and so it is perhaps not surprising that plants in grow bags, pots, or hanging baskets are susceptible. Sunken, blackish patches discolor the base of the fruit and it may rot as a consequence. There is no cure. Prevent it by attending to the correct watering, feeding, and mulching.

BLOSSOM END ROT

CHLOROSIS

Chlorosis is particularly noticeable in acid-loving plants, such as blueberries, which may be growing in soils that are too alkaline for their tastes. Plants are unable to take up enough manganese and iron from the soil and leaves turn yellow, particularly between the veins. Prevent it by matching plants to the right growing conditions. You can lower the pH by adding sulfur to the soil and using an acidic, water-soluble fertilizer.

SPUR OR CANE BLIGHT

Small purplish spots may appear on the canes of raspberries, loganberries, and other hybrid berries in summer. The spots eventually die, killing buds and spurs emerging from the diseased area or the entire cane. Avoid this problem by planting resistant cultivars such as 'Amity'. Control by cutting out any affected canes. Spray with a systemic fungicide every 2 weeks if necessary from the time the flower buds start to open until petal fall.

LATE BLIGHT

This is most troublesome on potatoes and tomatoes. It is prevalent in damp summers, when spores of the fungus *Phytophthora infestans* cause blotches on foliage. In certain conditions it spreads rapidly, completely rotting the foliage. Brown patches on potatoes spread into the hearts of the tubers. The best way to prevent it is to grow blight-resistant cultivars of potato, such as 'Wilja'. You can also spray with a copper fungicide at 2-week intervals from midsummer onward.

TOMATO BLIGHT   POTATO BLIGHT

FIREBLIGHT

This fast-spreading bacterial disease attacks apples, quinces, pears, and related ornamental plants. It attacks through open flowers and then spreads down the branch, causing it to blacken and curl at the tip. Avoid by planting resistant cultivars such as 'Moonglow' pears and 'Liberty' and 'Prima' apples, encouraging slow-growing branches that are less susceptible to attack, and spraying with streptomycin when flowers are open. Prune off infected branches, cutting them down to a 5-in (12-cm) long stub and sterilizing tools with 1 part chlorine bleach in 9 parts water. The following winter, remove the stub and any disease that may linger in it.

CLUBROOT

The spores of clubroot can remain active in the soil for up to 20 years, causing galls on the roots of the cabbage family (which includes rutabagas and turnips). Roots become distorted and swollen and may rot. Leaves turn yellow, red, or purple. There is no cure; crop rotation is the best defense. Do not compost roots, and lime soil to create a pH of 7–7.5 (see page 161).

CLUBROOT

DOWNY MILDEW

Many crops, including spinach, cabbages, onions, peas, grapes, and especially lettuce, may be affected. In cool humid conditions, fluffy white fungal growths develop on the undersides of leaves, foliage is discolored, and growth is stunted. Start with disease-free plants, provide good air circulation, and use fungicides if necessary.

DOWNY MILDEW

ROOT ROT

In wet soils or even in planters that are overwatered, many crops will suffer from root rot caused by fungus diseases. Avoid root rot by correcting poorly drained soils and by letting potted plants dry out slightly between waterings.

BROWN ROT

This fungus disease can do what the name infers to the ripening fruit of stone fruit such as apricots, cherries, peaches, nectarines, and plums. The disease also makes flowers rot and causes cankers on stems. Look for resistant cultivars. Spray with preventative fungicides when the tree flowers and as the fruit matures and begins to ripen. Cut off cankers. Remove and destroy all infected fruit.

GRAY MOLD/*BOTRYTIS*

Many fruit and vegetables, including zucchini and squash, peas, beans, lettuce, figs, grapes, raspberries, and especially strawberries, may be affected by this disease. It is worse in damp summers. Buds, fruit, leaves, and stems can all become covered with gray, fluffy mold. It often attacks plants already suffering from diseases such as downy mildew. Some strains are resistant to fungicides, but you can try spraying soft fruit at flowering time, repeating every 2 weeks.

GRAY MOLD/*BOTRYTIS*

DAMPING OFF

Potted seedlings that rot where they emerge from the soil are victims of damping off fungus. You can avoid this disease by planting in sterile, peat-based potting mix and cleaning recycled pots with a 10 percent solution of bleach. Sow frugally so the seedlings are not bunched up, limiting air circulation.

SOOTY MOLD

Sooty mold forms on the sticky liquid that aphids excrete. It weakens a plant because it blocks out light from leaves and prevents the plant from photosynthesizing. You can wash it off with soapy water.

PARSNIP CANKER

The shoulders of affected parsnips discolor and rot. The disease may also spread into the root, especially where there are lesions caused by carrot rust fly. The disease shows as black or orange patches on the flesh. It is worse in wet seasons. There is no cure, but you can prevent outbreaks by rotating crops, improving drainage, and planting canker-resistant varieties such as 'Andover', 'Avonresister', and 'Cobham Improved Marrow'.

PARSNIP CANKER

NUTRIENT DEFICIENCES

Insufficient nutrient availability can mimic disease symptoms. Lack of nitrogen slows growth and yellows older leaves. Lack of phosphorus causes leaves to turn bronze and stunts flower and fruit production. Inadequate potassium also causes yellowing of leaves. A soil test can help you to identify these deficiencies.

PEACH LEAF CURL

Peaches, nectarines, and almonds may all be attacked by the fungus *Taphrina deformans*. It distorts and blisters foliage, which drops and is replaced by a second healthy crop of leaves. Repeated attacks weaken trees. Protect wall-trained trees with a light plastic shelter to keep off rain that contains the spores from midwinter to midspring. Spray with a copper-based fungicide in autumn, after leaf fall, and again when buds swell from late winter.

PEACH LEAF CURL

SOUTHERN BLIGHT

This may attack Jerusalem artichokes, carrots, parsnips, okra, and celery. White fluffy mold gathers on the bottoms of the stems, killing plants if severe. Affected plants should be dug up and destroyed. The mold can attack stored carrots and parsnips. Keep stored crops cool and dry. On celery plants, southern blight is most likely to form on the crown. There is no cure. Destroy affected plants and practice a very strict crop rotation.

POWDERY MILDEW

Powdery mildew attacks a wide range of crops, including cabbages, zucchini, peas, apples, pears, cherries, gooseberries, peaches, plums, grapes, and strawberries. The mildew, which coats the leaves and stems, is most likely to be a problem in hot seasons. The only certain control is to grow resistant cultivars and spray with a systemic fungicide before the disease appears, continuing at 2-week intervals.

POWDERY MILDEW ON FRUIT AND SHOOT

RUST

Powdery brownish spots or streaks appear on leeks, onions, beans, asparagus, and corn, but the disease is rarely fatal. Destroy affected leaves and practice crop rotation. Water at the base of the plant rather than over the leaves. Look for rust-resistant cultivars such as 'Jersey Giant' asparagus.

RUST ON LEEKS

Species of *Ribes*, particularly black currants, are susceptible to white pine blister rust, which also attacks 5-needled pines. It causes rust patches on currant leaves but is not usually fatal. However, it can kill nearby pines and, for that reason, planting currants and even related gooseberries is banned in some parts of North America. Be sure to grow disease-resistant cultivars of currants or keep a distance of 900ft (275m) between currant bushes and plantings of 5-needled pines.

SCAB ON APPLES

SCAB

Apples, pears, and citrus fruit can all develop scab. It appears as black, scabby patches on fruit and foliage, and fruit may remain small and distorted. It is worse in mild, damp summers. Plant scab-resistant varieties such as the apple 'Jonathan' and the pear 'Beurré Hardy'. Clear away fallen leaves in autumn. Potato scab produces corky growths on tubers and is most common on light soils.

VERTICILLIUM AND *FUSARIUM* WILT

These soil-borne fungus diseases attack a wide variety of crops, clogging up stems, causing leaves to discolor, and plants to wilt and die. Wilts are present if a cut stem is dark inside. Destroy infected plants and grow only wilt-resistant cultivars.

FRUIT VIRUSES

Viruses infect fruit bushes and trees causing mottled, deformed leaves and stunting overall growth. There is no cure; avoid by buying certified disease-free stock. Use insecticidal soap to keep plants free of disease-carrying aphids and leafhoppers.

MOSAIC VIRUS

The virus attacks zucchini, squash, melons, tomatoes, and other crops. It is spread by aphids. Foliage is mottled with yellow and the fruit may also be affected, with stunted growth. Destroy badly affected plants and control aphids, which transmit the virus.

BIOLOGICAL CONTROL

THERE IS RATHER A GHASTLY FASCINATION in peering through a magnifying glass at a purposeful little ladybug scooping up garden pests and cramming them into its mouth with all the delight of a five-year-old at a birthday party. The brown and black ladybug called *Cryptolaemus montrouzieri* is one of several predators that, given the right conditions, can be highly effective in demolishing pests such as aphids, whitefly, and mites. The predators work best in a controlled environment such as a greenhouse, which is where pest attacks are often the most severe.

ENCARSIA FORMOSA
This tiny wasp, which lays its eggs in whitefly larvae, will control the pest in a greenhouse, but it is effective only in the right conditions.

To use biological controls effectively, you have to understand the life cycle of the pest as well as the predator. Whitefly have young offspring that suck in sap at one end and excrete a sticky syrup called honeydew at the other. Only a day or two after maturing, the adult whitefly starts to lay a frightening number of eggs. Having hatched, the larva plugs into a leaf vein to feed, and stays at the same trough until it pupates and itself becomes a fly. Then the whole revolting cycle starts again.

ENCARSIA FORMOSA, a minute wasp, is the most effective control against whitefly. Its method of attack is grisly. The adult lays its eggs inside the larva of the whitefly and the young eat their way out from the inside, emerging after about three weeks as fully fledged wasps. To operate productively, the wasp needs night temperatures above 50°F (10°C) and it is most effective in day temperatures of 65°F (18°C) and above. If the temperature is low, the wasp cannot breed as fast as the whitefly. *Encarsia* works best if introduced three times at intervals every 2 weeks in spring. Then the wasps attack the whitefly where it hurts most – right in the middle of its reproductive cycle. The wasps are powerless against clouds of whitefly on the wing, the point at which most gardeners start to think about biological control.

PHYTOSEIULUS PERSIMILIS, a mite itself, will control other mites and feeds on its prey at any stage, juvenile or adult, but, as with *Encarsia*, the conditions have to be right for it to keep up with its prey.

COMMON LADYBUGS, whether adult or in their larval form, can dispatch prodigious numbers of aphids – biological control can work with indigenous predators as well as with introduced ones.

HOVERFLIES, and their larvae, will help to keep down aphids. Plant pot marigolds and nasturtiums to attract them to the vegetable patch.

LACEWINGS are more likely to visit gardens with a wide range of plants. Their larvae will devour huge quantities of aphids.

ICHNEUMONS are a type of leggy, four-winged wasp that preys on caterpillars. You can encourage them to the garden by planting goldenrod and fennel.

CENTIPEDES are excellent predators. Slugs are their preferred diet, but they will make do with other pests.

GROUND BEETLES are also keen on slug breakfasts. Remember these friends before you start spraying your foes. If you must spray, use an insecticide specific to the job.

LACEWING

LACEWING LARVA

LACEWINGS
Lacewing larvae are also voracious aphid eaters. Growing flowers among the vegetables will help to attract the adults to the garden.

LADYBUG

LADYBUG LARVA

LADYBUGS
Adult ladybugs eat huge numbers of aphids, but their larvae have an even greater appetite and will make short shrift of 50 aphids a day.

HOVERFLY
Hoverflies provide their young with a ready meal by laying their eggs within aphid colonies. Increase the numbers of hoverflies visiting the garden by planting pot marigolds and nasturtiums.

WEEDS

NEW GARDENERS NEED TO know what weeds look like, especially in their seedling or underground forms. Bindweed roots look quite important if you are a novice, and you may be tempted to replant them tenderly in finely sifted soil. If you do, their gratitude will be boundless, as will the time you spend weeding. On the other hand, if you think a plant is pretty, keep it, even if know-it-alls tell you it is a weed. Corydalis, the weed with ferny leaves and yellow flowers that grows in walls, is a case in point. Daisies are enchanting. So, in the proper place, is speedwell. Call it by its scientific name, veronica, if it makes you feel better about it.

PERENNIALS

GOUTWEED
Aegopodium podagraria
The worst weeds are perennial ones such as goutweed, which thrives in a wide range of soils and often arrives entangled in the roots of the clumps of asters, daylilies or goldenrods that gardeners give away in suspiciously large quantities. It spreads both by seed and by means of its shallow network of creeping rhizomes. These will manage to sprout new plants from any small piece that you have left in the ground. Digging and pulling weakens it eventually, but it can be difficult to control among permanent plantings, for instance in a fruit garden.

GOUTWEED

CANADA THISTLE
Cirsium arvense
Canada thistle is another horror that often arrives woven, unnoticed, through the roots of other plants. A systemic weedkiller is the most effective way of attacking it. Systemic weedkillers travel down through leaves and stems into the roots of pernicious weeds. They do not work immediately, but they are very effective. The active ingredient breaks down rapidly in the soil. They work best if you apply them when the target weed is growing strongly. Holding fire in this way tests the nerves, but is the most effective strategy.

CANADA THISTLE

BINDWEED
Convolvulus arvensis
Bindweed makes its presence known in the second half of summer. Having hauled itself unnoticed through raspberry canes, it opens a succession of trumpet flowers. If it were not such a bully, it would be a very decorative climber. It dies down each winter to a tangle of fleshy white roots that travel yards in a season. Dig it out, or kill it with glyphosate. If digging, be sure to extract every last piece, as tiny lengths of root will grow into new plants.

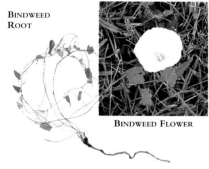

BINDWEED ROOT

BINDWEED FLOWER

QUACKGRASS
Elymus repens
Quackgrass, which can grow up to 30in (75cm), is supported by a deep subterranean network of rhizomes, by which it spreads rapidly through the ground. It flowers in late summer and can also spread by seed. Its greatest friend is the rototiller, which chops up its rhizomes and spreads them about very efficiently. Dig out every piece of rhizome, which will sprout afresh if left, or use a non-residual weedkiller, if necessary.

QUACKGRASS

DOCK
Rumex sp.
Docks are well anchored with long tap roots. Once dug up, they are done for, but if you merely snap off the roots, they will resprout, as will dandelions. There is immense satisfaction in drawing a large dock intact from the soil. Do not allow it to set seed, which it sheds prolifically, and tackle docks when young, before the root is too entrenched. There is little need to use herbicide.

DOCK

PERENNIAL STINGING NETTLE
Urtica dioica
These are a sign of fertile ground and have some use in the garden as fodder for moth and butterfly caterpillars and nettle aphids, on which predatory ladybugs feed. Nettles can also be turned into a liquid feed. Soak about 2lb (1kg) of them in a barrel of water. You can use the liquid after three weeks. If you cannot learn to love them, dig them out or spray them with glyphosate when they are in flower.

PERENNIAL STINGING NETTLE

ANNUALS

SHEPHERD'S PURSE
Capsella bursa-pastoris
Annual weeds are not so sinister as perennials, since they can easily be kept in check by hand-weeding or hoeing. Shepherd's purse may be in flower for much of the year and is therefore a prolific self-seeder. Deal with plants before they set seed.

SHEPHERD'S PURSE

HAIRY BITTERCRESS
Cardamine hirsuta
This is a landcress which, when young, you can mix in salads. It has a peppery taste, not unlike watercress. That is one way of keeping on top of it. It has a

staggeringly explosive mechanism for dispersing seeds. Catch it before it lets them fly. Its roots are not usually difficult to pull from the soil.

HAIRY BITTERCRESS

ANNUAL MEADOW GRASS
Poa annua
This is most likely to be a problem where there are grass paths through a kitchen garden, but it is easy to pull out. It can be suppressed to a large extent by heavy mulching. As with most annual weeds, the trick is to deal with it before rather than after it has seeded.

ANNUAL MEADOW GRASS

GROUNDSEL
Senecio vulgaris
Each plant of groundsel, with its yellow flowers, can produce up to 500 seeds, so the best time to pull or hoe it is before it sheds them. Hoeing is best done in hot, dry weather, when plants die quickly. You do not have to uproot annual weeds, just cut off their heads.

GROUNDSEL

LAMB'S QUARTERS
Chenopodium album
Lamb's quarters, with its succulent leaves and green bobbly flowers, can carry up to 28,000 seeds on one plant. Weed seeds germinate in the top 2in (5cm) of soil, so mulches need to be deeper than that if they are going to suppress weeds.

LAMB'S QUARTERS

COMMON CHICKWEED
Stellaria media
Common chickweed is one of the most persistent weeds in vegetable gardens, flowering for most of the year. Seeds will germinate in autumn, and the plants continue to grow all winter in mild areas. Control it by hand-weeding or hoeing.

CHICKWEED

SPEEDWELL
Veronica persica
The common field speedwell is one of the large family of speedwells which, although very pretty, may spread rapidly to become a weed in the kitchen garden. Control it by pulling or hoeing.

SPEEDWELL

THE KITCHEN GARDEN CALENDAR

SPRING

These recommendations are for cool climates; consult your Cooperative Extension Service for specifics in your area.

	EARLY SPRING	MIDSPRING	LATE SPRING
THROUGHOUT SPRING • Hoe regularly between crops to keep down weeds. • Mulch between plants and around trees and bushes to suppress weeds and conserve moisture in the soil. • Water if necessary, especially newly planted crops.	**VEGETABLES** • When snow melts or spring rains arrive, watch where the water drains to identify overly wet areas that need improvement before proceeding to plant. • Continue to force Belgian endive. • Sow broccoli, cabbages, celeriac, celery, eggplants, leeks, lettuce, onions, peppers, and tomatoes indoors. **FRUIT** • Plant and prune fruit trees and bushes; thin out crowded raspberry and blackberry thickets. • Where mildew has been a problem, spray gooseberries just before the flowers open and continue spraying every 2 weeks. • Hand-pollinate early-flowering fruit such as peaches and apricots if insects are not on the wing. • Prune out some of the old wood on sour cherries if not already done. • Spray fruit trees before leaf break. • Check blackberries, loganberries, and tayberries. Tie in to wires as necessary. • Mulch young trees, raspberry canes, and fruit bushes. • Set out young plantlets grown from strawberry runners.	**VEGETABLES** • Sow arugula, beets, broad beans, broccoli, winter cabbages, carrots, kohlrabi, leeks, parsley, parsnips, peas, radishes, red chicory, rutabagas, salsify, scallions, scorzonera, spinach, and turnips. • Plant out broccoli, cabbages, cauliflowers, lettuce, Jerusalem artichokes, onion sets, potatoes and seedlings of leeks, parsley, rhubarb, and shallots. • Sow Brussels sprouts, cucumbers, eggplants, melons, peppers, pumpkins, squash, sweet corn, tomatoes and zucchini indoors. **FRUIT** • Pick flowers off new young June-bearing strawberry plants, which should not be allowed to fruit in their first year. Remove flowers on everbearing and day-neutral strawberries for 6 weeks after planting. • Finish planting raspberries and blueberries, if this was not done in early spring. • Check fig trees, and prune new growth if necessary. • Hand-pollinate wall-trained peaches and nectarines if necessary. If the weather is very dry, spray the trees with a fine mist of water that will help the fruit to set.	**VEGETABLES** • Plant globe artichokes, cardoons and brassica seedlings. • Stake peas. • Sow beets, cabbages, carrots, cauliflower, chard, kohlrabi, parsley, parsnips, peas, rutabagas, scallions, and turnips. Start succession sowings of arugula, red chicory, endive, lettuce, radishes, spinach, and other salad crops. • If the threat of frost has passed, sow or transplant snap and scarlet runner beans, Brussels sprouts, celeriac, celery, cucumbers, eggplants, melons, peppers, squash, sweet corn, tomatoes, and zucchini. **FRUIT** • Pull out any new young raspberry canes that come up a long way from the original rows. • Continue to water if necessary, especially wall-trained trees or container plants. • Weed strawberries and put straw around the plants, together with a sprinkling of slug pellets if slugs are known to be a problem. • Put netting over soft fruit. • Start to thin out new shoots on wall-trained peaches, apricots, and plums.

SUMMER

	EARLY SUMMER	MIDSUMMER	LATE SUMMER
THROUGHOUT SUMMER • Hoe regularly between crops to keep weeds down. • Mulch around plants to suppress weeds and conserve moisture. • Water if necessary, especially newly planted crops. • Mound up soil around potatoes.	**VEGETABLES** • Sow arugula, snap and scarlet runner beans, beets, broccoli, carrots, chard, chicory, cucumbers, endive, Florence fennel, kohlrabi, lettuce, parsley, peas, radishes, rutabagas, scallions, squash, and zucchini. • Plant out cucumbers, peppers, and sweet corn into prepared ground. • Transplant broccoli, Brussels sprouts, cauliflowers, eggplants, leeks, and zucchini.	**VEGETABLES** • Watch for blight on midseason potatoes and spray if necessary. • Hill up Brussels sprouts and other brassicas on exposed, windy sites. • Remove sideshoots from tomatoes. • Harvest beans, squash, and zucchini to encourage additional fruit to set. • Lift garlic and dry off the bulbs. • Sow arugula, beets, broccoli, carrots, chard, chicory, endive, Florence fennel, kohlrabi, lettuce, parsley, peas, radishes, and turnips.	**VEGETABLES** • Lift onions and shallots and dry them before storing them. • Cut off and destroy the top growth of potatoes if it is blighted. • Sow kohlrabi, oriental salad leaves, radishes, spinach, and turnips. • Sow curly endive under glass. • Plant garlic.

SUMMER CONTINUED

FRUIT
- Pick strawberries, raspberries, currants, and gooseberries regularly.
- Train in new shoots of blackberries, loganberries, and other bramble berries.
- Tie in selected shoots of wall-trained peaches and nectarines, and thin the fruit if necessary.
- Remove strawberry runners unless needed to make new plants.
- Pinch out shoots on wall-trained plums and sour cherries that are growing in the wrong direction.

FRUIT
- Train in the canes of blackberries and hybrid berries. If you want to propagate them, tip layer the shoots.
- Thin apples and other large tree fruit if they have not already thinned themselves naturally.
- When raspberries and other bramble berries have fruited, cut out old canes and tie in new ones.
- Continue to train and tie in tree fruit growing espaliered against walls.

FRUIT
- Continue to cut out old raspberry canes that have fruited and tie in the new canes.
- Remove upright suckers from freestanding trees.
- Plant out well-rooted runners in new strawberry beds.
- Remove any diseased or damaged branches on fruit trees or bushes. Wait until the dormant season for other pruning.
- When espaliered peaches have finished fruiting, cut out the stems on which the fruit was borne and tie in new shoots to replace them.

AUTUMN

	EARLY AUTUMN	MID-AUTUMN	LATE AUTUMN

THROUGHOUT AUTUMN
- Store root vegetables such as beets, carrots, rutabagas, and turnips as you lift them. Keep them in a cool, frost-free place.
- Dig and manure ground once it has been cleared of crops.
- Clean out, shred, and compost garden debris to eliminate overwintering pests. Destroy any diseased plant remains.

EARLY AUTUMN

VEGETABLES
- Cure pumpkins and winter squash before storing them.
- Continue to hill up brassicas.
- Sow oriental salad leaves, radishes, and spinach.

FRUIT
- After fruiting cut out at the base old canes of blackberries, loganberries, and tayberries. Tie in new canes.
- Weed around fruit trees growing in grass to keep the soil clear.
- Cut off and destroy any mildewed top growth on gooseberries.
- Order new fruit trees and bushes.
- Harvest apples promptly, and freeze or dry the extras.
- Cut out dead wood on wall-trained sour cherries and tie in new shoots.

MID-AUTUMN

VEGETABLES
- Sow lettuce in a cold or hot frame for winter salads.
- Clear away bean sticks, tomato stakes, rotting vegetation, etc.
- Cut down stems of asparagus and Jerusalem artichokes.

FRUIT
- Store sound fruit in wooden boxes.
- Take cuttings, if necessary, from gooseberry and currant bushes.
- Prepare ground for planting new trees and bushes.
- Tidy up alpine strawberry plants, removing dead leaves.
- Prune gooseberries and currants after the leaves have fallen.
- Mow leaves off strawberries, rake them up, and destroy them.

LATE AUTUMN

VEGETABLES
- In cold areas, protect crowns of globe artichokes by packing them with straw.
- Once the ground is solidly frozen, mulch perennial crops such as strawberries to prevent frost from heaving them up.

FRUIT
- Rake up fallen leaves from fruit trees and destroy them if trees are prone to disease.
- Pull mulch away from tree trunks and shrub bases to discourage nesting mice, which may damage the bark.

WINTER

	EARLY WINTER	MIDWINTER	LATE WINTER

THROUGHOUT WINTER
- Dig and manure ground whenever conditions are suitable and prepare it for spring planting.
- Force plants such as Belgian endive and rhubarb from midwinter.
- Inspect stored apples, pears, potatoes, root crops, and winter squash regularly and take out any that are starting to go rotten.
- Use nonskid cat litter instead of salt on slippery garden areas.

EARLY WINTER

VEGETABLES
- Store carrots and rutabagas in a cool, frost-free place.
- Start basil indoors on a sunny windowsill.

FRUIT
- Check stakes and ties on fruit trees and loosen ties where necessary.

MIDWINTER

VEGETABLES
- Order vegetable and flower seeds, seed potatoes, and onion sets.
- Sow onion seeds indoors under lights to give them a strong start in the spring.

FRUIT
- Sprinkle small quantities of wood ashes around strawberries, gooseberries, and currants.

LATE WINTER

VEGETABLES
- Prepare seedbeds for early sowings.
- Sow celeriac, eggplants, leeks, lettuce, and onions in a frost-free greenhouse or indoors.
- Start onions and slow-germinating herbs or peppers indoors under lights.
- Sow salad greens in a cold frame.

FRUIT
- Do major structural pruning on fruit trees while they are still dormant.

STAR PLANTS

SOME VEGETABLES AND FRUIT in Part Two of this book (see pages 50–149) are starred, indicating they are particularly good choices for a decorative kitchen garden. This list acts as a quick reference to these star plants and includes some other cultivars recommended for their looks.

VEGETABLES

CABBAGES Savoy types, especially 'Julius', with swirling, crinkled outer leaves. Red cabbage: 'Super Red'.

ORIENTAL BRASSICAS Mizuna: deeply cut leaves. Bok choi: shiny foliage on snow-white stems.

KALE 'Chou Palmier': elegant, upright variety with nearly black leaves. 'Dwarf Green Curled': spreading, curly leaves. 'Russian Red': purple leaves with striking red ribs.

CHARD 'Rhubarb Chard': scarlet ribs. 'Burgundy Chard': purplish red stems.

LETTUCE 'Little Gem': small semicos. 'Iceberg': crunchy texture. 'Lollo Rossa': frilly leaves tinged with red. 'Red Salad Bowl': lasts all summer if picked regularly.

CHICORY AND ENDIVE 'Chioggia': striking red and white leaves. 'Green Curled': pretty, frilly head.

ZUCCHINI All are decorative, especially 'Cocozellé', with dark green fruit with paler stripes.

PUMPKINS AND SQUASH All are decorative, especially 'Turk's Turban', intricately shaped and marked.

HOT PEPPERS 'Yellow Cayenne Hybrid': good in containers. 'Jalapeño': bullet-shaped fruit. 'Super Cayenne Hybrid': prolific cayenne type.

SWEET CORN All are decorative.

GLOBE ARTICHOKES AND CARDOONS All are decorative, especially 'Green Globe', a classic artichoke with flat, rounded head.

TOMATOES All are decorative, especially 'Tigerella', with striped fruit, and 'Taxi', with bright yellow fruit.

RUNNER BEANS All are decorative, especially 'Painted Lady', with red and white flowers, and 'White Dutch Runner', with white flowers.

SNAP BEANS 'Purple Queen': purple pods. 'Kinghorn Wax': yellow pods. 'Blue Lake': climbing variety.

PEAS 'Novella': self-supporting, makes a low informal hedge.

BROAD BEANS All are decorative.

LEEKS All are decorative, especially the traditional, purplish blue French cultivar 'Bleu de Solaise'/'St. Victor'.

FLORENCE FENNEL All are decorative.

ASPARAGUS All are decorative.

CARROTS All are decorative.

BEETS All are decorative, especially glossy-leaved cultivars when grown next to orange pot marigolds.

FRUIT

APPLES All are decorative, especially when trained as cordons and espaliers or grown as standards or half-standards as specimens in a lawn.

PEARS All are decorative, especially when trained as cordons, fans, and espaliers, or grown as specimens in a lawn.

PLUMS Decorative trained as fans.

PEACHES AND NECTARINES Decorative trained as fans.

APRICOTS Decorative trained as fans.

CITRUS FRUIT Decorative as specimens in large tubs.

FIGS Decorative trained as fans on a wall.

MULBERRIES Decorative grown as specimens in a lawn.

MEDLARS AND QUINCES Good lawn specimens.

HAZELNUTS Decorative in early spring, when covered with catkins, and in autumn, with butter-colored leaves.

BLACKBERRIES 'Oregon Thornless': leaves deeply cut like parsley.

STRAWBERRIES 'Baron Solemacher': neat alpine type that does not produce runners.

RED CURRANTS Decorative trained as double cordons.

GOOSEBERRIES Decorative grown as mop-headed standards.

GRAPES All vines are decorative in leaf.

MELONS Decorative in fruit.

KIWI AND PASSION FRUIT Decorative trained against supports; the kiwi has particularly good foliage.

BIBLIOGRAPHY

Baker, Harry: *The Fruit Garden Displayed*, London, 1986

Bunyard, Edward: *The Anatomy of Dessert*, London, 1929

Bunyard, Edward: *The Epicure's Companion*, London, 1937

Bunyard, George: *The Fruit Garden*, London, 1904

Creasy, Rosalind: *The Complete Book of Edible Landscaping*, San Francisco, 1982

Davidson, Alan: *Fruit*, London, 1991

Hogg, Robert: *The Fruit Manual*, London, 1875

Larkcom, Joy: *Vegetables for Small Gardens*, London, 1995

Larkcom, Joy: *The Vegetable Garden Displayed*, London, 1992

Larkcom, Joy: *Oriental Vegetables*, London, 1991

McVicar, Jekka: *Jekka's Complete Herb Book*, London, 1994

Morgan, Joan: *A Paradise out of a Common Field*, London, 1990

Phillips, Roger and Martyn Rix: *Vegetables*, London, 1993

Robinson, William: *The Vegetable Garden*, London, 1905

Sanders, Rosanne: *The English Apple*, Oxford, 1988

Wilson, Alan: *The Story of the Potato*, 1995

FURTHER READING

Gessert, Kate Rogers: *The Beautiful Food Garden*, Pownal VT; Storey Communications, 1987

Harrington, Geri: *Grow Your Own Chinese Vegetables*, Pownal, VT; Storey Communications, 1984

Hertzberg, Ruth, Janet Greene, and Beatrice Vaughan: *Putting Food By*, New York; Dutton, 1982

Hill, Lewis: *Cold-Climate Gardening*, Pownal, VT; Storey Communications, 1987

McClure, Susan: *The Harvest Gardener*, Emmaus, PA; Rodale Press, 1993

Nick, Jean M.A., and Fern Marshall Bradley (eds): *Growing Fruits and Vegetables Organically*, Emmaus, PA; Rodale Press, 1994

Pleasant, Barbara: *Warm-Climate Gardening*, Pownal, VT; Storey Communications, 1993

Smith, Miranda: *Backyard Fruits and Berries*, Emmaus, PA; Rodale Press, 1994

USEFUL ADDRESSES

Listed below are nurseries, seed suppliers, and specialty companies that offer a wide selection of vegetables, fruits, and berries. Several also have excellent display gardens. Request information on visiting them when you write for a catalog. Also presented are organizations you may wish to join, and public gardens with interesting vegetable gardens or fruit displays.

GENERAL NURSERIES

These companies offer a wide selection of vegetables, fruit, and berries.

W. Atlee Burpee & Co.
300 Park Ave.
Warminster, PA 18974

Henry Field's Seed & Nursery Co.
P.O. Box 700
415 N. Burnett St.
Shenandoah, IA 51602

Gurney Seed & Nursery Co.
110 Capital St.
Yankton, SD 57079

Park Seed Co.
Cokesbury Rd.
P.O. Box 31
Greenwood, SC
29647-0001

VEGETABLE SEEDS

The Cook's Garden
P.O. Box 535
Londonderry, VT 05148
Seeds for gourmet vegetables and salad plants

Johnny's Selected Seeds
310 Foss Hill Rd.
Albion, ME 04910
Vegetable seeds; oriental vegetables; seed potatoes

Pinetree Garden Seeds
Box 300
New Gloucester, ME
04260-3400
Vegetable seeds; oriental and other ethnic selections

Shepherd's Garden Seeds
30 Irene St.
Torrington, CT 06790
Seeds for gourmet vegetables and salad plants

Territorial Seed Co.
P.O. Box 157
Cottage Grove, OR
97424-0061
Vegetable seeds; emphasis on types for year-round gardening

Tomato Growers Supply Co.
P.O. Box 2237
Ft. Myers, FL 33902
Exhaustive selection of tomatoes and peppers

Vermont Bean Seed Co.
Garden Lane
P.O. Box 308
Bomoseen, VT
05732-0308
Extensive selection of beans and other vegetables

SPECIALTY NURSERIES

Bear Creek Nursery
P.O. Box 411
Northport, WA 99157
Extensive tree fruit and berry listing, rootstocks, nut trees

Edible Landscaping
P.O. Box 77
Afton, VA 22920
Unusual fruits and berries

J.E. Miller Nurseries Inc.
5060 West Lake Rd.
Canandaigua, NY 14424
Fruits, berries, and nuts

Northwoods Nursery
28696 S. Cramer Rd.
Molalla, OR 97038
Tree fruits and berries, rootstocks, nut trees, citrus, nonhardy fruit

Ronniger's Seed Potatoes
Star Rt.
Moyie Springs, ID 83845
Potatoes, garlic, onions

St. Lawrence Nurseries
R.D. 5, Box 324
Potsdam-Madrid Rd.
Potsdam, NY 13676
Hardy fruits and nuts

Stark Bros. Nurseries & Orchards Co.
Highway 54
Louisiana, MO 63353
Tree fruits

ORGANIZATIONS

North American Fruit Explorers
Route 1, Box 94
Chapin, IL 62628
Information on unusual fruits and nuts for home gardeners

Seed Saver's Exchange
3076 North Winn Rd.
Decorah, IA 52101
Preservation of heirloom vegetables, fruit, nuts, and berries; demonstration garden

GARDENS

The following gardens have demonstration vegetable gardens as well as other features, as listed. Send a self-addressed, stamped envelope to the addresses listed for more information and directions.

Berkshire Botanical Garden
P.O. Box 826
Stockbridge, MA 01262
Orchard and vineyard

Callaway Gardens
U.S. Highway 27
P.O. Box 2000
Pine Mountain, GA
31822-2000
Vegetable garden

Chicago Botanical Garden
P.O. Box 400
Glencoe, IL 60022-0400
Demonstration fruit and vegetable garden

Colonial Williamsburg
P.O. Box C
134 N. Henry St.
Williamsburg, VA
23187-1776
Demonstration colonial garden

Fetzer Vineyards
13500 S. Highway 101
Hopland, CA 95449
Organic vegetable garden and vineyard

Fullerton Arboretum
California State University
Fullerton, CA 92634
Subtropical fruit grove

Longwood Gardens
P.O. Box 501, Route 1
Kennett Square, PA 19348
Demonstration home vegetable garden

Minnesota Landscape Arboretum
3675 Arboretum Drive, Box 39
Chanhassen, MN 55317
Demonstration vegetable garden

Monticello
P.O. Box 316
Charlottesville, VA 22902
Historic vegetable garden

Montréal Botanic Garden
4101 Sherbrook Street E.
Montréal, PQ HIX 2B2
Canada
Demonstration vegetable garden

New York Botanical Garden
Bronx, NY 10458-5126
Demonstration vegetable garden

Quail Botanical Gardens Foundation
230 Quail Gardens Dr.
Encinitas, CA 92024
Demonstration garden of subtropical fruit

Rodale Institute Research Center
611 Siegfriedale Rd.
Kutztown, PA
19530-9749
Organic garden and orchard

Stonecrop Gardens
RR2, Box 371
Cold Spring, NY 10516
Demonstration vegetable garden

Strybing Arboretum & Botanical Gardens
9th Avenue & Lincoln Way
San Francisco, CA 94122
Demonstration vegetable planting in Children's Garden

INDEX

Page numbers in *italics* indicate photographs or illustrations.

ACKNOWLEDGMENTS

AUTHOR'S ACKNOWLEDGMENTS

Without the generosity of garden owners, this book could not have come into being. I would particularly like to thank Tim and Darina Allen at Kinoith; Dr. and Mrs. A. J. Cox at Woodpeckers; Christine Forecast at Congham Hall; Rupert Golby and *Country Living* magazine for photographs of their garden at the Chelsea Flower Show; John and Caryl Hubbard at Chilcombe; Stewart and Jill Macphie at Glenbervie; Mr. and Mrs. R. Paice and their gardener Paul Williams at Bourton House; Nori and Sandra Pope at Hadspen Garden; Malcolm Seal and Anna Jamieson at Hill Cottage; and Lord and Lady Vestey and their gardener Neil Hewertson at Stowell Park, who have all allowed their gardens to be photographed. The design for the herb garden on pages 48–49 is adapted from one at Coton Manor, by kind permission of Mr. and Mrs. Ian Pasley-Turner. I would also like to acknowledge a debt to Rosemary Verey of Barnsley House, a pioneer of potagers, and to Joy Larkcom, whose writing has done so much to increase our knowledge of unfamiliar vegetables, particularly those from the orient.

Finally, I would like to thank the staff at Dorling Kindersley, particularly Thomas Keenes, for the clarity of his design, and Pamela Brown whose determination, good humour and expertise have made her an exemplary editor.

DORLING KINDERSLEY would like to thank Serena Dilnot, Nell Graville, and Heather Jones for editorial assistance; Claire Naylor, Joanne Long, and Laura Owen for design assistance; Dorothy Frame for the index; Sarah Ashun for photographic assistance; Suttons Seeds and Hyams & Cockerton for supplying plants, fruit and vegetables for photography.

PICTURE CREDITS
Additional commissioned photography by Steve Gorton: 4-5, 52-3, 59tl, 61, 63bl, 65tr, 81cl,tc, 85, 89cl,tr,bc, 101tr, 103br, 104tr, 116-7, 137tr, 157tr, 157tr, 159, 162, 196bc,tl,tr; and Andy Crawford: 7, 83cl, 87cl,bl, 88br

Additional photography: Peter Anderson, Andy Crawford, Geoff Dann, Philip Dowell, Andreas Einsiedel, Neil Fletcher, Frank Greenaway, Dave King, David Murray, Tim Ridley, Karl Shone, and Clive Streeter.

Dorling Kindersley would like to thank the following for their kind permission to reproduce their photographs:
Bruce Coleman Ltd: Dr. Frieder Sauer 195bc /Kim Taylor 195crb/ Elsoms Seeds: 21tr, 40bl, 54bl /Eric Crichton: 79br /Mary Evans Picture Library: 34bl, 46bl /Garden Picture Library: Gillian McCalmont 135tr/Howard Rice 118-9c/Gary Rogers 44br, 119tr/Juliette Wade 109tc/John Glover: 182b /Holt Studios International: 192bl, 193l,cl,tc,cr,cl,bc /Jacqui Hurst: 68bl, 122, 141, 143tc, 184, 186br, 189cr National Institute of Agricultural Botany: 103bl,tr /Oxford Scientific Films: J.A.L. Cooke 195tr/Mark Hamblin 197br /Photos Horticultural: 26tr, 27t, 166b l/Harry Smith Horticultural Collection: 71bc, 83tc, 136bl, 140br /Suttons Seeds Ltd: 67tl /Steven Wooster: 42br, 153tr
Key to illustration positions: t = top; b = bottom; l = left; r = right; c = center

Picture Researcher: Lorna Ainger

Note
Preserving is not without dangers. Cleanliness, equipment, timing, acidity, and a wide variety of other factors are critical to getting results that are safe to eat. This book gives recipes and guidelines only. Preserves should be canned according to USDA standards. For additional information, contact your Department of Agriculture Cooperative Extension Service. Dorling Kindersley assumes no responsibility for the preserving of foods described in this book.